CRE·TIVE
HOMEOWNER®

BEST-SELLING
HOUSE PLANS

CREATIVE HOMEOWNER®, Upper Saddle River, New Jersey

COPYRIGHT © 2009

CREATIVE
HOMEOWNER®

A Division of Federal Marketing Corp.
Upper Saddle River, NJ

Home Plans Editor: Kenneth D. Stuts, CPBD

Design and Layout: iiCREATiVE (David Kroha, Cindy DiPierdomenico, Judith Kroha)

Cover Design: David Geer

Vice President and Publisher: Timothy O. Bakke
Production Coordinator: Sara M. Markowitz

Current Printing (last digit)
10 9 8 7 6 5 4 3 2 1

Best-Selling House Plans
Library of Congress Control Number: 2009923712
ISBN-10: 1-58011-470-9
ISBN-13: 978-1-58011-470-7

CREATIVE HOMEOWNER®
A Division of Federal Marketing Corp.
24 Park Way
Upper Saddle River, NJ 07458
www.creativehomeowner.com

Note: The homes as shown in the photographs and renderings in this book may differ from the actual blueprints. When studying the house of your choice, please check the floor plans carefully.

Contents

Getting Started

Maybe you can't wait to bang the first nail. Or you may be just as happy leaving town until the windows are cleaned. The extent of your involvement with the construction phase is up to you. Your time, interests, and abilities can help you decide how to get the project from lines on paper to reality. But building a house requires more than putting pieces together. Whoever is in charge of the process must competently manage people as well as supplies, materials, and construction. He or she will have to

- Make a project schedule to plan the orderly progress of the work. This can be a bar chart that shows the time period of activity by each trade.
- Establish a budget for each category of work, such as foundation, framing, and finish carpentry.
- Arrange for a source of construction financing.
- Get a building permit and post it conspicuously at the construction site.
- Line up supply sources and order materials.
- Find subcontractors and negotiate their contracts.
- Coordinate the work so that it progresses smoothly with the fewest conflicts.
- Notify inspectors at the appropriate milestones.
- Make payments to suppliers and subcontractors.

You as the Builder

You'll have to take care of every logistical detail yourself if you decide to act as your own builder or general contractor. But along with the responsibilities of managing the project, you gain the flexibility to do as much of your own work as you want and subcontract out the rest. Before taking this path, however, be sure you have the time and capabilities. Do you also have the

time and ability to schedule the work, hire and coordinate subs, order materials, and keep ahead of the accounting required to manage the project successfully? If you do, you stand to save the amount that a general contractor would charge to take on these responsibilities, normally 15 to 30 percent of the construction cost. If you take this responsibility on but mismanage the project, the potential savings will erode and may even cost you more than if you had hired a builder in the first place. A subcontractor might charge extra for hav-

Acting as the builder, above, requires the ability to hire and manage subcontractors.

Building a home, opposite, includes the need to schedule building inspections at the appropriate milestones.

ing to return to the site to complete work that was originally scheduled for an earlier date. Or perhaps because you didn't order the windows at the beginning, you now have to pay for a recent cost increase. (If you had hired a builder in the first place he or she would absorb the increase.)

Hiring a Builder to Handle Construction

A builder or general contractor will manage every aspect of the construction process. Your role after signing the construction contract will be to make regular progress payments and ensure that the work for which you are paying has been completed. You will also consult with the builder and agree to any changes that may have to be made along the way.

Leads for finding builders might come from friends or neighbors who have had contractors build, remodel, or add to their homes. Real-estate agents and bankers may have some names handy but are more likely familiar with the builder's ability to complete projects on time and budget than the quality of the work itself.

The next step is to narrow your list of candidates to three or four who you think can do a quality job and work harmoniously with you. Phone each builder to see whether he or she is interested in being considered for your project. If so, invite the builder to an interview at your home. The meeting will serve two purposes. You'll be able to ask the candidate about his or her experience, and you'll be able to see whether or not your personalities are compatible. Go over the plans with the builder to make certain that he or she understands the scope of the project. Ask if they have constructed similar houses. Get references, and check the builder's standing with the Better Business Bureau. Develop a short list of builders, say three, and ask them to submit bids for the project.

Contracts

Lump-Sum Contracts

A lump-sum, or fixed-fee, contract lets you know from the beginning just what the project will cost, barring any changes made because of your requests or unforeseen conditions. This form works well for projects that promise few surprises and are well defined from the outset by a complete set of contract documents. You can enter into a fixed-price contract by negotiating with a single builder on your short list or by obtaining bids from three or four builders. If you go the latter route, give each bidder a set of documents and allow at least two weeks for them to submit their bids. When you get the bids, decide who you want and call the others to thank them for their efforts. You don't have to accept the lowest bid, but it probably makes sense to do so since you have already honed the list to builders you trust. Inform this builder of your intentions to finalize a contract.

Cost-Plus-Fee Contracts

Under a cost-plus-fee contract, you agree to pay the builder for the costs of labor and materials, as verified by receipts, plus a fee that represents the builder's overhead and profit. This arrangement is sometimes referred to as "time and materials." The fee can range between 15 and 30 percent of the incurred costs. Because you ultimately pick up the tab—whatever the costs—the contractor is never at risk, as he is with a lump-sum contract. You won't know the final total cost of a cost-plus-fee contract until the project is built and paid for. If you can live with that uncertainty, there are offsetting advantages. First, this form allows you to accommodate unknown conditions much more easily than does a lump-sum contract. And rather than being tied down by the project documents, you will be free to make changes at any point along the way. This can be a trap, though. Watching the project take shape will spark the desire to add something or do something differently. Each change costs more, and the accumulation can easily exceed your budget. Because of the uncertainty of the final tab and the built-in advantage to the contractor, you should think twice before entering into this form of contract.

Contract Content

The conditions of your agreement should be spelled out thoroughly in writing and signed by both parties, whatever contractual arrangement you make with your builder. Your contract should include provisions for the following:

- The names and addresses of the owner and builder.
- A description of the work to be included ("As described in the plans and specifications dated . . .").
- The date that the work will be completed if time is of the essence.
- The contract price for lump-sum contracts and the builder's allowed profit and overhead costs for changes.
- The builder's fee for cost-plus-fee contracts and the method of accounting and requesting payment.
- The criteria for progress payments (monthly, by project milestones) and the conditions of final payment.
- A list of each drawing and specification section that is to be included as part of the contract.
- Requirements for guarantees. (One year is the standard period for which contractors guarantee the entire project, but you may require specific guarantees on

When submitting bids, all of the builders should base their estimates on the same specifications. Once the work begins, communicate with your builder to keep the work proceeding smoothly.

Inspect your newly built home, if possible, before the builder closes it up and finishes it.

certain parts of the project, such as a 20-year guarantee on the roofing.)
- Provisions for insurance.
- A description of how changes in the work orders will be handled.

The builder may have a standard contract that you can tailor to the specifics of your project. These contain complete specific conditions with blanks that you can fill in to fit your project and a set of "general conditions" that cover a host of issues from insurance to termination provisions. It's always a good idea to have an attorney review the draft of your completed contract before signing it.

Working with Your Builder

The construction phase officially begins when you have a signed copy of the contract and copies of any insurance required from the builder. It's not unheard of for a builder to request an initial payment of 10 to 20 percent of the total cost to cover mobilization costs, those costs associated with obtaining permits and getting set up to begin the actual construction. If you agree to this, keep a careful eye on the progress of the work to ensure that the total paid out at any one time doesn't get too far out of sync with the actual work completed.

What about changes? From here on, it's up to you and your builder to proceed in good faith and to keep the channels of communication open. Even so, changes of one sort or another beset every project, and they usually add to its cost.

Light at the End of the Tunnel.

The builder's request for a final inspection marks the end of the construction phase—almost. At the final inspection meeting, you and the builder will inspect the work, noting any defects or incomplete items on a "punch list." When the builder tidies up the punch list items, you should reinspect. Sometimes, builders go on to another job and take forever to clean up the last few details, so only after all items on the list have been completed satisfactorily should you release the final payment, which often accounts for the builder's profit.

Some Final Words

Having a positive attitude is important when undertaking a project as large as building a home. A positive attitude can help you ride out the rigors and stress of the construction process.

Stay Flexible. Expect problems, because they certainly will occur. Weather can upset the schedule you have established for subcontractors. A supplier may get behind on deliveries, which also affects the schedule. An unexpected pipe may surprise you during excavation. Just as certain, every problem that comes along has a solution if you are open to it.

Be Patient. The extra days it may take to resolve a construction problem will be forgotten once the project is completed.

Express Yourself. If what you see isn't exactly what you thought you were getting, don't be afraid to look into changing it. Or you may spot an unforeseen opportunity for an improvement. Changes usually cost more money, though, so don't make frivolous decisions.

Finally, watching your home go up is exciting, so stay upbeat. Get away from your project from time to time. Dine out. Take time to relax. A positive attitude will make for smoother relations with your builder. An optimistic outlook will yield better-quality work if you are doing your own construction. And though the project might seem endless while it is under way, keep in mind that all the planning and construction will fade to a faint memory at some time in the future, and you will be getting a lifetime of pleasure from a home that is just right for you.

Ten Steps You Should Do Before Submitting Your Plans For a Permit

1. Check Your Plans to Make Sure That You Received What You Ordered

You should immediately check your plans to make sure that you received exactly what you ordered. All plans are checked for content prior to shipping, but mistakes can happen. If you find an error in your plans call 1-800-523-6789. All plans are drawn on a particular type of foundation and all details of the plan will illustrate that particular foundation. If you ordered an alternate foundation type. It should be included immediately after the original foundation. Tell your builder which foundation you wish to use and disregard the other foundation.

2. Check to Make Sure You Have Purchased the Proper Plan License

If you purchased prints, your plan will have a round red stamp stating, "If this stamp is not red it is an illegal set of plans." This license grants the purchaser the right to build one home using these construction drawings. It is illegal to make copies, doing so is punishable up to $150,000 per offense plus attorney fees. If you need more prints, call 1-800-523-6789. The House Plans Market Association monitors the home building industry for illegal prints.

It is also illegal to modify or redraw the plan if you purchased a print. If you purchased prints and need to modify the plan, you can upgrade to the reproducible master or CAD file — call 1-800-523-6789. If you purchased a reproducible master or CAD file you have the right to modify the plan and make up to 10 copies. A reproducible master or CAD files comes with a license that you must surrender to the printer or architect making your changes.

3. Complete the "Owner Selection" Portion of the Building Process

The working drawings are very complete, but there are items that you must decide upon. For example, the plans show a toilet in the bathroom, but there are hundreds of models from which to choose. Your individual selection should be made based upon the color, style, and price you wish to pay. This same thing is true for all of the plumbing fixtures, light fixtures, appliances, and interior finishes (for the floors. walls and ceilings) and the exterior finishes. The selection of these items are required in order to obtain accurate competitive bids for the construction of your home

4. Complete Your Permit Package by Adding Other Documents That May Be Required

Your permit department, lender, and builder will need other drawings or documents that must be obtained locally. These items are explained in the next three items.

5. Obtain a Heating & Cooling Calculation and Layout

The heating and cooling system must be calculated and designed for your exact home and your location. Even the orientation of your home can affect the system size. This service is normally provided free of charge by the mechanical company that is supplying the equipment and installation. However, to get an unbiased calculation and equipment recommendation, we suggest employing the services of a mechanical engineer.

6. Obtain a Site Plan

A site plan is a document that shows the relationship of your home to your property. It may be as simple as the document your surveyor provides, or it can be a complex collection of drawings such as those prepared by a landscape architect. Typically, the document prepared by a surveyor will only show the property boundaries and the footprint of the home. Landscape architects can provide planning and drawings for all site amenities, such as driveways and walkways, outdoor structures such as pools, planting plans, irrigation plans, and outdoor lighting.

7. Obtain Earthquake or Hurricane Engineering if You Are Planning to Build in an Earthquake or Hurricane Zone

If you are building in an earthquake or hurricane zone, your permit department will most likely require you to submit calculations and drawings to illustrate the ability of your home to withstand those forces. This information is never included with pre-drawn plans because it would penalize the vast majority of plan purchasers who do not build in those zones. A structural engineer licensed by the state where you are building usually provides this information.

8. Review Your Plan to See Whether Modifications Are Needed

These plans have been designed to assumed conditions and do not address the individual site where you are building. Conditions can vary greatly, including soil conditions, wind and snow loads, and temperature, and any one of these conditions may require some modifications of your plan. For example, if you live in an area that receives snow, structural changes may be necessary. We suggest:

(i)Have your soil tested by a soil-testing laboratory so that subsurface conditions can be determined at your specific building site. The findings of the soil-testing laboratory should be reviewed by a structural engineer to determine if the existing plan foundation is suitable or if modifications are needed.

(ii)Have your entire plan reviewed by your builder or a structural engineer to determine if other design elements, such as load bearing beams, are sized appropriately for the conditions that exist at your site.

Now that you have the complete plan, you may discover items that you wish to modify to suit your own personal taste or decor. To change the drawings, you must have the reproducible masters or CAD files (see item 2). We can make the changes for you. For complete information regarding modifications, including our fees, go to www.ultimateplans.com and click the "resources" button on the home page; then click on "our custom services."

9. Record Your Blueprint License Number

Record your blueprint license number for easy reference. If you or your builder should need technical support, the license number is required.

10. Keep One Set of Plans as Long as You Own the Home

Be sure to file one copy of your home plan away for safe keeping. You may need a copy in the future if you remodel or sell the home. By filing a copy away for safe keeping, you can avoid the cost of having to purchase plans later.

Plan #351013

Dimensions: 30' W x 36' D

Levels: 1

Heated Square Footage: 800

Bedrooms: 2

Bathrooms: 1

Foundation: Crawl space or basement

Materials List Available: Yes

Price Category: B

The design and layout of this home bring back the memories of days gone by and places in which we feel comfortable.

Features:

- **Living Room:** When you enter this room from the front porch, you can feel the warmth from its fireplace.

- **Kitchen:** This kitchen features a raised bar and is open to the living room.

- **Bedrooms:** Two equally sized bedrooms share a common bathroom located in the hall.

- **Screened Porch:** Located in the rear of the home and accessible from bedroom 1 and the kitchen, this area is for relaxing.

CAD FILE AVAILABLE

Images provided by designer/architect.

Copyright by designer/architect.

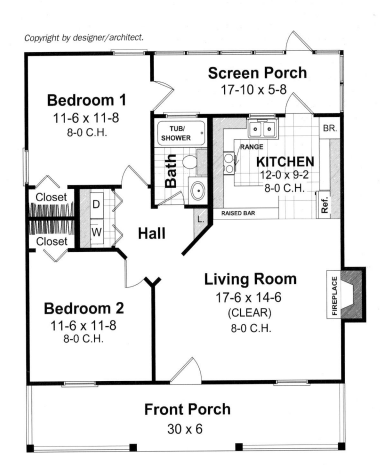

Bedroom 1
11-6 x 11-8
8-0 C.H.

Screen Porch
17-10 x 5-8

TUB/SHOWER

BR.

RANGE

Bath

KITCHEN
12-0 x 9-2
8-0 C.H.

Closet

D

W

RAISED BAR

Ref.

L.

Closet

Hall

Living Room
17-6 x 14-6
(CLEAR)
8-0 C.H.

FIREPLACE

Bedroom 2
11-6 x 11-8
8-0 C.H.

Front Porch
30 x 6

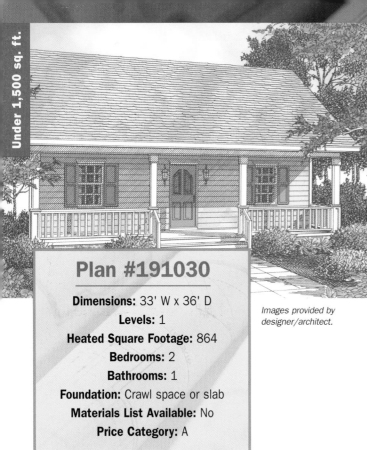

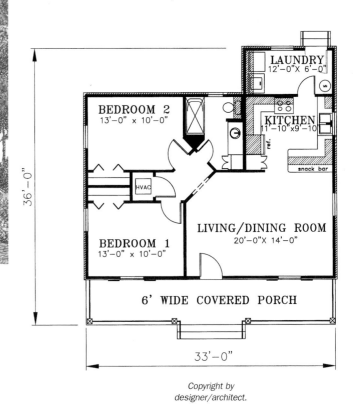

Plan #191030

Dimensions: 33' W x 36' D
Levels: 1
Heated Square Footage: 864
Bedrooms: 2
Bathrooms: 1
Foundation: Crawl space or slab
Materials List Available: No
Price Category: A

Images provided by designer/architect.

BEDROOM 2
13'-0" x 10'-0"

LAUNDRY
12'-0" X 6'-0"

KITCHEN
11-10"x9-10

ref.

snack bar

BEDROOM 1
13'-0" x 10'-0"

LIVING/DINING ROOM
20'-0" X 14'-0"

HVAC

36'-0"

6' WIDE COVERED PORCH

33'-0"

Copyright by designer/architect.

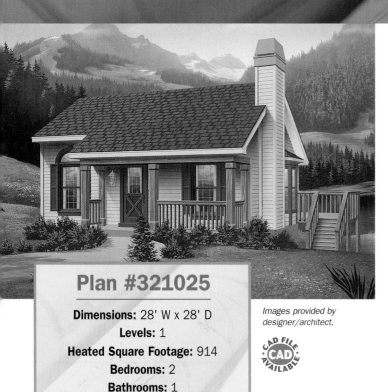

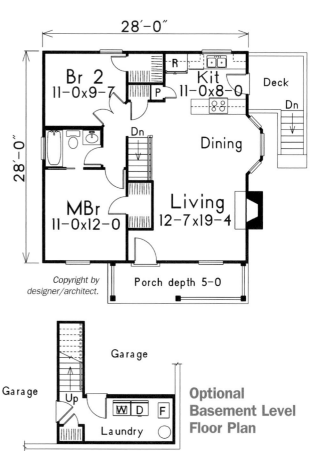

Plan #321025

Dimensions: 28' W x 28' D
Levels: 1
Heated Square Footage: 914
Bedrooms: 2
Bathrooms: 1
Foundation: Walkout
Materials List Available: Yes
Price Category: A

Images provided by designer/architect.

CAD FILE AVAILABLE

28'-0"

Br 2
11-0x9-7

Kit
11-0x8-0

R

P

Deck

Dn

28'-0"

Dn

Dining

MBr
11-0x12-0

Living
12-7x19-4

Copyright by designer/architect.

Porch depth 5-0

Garage

Garage

Up

W D F

Laundry

Optional Basement Level Floor Plan

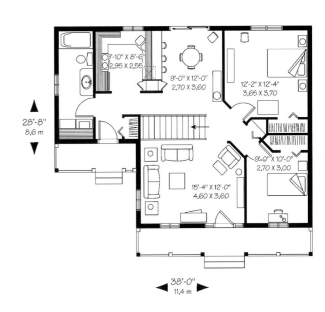

Copyright by designer/architect.

28'-8"
8,6 m

9'-10" X 8'-6"
2,95 X 2,55

9'-0" X 12'-0"
2,70 X 3,60

12'-2" X 12'-4"
3,65 X 3,70

15'-4" X 12'-0"
4,60 X 3,60

9'-0" X 10'-0"
2,70 X 3,00

38'-0"
11,4 m

Plan #181218

Dimensions: 38' W x 28'8" D

Levels: 1

Heated Square Footage: 946

Bedrooms: 2

Bathrooms: 1

Foundation: Basement

Materials List Available: Yes

Price Category: A

Images provided by designer/architect.

CAD FILE AVAILABLE

Plan #131034

Dimensions: 40' W x 32' D

Levels: 2 (upper unfinished)

Heated Square Footage: 1,040

Bedrooms: 5 or 4

Bathrooms: 2½

Foundation: Crawl space, slab, or basement

Materials List Available: Yes

Price Category: C

Images provided by designer/architect.

Main Level Floor Plan

MSTR BEDRM
14'-0" x 11'-4"

BATH

KIT
16'-0" x

STEPPED CLG
DINING
11'-4"

WICL

LAV

BEDRM #2
10'-0" x
9'-0"

BEDRM #3
9'-4" x
10'-0"

STEPPED CLG
LIVING RM
17'-0" x 13'-8"

COVERED PORCH

Optional Upper Level Floor Plan

Optional Main Level Floor Plan

MSTR BEDRM
14'-0" x 14'-0"

BUILT-IN OR CLOS.

BATH

WICL

MSTR BATH

BEDRM #2
9'-4" x
10'-0"

COV PORCH

OPT BATH DORMER

BALCONY

CL

BEDRM #3
14'-0" x 12'-0"

BEDRM #4
12'-8" x 12'-0"

WICL

Copyright by designer/architect.

Plan #401005

Dimensions: 24' W x 28' D

Levels: 2

Heated Square Footage: 1,073

Main Level Sq. Ft.: 672

Upper Level Sq. Ft.: 401

Bedrooms: 3

Bathrooms: 1½

Foundation: Basement

Materials List Available: Yes

Price Category: B

Images provided by designer/architect.

Main Level Floor Plan

Upper Level Floor Plan

Copyright by designer/architect.

Rear Elevation

Left Side Elevation

Scalloped fascia boards in the steep gable roof and the fieldstone chimney detail enhance this chalet.

Features:

- Outdoor Living: The front-facing deck and covered balcony are ideal outdoor living spaces.

- Living Room: The fireplace is the main focus in this living room, separating it from the dining room.

- Bedrooms: One bedroom is found on the first floor; two additional bedrooms and a full bath are upstairs.

- Storage: You'll find three large storage areas on the second floor.

Plan #131004

Dimensions: 59'4" W x 35'8" D

Levels: 1

Heated Square Footage: 1,097

Bedrooms: 3

Bathrooms: 2

Foundation: Crawl space, slab, or basement

Materials List Available: Yes

Price Category: C

You'll love the extra features you'll find in this charming but easy-to-build ranch home.

Features:

- Porch: This full-width porch is graced with impressive round columns, decorative railings, and ornamental moldings.

- Living Room: Just beyond the front door, the living room entrance has a railing that creates the illusion of a hallway. The 10-ft. tray ceiling makes this room feel spacious.

- Dining Room: Flowing from the living room, this room has a 9-ft.-high stepped ceiling and leads to sliding glass doors that open to the large rear patio.

- Kitchen: This kitchen is adjacent to the dining room for convenience and has a large island for efficient work patterns.

- Master Suite: Enjoy the privacy in this bedroom with its private bathroom.

This home, as shown in the photograph, may differ from the actual blueprints. For more detailed information, please check the floor plans carefully.

Images provided by designer/architect.

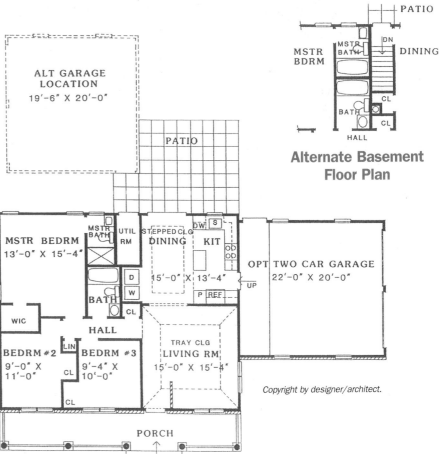

Alternate Basement Floor Plan

Copyright by designer/architect.

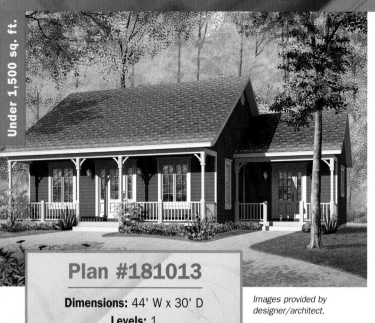

Images provided by designer/architect.

Plan #181013

Dimensions: 44' W x 30' D

Levels: 1

Heated Square Footage: 1,147

Bedrooms: 3

Bathrooms: 1

Foundation: Full basement

Materials List Available: Yes

Price Category: B

CAD FILE AVAILABLE

Copyright by designer/architect.

44'-0"
13,2 m

Plan #431004

Dimensions: 41' W x 30' D

Levels: 2

Heated Square Footage: 1,156

Main Level Sq. Ft.: 810

Upper Level Sq. Ft.: 346

Bedrooms: 2

Bathrooms: 2

Foundation: Crawl space

Material List Available: Yes

Price Category: B

Images provided by designer/architect.

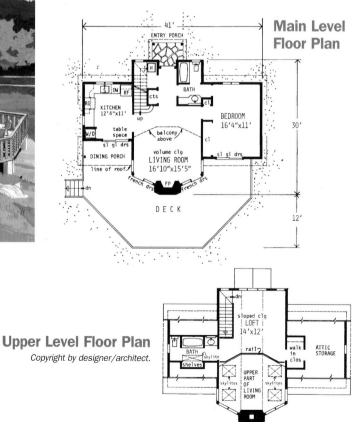

Main Level Floor Plan

Upper Level Floor Plan
Copyright by designer/architect.

SMARTtip

Tile for a Creative Fireplace

Tile on a fireplace face can offer a low-cost and unique alternative to masonry. Use reproduction tiles for an Arts and Crafts look, add European flair with painted ceramic tiles, drama with a mosaic design, or sleek contemporary styling with granite, terrazzo, or limestone tiles.

Plan #341018

Dimensions: 53'6" W x 35' D

Levels: 1

Heated Square Footage: 1,191

Bedrooms: 3

Bathrooms: 2

Foundation: Crawl space, slab, or basement

Materials List Available: Yes

Price Category: B

Images provided by designer/architect.

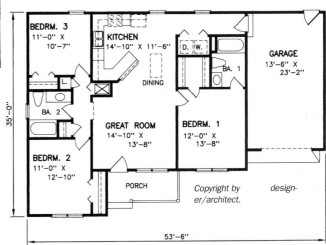

Plan #121144

Dimensions: 40' W x 48'8" D

Levels: 1

Heated Square Footage: 1,195

Bedrooms: 3

Bathrooms: 2

Foundation: Basement; crawl space for fee

Material List Available: Yes

Price Category: B

Images provided by designer/architect.

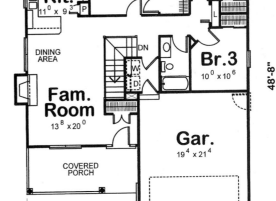

Copyright by designer/architect.

Plan #341173

Dimensions: 57' W x 33'10" D

Levels: 1

Heated Square Footage: 1,220

Bedrooms: 3

Bathrooms: 2

Foundation: Crawl space; slab or basement for fee

Material List Available: No

Price Category: B

Images provided by designer/architect.

Features:

- **Family Room:** This spacious family room lies just inside the wide front porch, which features a transom window over the front door.

- **Kitchen/Dining Area:** Sunlight brightens this area, which also includes a pantry. The laundry area is conveniently located nearby, so multi-tasking is a breeze.

- **Master Suite:** Spacious and inviting, this master suite includes a walk-in closet, a dual-sink vanity, and a garden tub.

- **Secondary Bedrooms:** Separated from the master suite for privacy, these two bedrooms share a bath.

This lovely home has several family-friendly features.

CAD FILE AVAILABLE

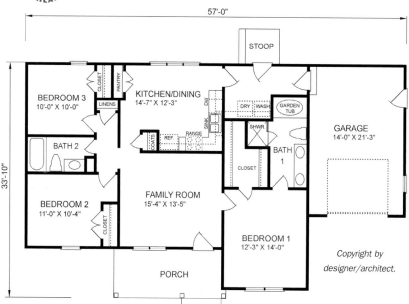

Copyright by designer/architect.

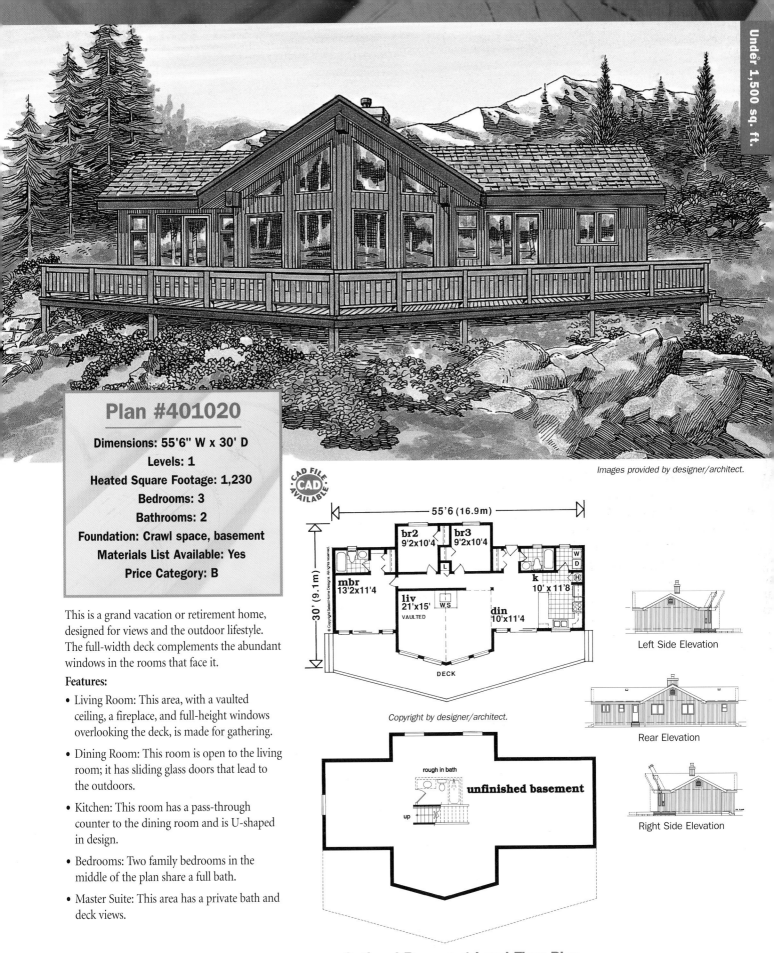

Images provided by designer/architect.

Plan #401020

Dimensions: 55'6" W x 30' D
Levels: 1
Heated Square Footage: 1,230
Bedrooms: 3
Bathrooms: 2
Foundation: Crawl space, basement
Materials List Available: Yes
Price Category: B

This is a grand vacation or retirement home, designed for views and the outdoor lifestyle. The full-width deck complements the abundant windows in the rooms that face it.

Features:

- Living Room: This area, with a vaulted ceiling, a fireplace, and full-height windows overlooking the deck, is made for gathering.

- Dining Room: This room is open to the living room; it has sliding glass doors that lead to the outdoors.

- Kitchen: This room has a pass-through counter to the dining room and is U-shaped in design.

- Bedrooms: Two family bedrooms in the middle of the plan share a full bath.

- Master Suite: This area has a private bath and deck views.

CAD FILE AVAILABLE

55'6 (16.9m)

30' (9.1m)

br2 9'2"x10'4

br3 9'2"x10'4

mbr 13'2"x11'4

liv 21'x15' VAULTED

din 10'x11'4

k 10' x 11'8

W D

DECK

© Copyright by Select Home Designs. All rights reserved.

Copyright by designer/architect.

Left Side Elevation

Rear Elevation

Right Side Elevation

rough in bath

unfinished basement

up

Optional Basement Level Floor Plan

Plan #341028

Dimensions: 40' W x 32' D

Levels: 1

Heated Square Footage: 1,248

Bedrooms: 3

Bathrooms: 2

Foundation: Crawl space; slab or basement for fee

Material List Available: Yes

Price Category: B

Images provided by designer/architect.

This home's efficient layout and comfortable living spaces all add up to a charming design that is perfect for many first-time homebuyers.

CAD FILE AVAILABLE

Features:

- **Living Room:** This spacious living room features a fireplace and twin windows.

- **Kitchen/Dining Room:** This kitchen/dining room provides a pantry and convenient access to the deck at the back of the home.

- **Master Suite:** You will love this master suite's dual-sink vanity and spacious walk-in closet.

- **Utility Room:** A separate utility room reduces the noise created by the washer and dryer.

Copyright by designer/architect.

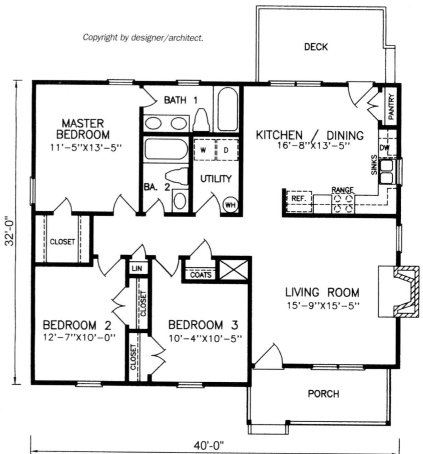

Plan #371005

Dimensions: 52'6" W x 45'8" D

Levels: 1½

Heated Square Footage: 1,250

Bedrooms: 2

Bathrooms: 2

Foundation: Crawl space, slab, or basement

Materials List Available: No

Price Category: B

This quaint country home feels much larger because of the cathedral ceiling in the living room and an upstairs loft. This is the perfect vacation getaway or a home for a small family.

Features:

- Front Porch: This large front porch is perfect for relaxing and entertaining.

- Living Room: This room is an open area and is great for having guests over.

- Loft: This area overlooks the living room and has an optional bath.

- Master Suite: This area has a large walk-in closet and its own private bath.

Images provided by designer/architect.

Copyright by designer/architect.

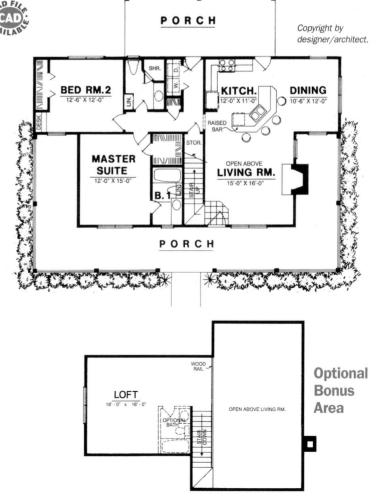

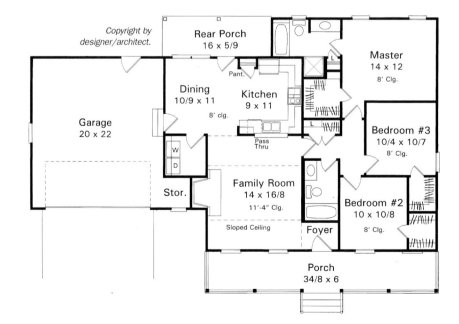

Images provided by designer/architect.

Plan #251001

Dimensions: 61'3" W x 40'6" D
Levels: 1
Heated Square Footage: 1,253
Bedrooms: 3
Bathrooms: 2
Foundation: Crawl space or slab
Materials List Available: Yes
Price Category: B

This charming country home has a classic full front porch for enjoying summertime breezes.

Features:

- Ceiling Height: 8 ft.

- Foyer: Guests will walk through the front porch into this foyer, which opens to the family room.

- Screened Porch: A second porch is screened and is located at the rear of the home off the dining room, so your guests can step out for a bit of fresh air after dinner.

- Family Room: Family and friends will be drawn to this large open space, with its handsome fireplace and sloped ceiling.

- Kitchen: This open and airy kitchen is a pleasure in which to work. It has ample counter space and a pantry.

- Master Bedroom: This master bedroom features a large walk-in closet. It has its own master bath with a single vanity, a tub, and a walk-in shower.

- Garage: This attached garage provides plenty of extra storage space, as well as parking for two cars.

CAD FILE AVAILABLE · CAD

Plan #341019

Dimensions: 44' W x 32' D

Levels: 1

Heated Square Footage: 1,258

Bedrooms: 3

Bathrooms: 2

Foundation: Crawl space or slab (basement for fee)

Materials List Available: Yes

Price Category: B

This quaint country home has a little something for everyone.

CAD FILE AVAILABLE

Features:

- Kitchen: This U-shaped kitchen has plenty of counter space and opens to the dining area.

- Family Room: This large gathering area welcomes you home and features a vaulted ceiling.

- Master Suite: This suite features a private bathroom with double vanities and a walk-in closet.

- Bedrooms: Two secondary bedrooms have large closets and share a hall bathroom.

Images provided by designer/architect.

Copyright by designer/architect.

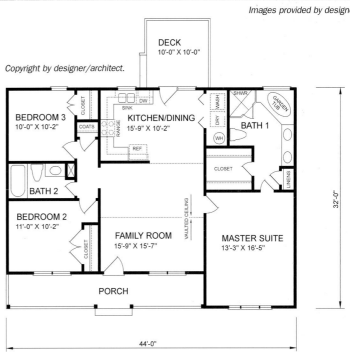

SMARTtip

Resin Outdoor Furniture

Resin furniture is made of molded plastic. Most resin pieces are quite affordable, but lacquered resin with brass fittings is a high-end item. Resin doesn't corrode and cleans easily, but a scratched finish cannot be repaired. Lacquered resin can be touched up, however.

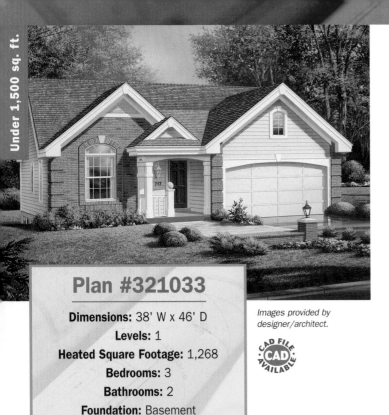

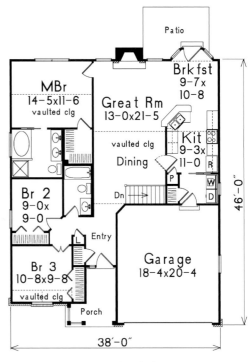

Patio

MBr
14-5x11-6
vaulted clg

Brkfst
9-7x
10-8

Great Rm
13-0x21-5

vaulted clg

Kit
9-3x
11-0

Dining

Br 2
9-0x
9-0

Dn

W
D

Entry

Br 3
10-8x9-8
vaulted clg

Garage
18-4x20-4

Porch

46'-0"

38'-0"

Images provided by designer/architect.

Copyright by designer/architect.

Plan #321033

Dimensions: 38' W x 46' D

Levels: 1

Heated Square Footage: 1,268

Bedrooms: 3

Bathrooms: 2

Foundation: Basement

Materials List Available: Yes

Price Category: D

CAD FILE AVAILABLE

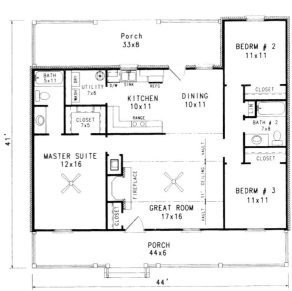

Porch
33x8

BEDRM # 2
11x11

CLOSET

BATH
5x11

WASH DRY

UTILITY
7x6

D/W SINK REFG

KITCHEN
10x11

DINING
10x11

CLOSET

BATH # 2
7x8

CLOSET
7x5

RANGE

CLOSET

MASTER SUITE
12x16

FIREPLACE

GREAT ROOM
17x16

VAULT 11' CEILING

BEDRM # 3
11x11

CLOSET

PORCH
44x6

41'

44'

Images provided by designer/architect.

Copyright by designer/architect.

Plan #171001

Dimensions: 44' W x 41' D

Levels: 1

Heated Square Footage: 1,277

Bedrooms: 3

Bathrooms: 2

Foundation: Crawl space or slab

Material List Available: Yes

Price Category: B

Plan #371093

Dimensions: 50' W x 45' D

Levels: 1

Heated Square Footage: 1,300

Bedrooms: 3

Bathrooms: 2

Foundation: Crawl space, slab, or basement

Material List Available: No

Price Category: B

Images provided by designer/architect.

Copyright by designer/architect.

Optional Basement Level Floor Plan

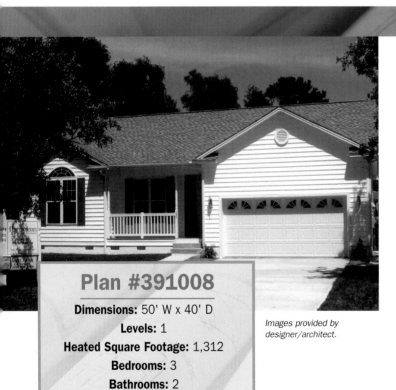

Plan #391008

Dimensions: 50' W x 40' D

Levels: 1

Heated Square Footage: 1,312

Bedrooms: 3

Bathrooms: 2

Foundation: Crawl space, slab, or basement

Materials List Available: Yes

Price Category: B

Images provided by designer/architect.

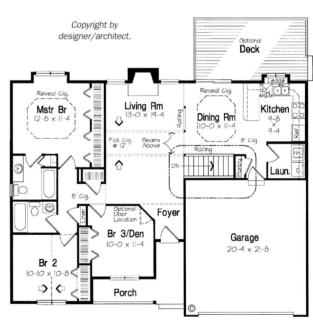

Copyright by designer/architect.

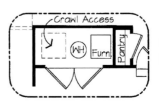

Crawl Space Option

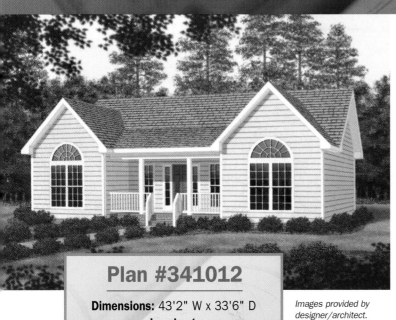

Copyright by designer/architect.

DECK

BEDROOM 3
11'-7"X10'-5"

CLOSET

DINING ROOM
11'-5"X9'-2"

KITCHEN
9'-0"X9'-2"

W.
D.

SINKS
DW

RANGE
REF.
PANTRY

COAT

BATH 2

LINEN

CLOSET

WH

BA. 1

LINEN

CLOSET

LIVING ROOM
17'-4"X18'-1"

MASTER BEDROOM
12'-9"X15'-1"

BEDROOM 2
11'-7"X11'-1"

PORCH

VAULTED CEILING

VAULTED CEILING

33'-6"

43'-2"

Plan #341012

Dimensions: 43'2" W x 33'6" D

Levels: 1

Heated Square Footage: 1,316

Bedrooms: 3

Bathrooms: 2

Foundation: Crawl space, slab, or basement

Materials List Available: Yes

Price Category: B

Images provided by designer/architect.

CAD FILE AVAILABLE

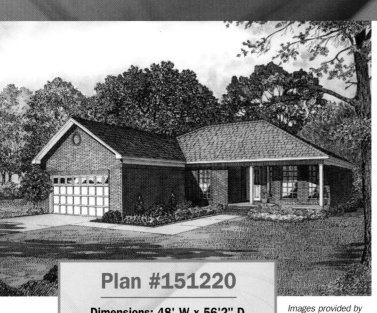

48'-0"

PATIO
10'-0" X 7'-8"

MASTER SUITE
11'-0" X 15'-4"

BATH
5'-0" X 14'-8"

BEDROOM 2
10'-0" X 12'-4"

KIT.
10'-2" X 14'-8"

DINING RM.
10'-2" X 11'-0"

M. BATH
6'-0" X 8'-6"

CLST
9'-4" X 5'-8"

LAU
6'-10" X 5'-8"

LIVING ROOM
16'-6" X 15'-4"
9' BOX CEILING

STORAGE
16'-4" X 3'-0"

BEDROOM 3
9'-4" X 11'-0"

COVERED PORCH
17'-4" X 6'-0"

6" COLUMNS

GARAGE
20'-10" X 20'-0"

56'-2"

Copyright by designer/architect.

Plan #151220

Dimensions: 48' W x 56'2" D

Levels: 1

Heated Square Footage: 1,325

Bedrooms: 3

Bathrooms: 2

Foundation: Crawl space or slab

Materials List Available: No

Price Category: B

Images provided by designer/architect.

CAD FILE AVAILABLE

48'-2"

50'-4"

GRILLING PORCH
10'-4" X 8'-6"

BRKFST. ROOM
9'-0" X 9'-0"

BEDROOM 3
10'-6" X 9'-2"

BEDROOM 2
14'-8" X 10'-0"

DINING ROOM
10'-0" X 9'-6"

KIT. DW
9'-0" X 11'-2"

BATH

MASTER SUITE
16'-2" X 11'-0"
9' BOXED CEILING

GREAT ROOM
13'-0" X 17'-0"

8" COLUMNS

BATH

STRG.
6'-2" X 5'-0"

LAU.
7'-2" X 9'-4"

PRCH

GARAGE
20'-10" X 20'-0"

GAS - FIREPLACE

Illustration provided by designer/architect.

CAD FILE AVAILABLE

Copyright by designer/architect.

Plan #151039

Dimensions: 48'2" W x 50'4" D
Levels: 1
Heated Square Footage: 1,353
Bedrooms: 3
Bathrooms: 2
Foundation: Crawl space, slab
Materials List Available: Yes
Price Category: B

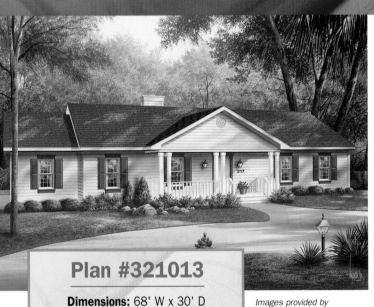

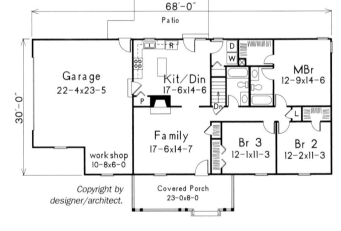

68'-0"

Patio

30'-0"

Garage
22-4x23-5

Kit/Din
17-6x14-6

D W

MBr
12-9x14-6

Family
17-6x14-7

Br 3
12-1x11-3

Br 2
12-2x11-3

workshop
10-8x6-0

Covered Porch
23-0x8-0

Copyright by designer/architect.

Images provided by designer/architect.

CAD FILE AVAILABLE

Plan #321013

Dimensions: 68' W x 30' D
Levels: 1
Heated Square Footage: 1,360
Bedrooms: 3
Bathrooms: 2
Foundation: Crawl space, slab, or basement
Materials List Available: Yes
Price Category: B

SMARTtip

Glass Doors and Fire Safety

Professionals recommend keeping glass doors open while a fire is burning. When the doors are left completely open, the burning flame has a more realistic appearance and the glass doesn't become soiled by swirling ashes. When the doors are closed, heat from a large hot fire can break the glass.

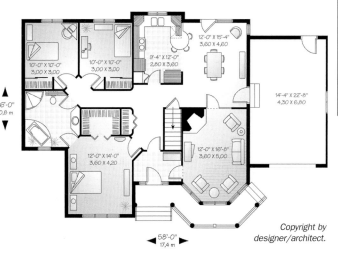

Plan #181024

Dimensions: 58' W x 36' D
Levels: 1
Heated Square Footage: 1,370
Bedrooms: 3
Bathrooms: 1
Foundation: Full basement
Materials List Available: Yes
Price Category: B

Images provided by designer/architect.

Copyright by designer/architect.

SMARTtip

Neoclassical Style

Instead of expensive hand-crafted plasterwork, look into the many prefabricated moldings, ceiling medallions, pillars, cornices, and the like that are made of lightweight molded plastic. They can be faux painted to resemble marble or stone and are fairly easy to install yourself.

Plan #151010

Dimensions: 38'4" W x 68'6" D
Levels: 1
Heated Square Footage: 1,379
Bedrooms: 3
Bathrooms: 2
Foundation: Crawl space, slab
CompleteCost List Available: Yes
Price Category: B

Images provided by designer/architect.

Copyright by designer/architect.

Images provided by designer/architect.

Plan #131014

Dimensions: 48' W x 43'4" D
Levels: 1
Heated Square Footage: 1,380
Bedrooms: 3
Bathrooms: 2
Foundation: Crawl space, slab, or basement
Materials List Available: Yes
Price Category: C

The exterior of this home looks formal, thanks to its twin dormers, gables, and the bay windows that flank the columned porch, but the inside is contemporary in both design and features.

Features:

• Great Room: Centrally located, this great room has a 10-ft. ceiling. A fireplace, built-in cabinets, and windows that overlook the rear covered porch make it as practical as it is attractive.

• Dining Room: A bay window adds to the charm of this versatile room.

• Kitchen: This U-shaped room is designed to make cooking and cleaning jobs efficient.

• Master Suite: With a bay window, a walk-in closet, and a private bath with an oval tub, the master suite may be your favorite area.

• Additional Bedrooms: Located on the opposite side of the house from the master suite, these rooms share a full bath in the hall.

Living Room

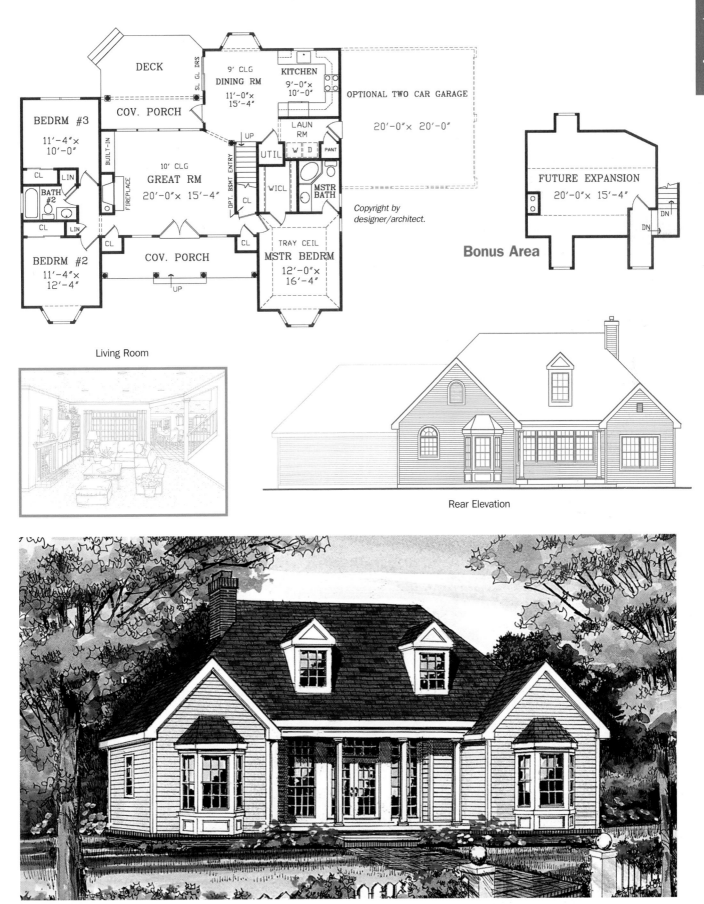

DECK

9' CLG
DINING RM
11'-0"×
15'-4"

KITCHEN
9'-0"×
10'-0"

SL GL DRS

COV. PORCH

OPTIONAL TWO CAR GARAGE
20'-0"× 20'-0"

BEDRM #3
11'-4"×
10'-0"

CL LIN

BATH
#2

CL LIN

CL

BEDRM #2
11'-4"×
12'-4"

BUILT-IN

FIREPLACE

10' CLG
GREAT RM
20'-0"× 15'-4"

UP

LAUN
RM
W D PANT

UTIL

DPT. BSMT ENTRY

WICL
CL

MSTR
BATH

Copyright by
designer/architect.

COV. PORCH
UP

CL

TRAY CEIL
MSTR BEDRM
12'-0"×
16'-4"

FUTURE EXPANSION
20'-0"× 15'-4"

DN

DN

Bonus Area

Living Room

Rear Elevation

Images provided by designer/architect.

41'-10"

48'-10"

WHP TUB/SHWR

DINING ROOM
11'-4" X 9'-2"

ATRIUM DOOR

DW

KITCHEN
15'-10" X 13'-8"

M. BATH
13'-8" X 10'-6"

KNEE SPACE

8" RND COL

REF

PAN

MASTER SUITE
9' BOXED CEILING
13'-8" X 11'-2"

GREAT ROOM
9' BOXED CEILING
17'-0" X 18'-8"

BEDROOM 3
9'-10" X 10'-0"

LAU.
6'-2" X 5'-6"

FOYER
4'-6" X 6'-0"

BATH

GARAGE
20'-10" X 20'-0"

PORCH
8" COLUMN

BEDROOM 2
9'-10" X 9'-8"

Copyright by designer/architect.

CAD FILE AVAILABLE

Plan #151059

Dimensions: 41'10" W x 48'10" D

Levels: 1

Heated Square Footage: 1,382

Bedrooms: 3

Bathrooms: 2

Foundation: Crawl space, slab; basement for fee

CompleteCost List Available: Yes

Price Category: B

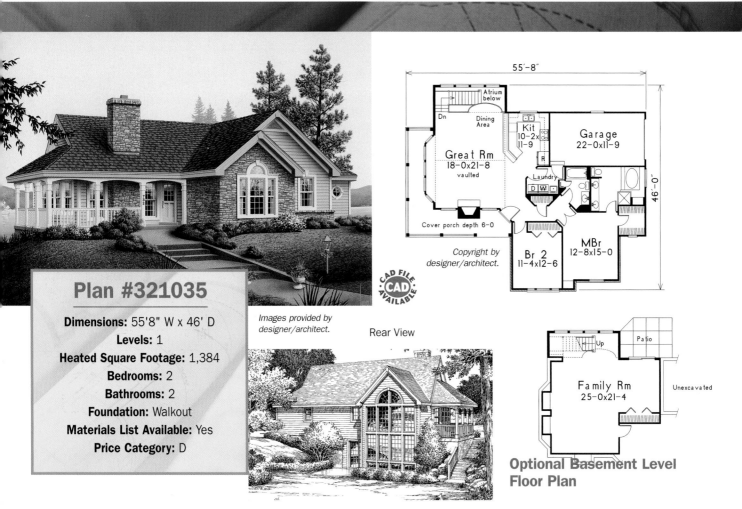

55'-8"

46'-0"

Atrium below

Dn

Dining Area

Kit
10-2x 11-9

Garage
22-0x11-9

Great Rm
18-0x21-8
vaulted

R

Laundry

D W

Cover porch depth 6-0

Copyright by designer/architect.

Br 2
11-4x12-6

MBr
12-8x15-0

CAD FILE AVAILABLE

Plan #321035

Dimensions: 55'8" W x 46' D

Levels: 1

Heated Square Footage: 1,384

Bedrooms: 2

Bathrooms: 2

Foundation: Walkout

Materials List Available: Yes

Price Category: D

Images provided by designer/architect.

Rear View

Up

Patio

Family Rm
25-0x21-4

Unexcavated

Optional Basement Level Floor Plan

Plan #121137

Dimensions: 42' W x 54' D

Levels: 1

Heated Square Footage: 1,392

Bedrooms: 3

Bathrooms: 2

Foundation: Basement; crawl space for fee

Material List Available: Yes

Price Category: B

Images provided by designer/architect.

CAD FILE AVAILABLE

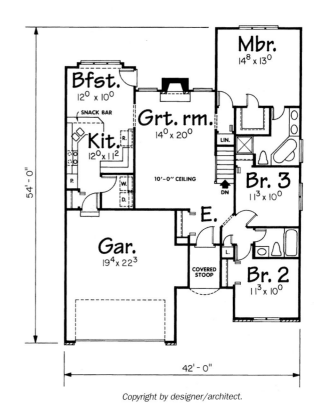

Copyright by designer/architect.

Plan #251003

Dimensions: 42' W x 42' D

Levels: 1

Heated Square Footage: 1,393

Bedrooms: 3

Bathrooms: 2

Foundation: Crawl space, or slab

Materials List Available: Yes

Price Category: B

Images provided by designer/architect.

Plan #151413

Dimensions: 32' W x 42' D
Levels: 1.5
Heated Square Footage: 1,400
Main Level Sq. Ft.: 948
Upper Level Sq. Ft.: 452
Bedrooms: 2
Bathrooms: 2
Foundation: Crawl space or slab
CompleteCost List Available: Yes
Price Category: B

Images provided by designer/architect.

Relax on the front porch of this lovely little cottage. It's a great starter home or a weekend getaway.

Features:

- Great Room: Enter from the front porch into this large room, with its vaulted ceiling and stone fireplace.

- Kitchen: This large kitchen has plenty of cabinets and counter space; there is even a raised bar.

- Grilling Porch: Just off the kitchen is this porch. Bedroom 1 has access to this area as well.

- Upper Level: Located on this level are a loft area, a full bathroom, and a bedroom.

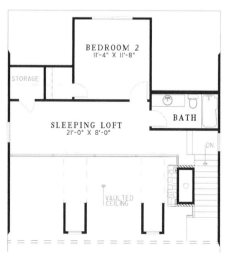

Main Level Floor Plan

GRILLING PORCH 15'-8" X 8'-0"

BEDROOM 1 12'-4" X 11'-4"

KITCHEN 15'-4" X 11'-10"

STACKED W/D

BATH

PAN

BALCONY LINE

GREAT RM. 17'-0" X 16'-2"

DINING 10'-6" X 13'-6"

VAULTED CEILING OPEN TO ABOVE

10'-9" WALL

UP

COVERED PORCH 32'-0" X 8'-0"

32'-0"

42'-0"

Upper Level Floor Plan

BEDROOM 2 11'-4" X 11'-8"

STORAGE

SLEEPING LOFT 21'-0" X 8'-0"

BATH

VAULTED CEILING

DN

Copyright by designer/architect.

Images provided by designer/architect.

Plan #321002

Dimensions: 72' W x 28' D

Levels: 1

Heated Square Footage: 1,400

Bedrooms: 3

Bathrooms: 2

Foundation: Crawl space, basement

Materials List Available: Yes

Price Category: D

If you're looking for a well-designed compact home with contemporary amenities, this could be the home of your dreams.

Features:

- **Porch:** Just the right size for some rockers and a swing, this porch could become your outdoor living area when the weather is fine.

- **Living Room:** A vaulted ceiling adds to the spacious feeling in this room, where friends and family are sure to gather.

- **Kitchen:** This space-saving design, in combination with the ample counter and cabinet space, makes cooking a pleasure.

- **Utility Room:** This large room is fitted with cabinets for extra storage space. You'll find storage space in the large garage, too.

- **Master Bedroom:** This room is somewhat secluded for privacy, making it an ideal place for some quiet time at the end of the day.

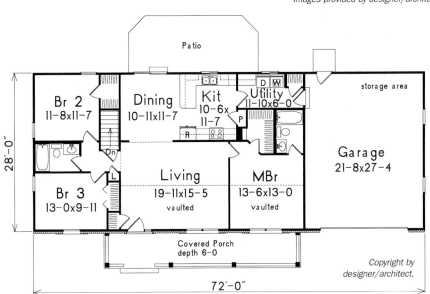

Copyright by designer/architect.

SMARTtip

Fabric Draping Ability

Test a fabric's draping ability by looking at a large piece in a fabric store. Gather at least two to three yards of material, holding one end in your hand. Check how it drapes. Does it fall into folds easily? Also look at the pattern when it is gathered. Does the design become lost in the folds? Ask a salesclerk or a friend to hold the fabric, and look at it from a few feet away.

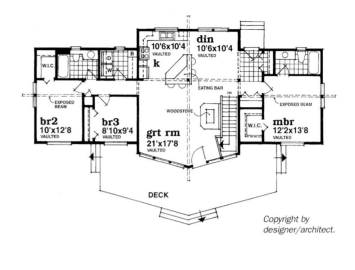

Images provided by designer/architect.

Copyright by designer/architect.

Rear Elevation

Plan #401033

Dimensions: 62' W x 29' D

Levels: 1

Heated Square Footage: 1,405

Bedrooms: 3

Bathrooms: 2

Foundation: Crawl space or basement

Materials List Available: Yes

Price Category: B

Images provided by designer/architect.

Plan #401025

Dimensions: 70' W x 34' D

Levels: 1

Heated Square Footage: 1,408

Bedrooms: 3

Bathrooms: 2

Foundation: Crawl space, basement

Materials List Available: Yes

Price Category: B

Optional Floor Plan

Copyright by designer/architect.

Rear Elevation

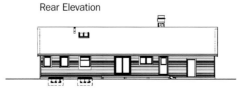

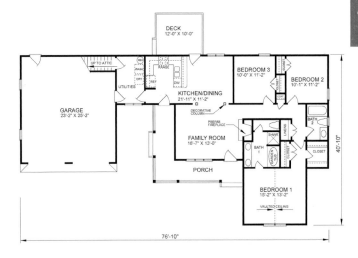

Plan #341128

Dimensions: 76'10" W x 40'10" D

Levels: 1

Heated Square Footage: 1,410

Bedrooms: 3

Bathrooms: 2

Foundation: Crawl space, slab, basement, or walkout

Material List Available: Yes

Price Category: B

Images provided by designer/architect.

CAD FILE AVAILABLE **CAD**

Copyright by designer/architect.

Plan #341064

Dimensions: 58'6" W x 36'9" D

Levels: 1

Heated Square Footage: 1,418

Bedrooms: 3

Bathrooms: 2

Foundation: Crawl space, slab, basement, or walkout

Materials List Available: Yes

Price Category: B

Images provided by designer/architect.

Copyright by designer/architect.

Plan #121009

Dimensions: 50' W x 58' D
Levels: 1
Heated Square Footage: 1,422
Bedrooms: 3
Bathrooms: 2
Foundation: Basement;
crawl space or slab for fee
Materials List Available: Yes
Price Category: B

This amenity-filled home is perfect for the growing family or as a retirement retreat.

Features:

• Ceiling Height: 8 ft. unless otherwise noted.

• Great Room: This inviting space is the perfect place for gatherings of all sizes. It shares 12-ft. ceilings with the dining room and kitchen.

• Dining Room: In addition to the 12-ft. ceiling, arched openings, and built-in book cases make this an elegant place to dine.

• Private Porch: After dinner, step through a door in the dining room to enjoy a summer breeze in this inviting porch.

• Master Suite: The boxed ceiling lends drama to this suite and a walk-in closet adds convenience. Luxury comes from the whirlpool bath.

• Garage: You won't be short of parking and storage space in this two-bay garage. As a bonus there is space for a workbench.

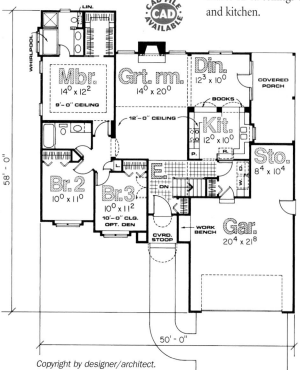

SMARTtip

Window Cornices

You can transform plain rooms by making jogs in cornice molding that will hold shades, blinds, and other window treatments. You can create individual pockets over each window or continue the molding past narrow wall sections between windows to form a more expansive detail. Housings below the cornice can be painted or papered.

Images provided by designer/architect.

Plan #341034

Dimensions: 50' W x 38'2" D

Levels: 1

Heated Square Footage: 1,445

Bedrooms: 3

Bathrooms: 2

Foundation: Crawl space, slab, or basement

Materials List Available: Yes

Price Category: B

This country charmer has a wraparound front porch.

Features:

- **Living Room:** This large gathering area welcomes you home and features a cathedral ceiling.

- **Kitchen:** This U-shaped kitchen has plenty of counter space and an exit onto the front porch.

- **Master Suite:** This suite features a walk-in closet and a private bathroom with double vanities.

- **Bedrooms:** Two secondary bedrooms have large closets and share a hall bathroom.

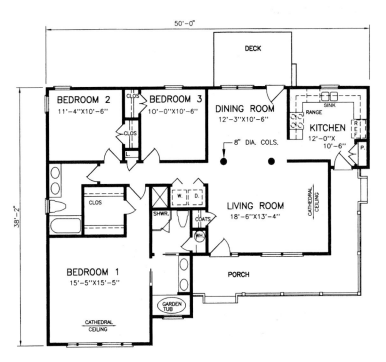

Copyright by designer/architect.

Images provided by designer/architect.

Plan #151035

Dimensions: 37'8" W x 38'4" D

Levels: 1.5

Heated Square Footage: 1,451

Main Level Sq. Ft.: 868

Upper Level Sq. Ft: 583

Bedrooms: 3

Bathrooms: 2

Foundation: Crawl space or slab

CompleteCost List Available: Yes

Price Category: B

Features:

- Den: The large stone fireplace is the focal point in this gathering area. Located just off the entry porch, the area welcomes you home.

- Kitchen: This efficiently designed kitchen has an abundance of cabinets and counter space. The eat-at counter, open to the den, adds extra space for family and friends.

- Grilling Porch: On nice days, overflow your dinner guests onto this rear covered grilling porch. From the relaxing area you can watch the kids play in the backyard.

- Upper Level: Two bedrooms, with large closets, and a full bathroom occupy this level. The dormers in each of the bedrooms add more space to these rooms.

Country living meets the modern day family in this well designed home.

Kitchen/Den

Porch

Kitchen

Master Bedroom

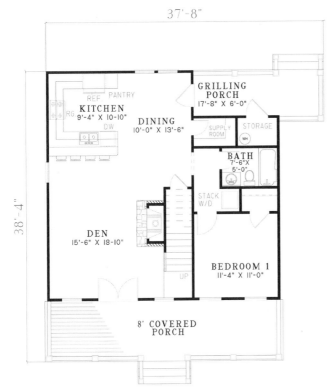

Main Level Floor Plan

37'-8"

38'-4"

GRILLING PORCH
17'-8" X 6'-0"

REF. PANTRY

KITCHEN
9'-4" X 10'-10"

RG

DW

DINING
10'-0" X 13'-6"

SUPPLY ROOM

STORAGE

WH

BATH
7'-6" X 5'-0"

STACK W/D

DEN
15'-6" X 18'-10"

UP

BEDROOM 1
11'-4" X 11'-0"

8' COVERED PORCH

Den

Upper Level Floor Plan

Images provided by designer/architect.

BATH
7'-8" X 7'-0"

6'4" WALL

6'4" WALL

LIN

R.A.

8' LINE

BEDROOM 2
13'-4" X 14'-6"

DN.

BEDROOM 3
11'-4" X 14'-5"

8' LINE

8' LINE

4' WALL

4' WALL

Dining Room

Plan #221016

Dimensions: 56' W x 42' D

Levels: 1

Heated Square Footage: 1,461

Bedrooms: 3

Bathrooms: 2

Foundation: Basement

Materials List Available: No

Price Category: B

Images provided by designer/architect.

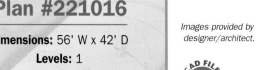

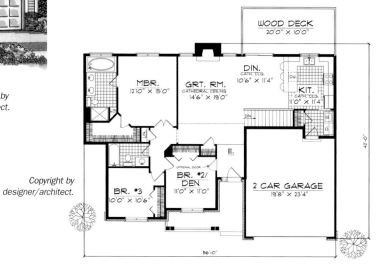

Rear Elevation

Copyright by designer/architect.

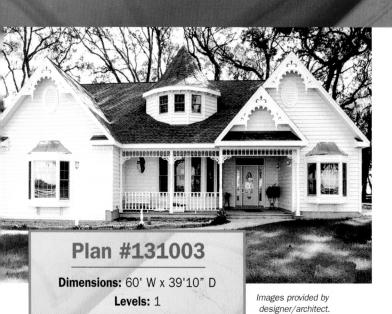

Plan #131003

Dimensions: 60' W x 39'10" D

Levels: 1

Heated Square Footage: 1,466

Bedrooms: 3

Bathrooms: 2

Foundation: Basement, crawl space, or slab

Materials List Available: No

Price Category: C

Images provided by designer/architect.

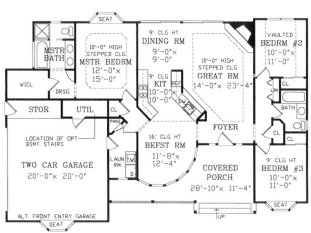

Copyright by designer/architect.

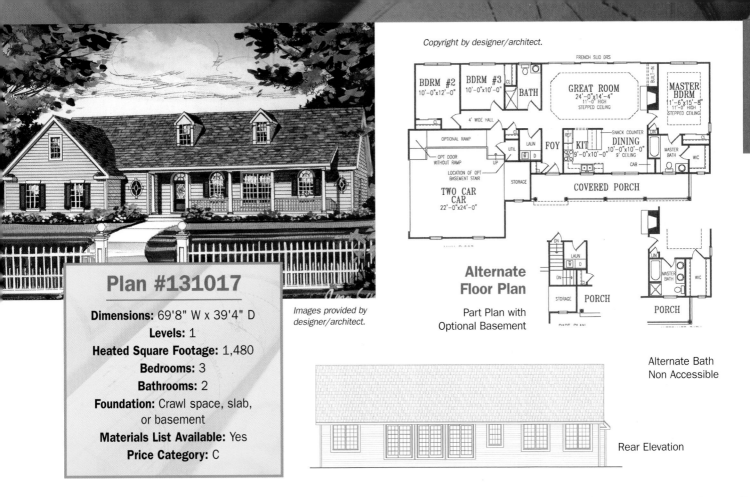

BDRM #2
10'-0"x12'-0"

BDRM #3
10'-0"x10'-0"

BATH

GREAT ROOM
24'-0"x14'-4"
11'-0" HIGH
STEPPED CEILING

FRENCH SLID DRS

MASTER BDRM
11'-6"x15'-8"
11'-0" HIGH
STEPPED CEILING

4' WIDE HALL

OPTIONAL RAMP

OPT DOOR
WITHOUT RAMP

LOCATION OF OPT
BASEMENT STAIR

UTIL

LAUN

UP

FOY

KIT
9'-0"x10'-0"

DINING
10'-0"x10'-0"
9' CEILING

SNACK COUNTER

MASTER BATH

WIC

TWO CAR
CAR
22'-0"x24'-0"

STORAGE

COVERED PORCH

Alternate Floor Plan

Part Plan with Optional Basement

DN

DN

W D

STORAGE

PORCH

PART PLAN

LIN

MASTER BATH

WIC

PORCH

Alternate Bath
Non Accessible

Images provided by designer/architect.

Rear Elevation

Plan #131017

Dimensions: 69'8" W x 39'4" D
Levels: 1
Heated Square Footage: 1,480
Bedrooms: 3
Bathrooms: 2
Foundation: Crawl space, slab, or basement
Materials List Available: Yes
Price Category: C

Plan #151797

Dimensions: 53' W x 41'10" D
Levels: 1
Heated Square Footage: 1,480
Bedrooms: 3
Bathrooms: 2
Foundation: Crawl space
CompleteCost List Available: Yes
Price Category: B

Images provided by designer/architect.

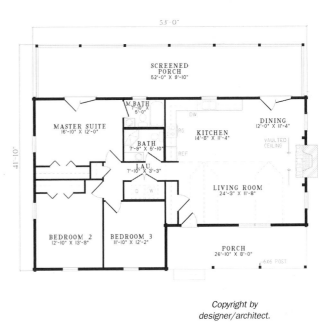

53'-0"

SCREENED PORCH
52'-0" X 9'-10"

M.BATH
5'-0"

MASTER SUITE
16'-10" X 12'-0"

BATH
7'-9" X 6'-10"

LAU.
7'-10" X 3'-3"

KITCHEN
14'-8" X 11'-4"

DINING
12'-0" X 11'-4"

VAULTED CEILING

LIVING ROOM
24'-3" X 11'-8"

41'-10"

BEDROOM 2
12'-0" X 13'-8"

BEDROOM 3
11'-10" X 12'-2"

PORCH
26'-10" X 8'-0"

6x6 POST

Copyright by designer/architect.

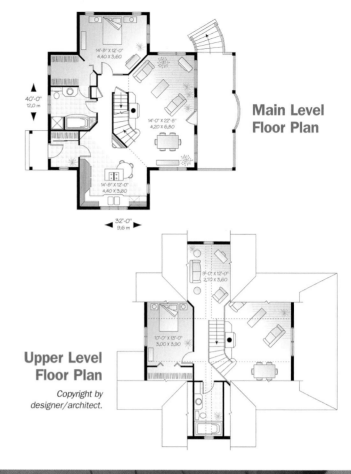

**Main Level
Floor Plan**

14'-8" X 12'-0"
4,40 X 3,60

40'-0"
12,0 m

14'-0" X 22'-8"
4,20 X 6,80

14'-8" X 12'-0"
4,40 X 3,60

32'-0"
9,6 m

9'-0" X 12'-0"
2,70 X 3,60

**Upper Level
Floor Plan**

10'-0" X 13'-0"
3,00 X 3,90

*Copyright by
designer/architect.*

Plan #181120

Dimensions: 32' W x 40' D
Levels: 2
Heated Square Footage: 1,480
Main Level Sq. Ft.: 1,024
Second Level Sq. Ft.: 456
Bedrooms: 2
Bathrooms: 2
Foundation: Basement, or walkout
Materials List Available: Yes
Price Category: C

*Images provided by
designer/architect.*

Plan #351020

Dimensions: 54' W x 48' D
Levels: 1
Heated Square Footage: 1,488
Bedrooms: 3
Bathrooms: 2
Foundation: Crawl space, slab,
or basement
Materials List Available: Yes
Price Category: D

*Images provided by
designer/architect.*

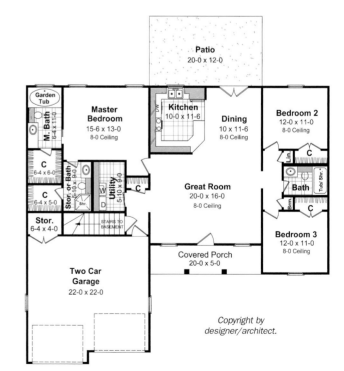

Patio
20-0 x 12-0

Garden
Tub

Master
Bedroom
15-6 x 13-0
8-0 Ceiling

Kitchen
10-0 x 11-6

Dining
10 x 11-6
8-0 Ceiling

Bedroom 2
12-0 x 11-0
8-0 Ceiling

M. Bath
6-4 x 11-0

C
6-4 x 6-0

C
6-4 x 5-0

Stor. or Bath
5-10 x 9-0

Utility
5-10 x 9-0

W
D

Great Room
20-0 x 16-0
8-0 Ceiling

Lin.

C

Bath

Tub/Shr.

C

Stor.
6-4 x 4-0

STAIRS TO
BASEMENT

Bedroom 3
12-0 x 11-0
8-0 Ceiling

Covered Porch
20-0 x 5-0

Two Car
Garage
22-0 x 22-0

*Copyright by
designer/architect.*

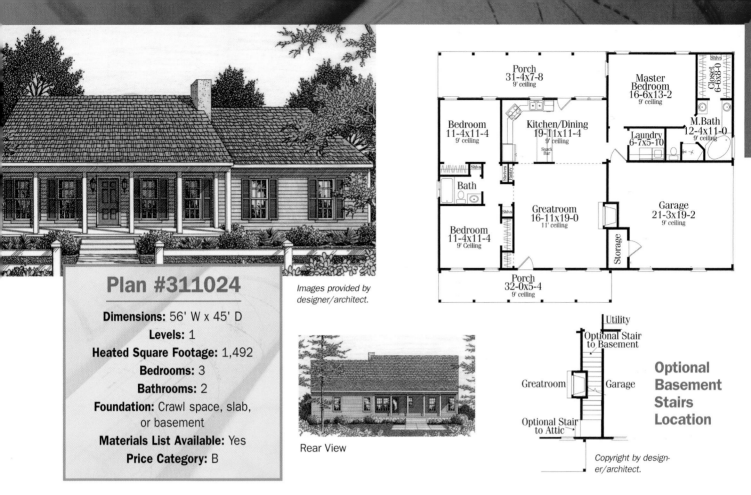

Porch
31-4x7-8
9' ceiling

Master Bedroom
16-6x13-2
9' ceiling

Closet
6-6x8-0

Bedroom
11-4x11-4
9' ceiling

Kitchen/Dining
19-11x11-4
9' ceiling

M.Bath
12-4x11-0
9' ceiling

Laundry
6-7x5-10

Bath

Greatroom
16-11x19-0
11' ceiling

Garage
21-3x19-2
9' ceiling

Bedroom
11-4x11-4
9' Ceiling

Storage

Porch
32-0x5-4
9' ceiling

Images provided by designer/architect.

Rear View

Utility

Optional Stair to Basement

Greatroom

Garage

Optional Stair to Attic

Optional Basement Stairs Location

Copyright by designer/architect.

Plan #311024

Dimensions: 56' W x 45' D

Levels: 1

Heated Square Footage: 1,492

Bedrooms: 3

Bathrooms: 2

Foundation: Crawl space, slab, or basement

Materials List Available: Yes

Price Category: B

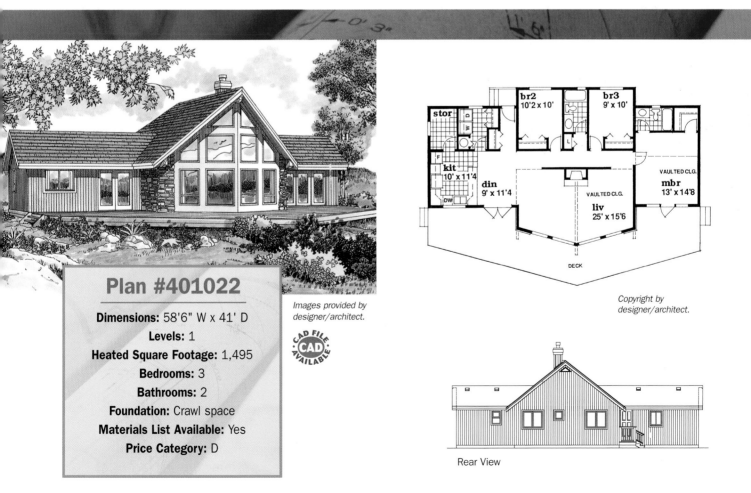

stor

br2
10'2 x 10'

br3
9' x 10'

W D

kit
10' x 11'4

F

DW

din
9' x 11'4

VAULTED CLG.

VAULTED CLG.

mbr
13' x 14'8

liv
25' x 15'6

DECK

Copyright by designer/architect.

Rear View

Plan #401022

Dimensions: 58'6" W x 41' D

Levels: 1

Heated Square Footage: 1,495

Bedrooms: 3

Bathrooms: 2

Foundation: Crawl space

Materials List Available: Yes

Price Category: D

Images provided by designer/architect.

CAD FILE AVAILABLE

Plan #131013

Dimensions: 50' W x 41'8" D

Levels: 1

Heated Square Footage: 1,489

Bedrooms: 3

Bathrooms: 2

Foundation: Crawl space, slab, basement, or walkout

Materials List Available: Yes

Price Category: C

Images provided by designer/architect.

You'll love the Victorian details on the exterior of this charming ranch-style home.

Features:

- Front Porch: This porch is large enough so that you can sit out on warm summer nights to catch a breeze or create a garden of potted ornamentals.

- Great Room: Running from the front of the house to the rear, this great room is bathed in natural light from both directions. The volume ceiling adds a luxurious feeling to it, and the fireplace creates a cozy place on chilly afternoons.

- Kitchen: Cooking will be a pleasure in this kitchen, thanks to the thoughtful layout and well-designed work areas.

- Master Suite: Enjoy the quiet in this room, where it will be easy to relax and unwind, no matter what the time of day. The walk-in closet gives you plenty of storage space, and you're sure to appreciate both the privacy and large size of the master bath.

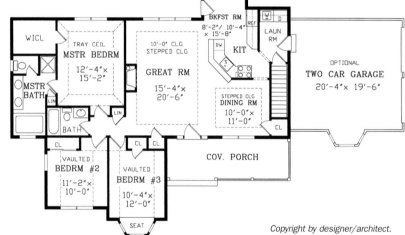

Copyright by designer/architect.

Rear Elevation

Plan #351021

Dimensions: 61' W x 47'4" D

Levels: 1

Heated Square Footage: 1,500

Bedrooms: 3

Bathrooms: 2

Foundation: Crawl space, slab, or basement

Materials List Available: Yes

Price Category: E

This lovely home provides a functional split-floor-plan layout with many of the features that your family desires.

Features:

- **Great Room:** This large gathering area, with a vaulted ceiling, has a gas log fireplace.

- **Kitchen:** This open kitchen layout has plenty of counter space for that growing family.

- **Master Suite:** This expansive master bedroom and bath has plenty of storage space in its separate walk-in closets.

- **Garage:** This two-car garage has a storage area.

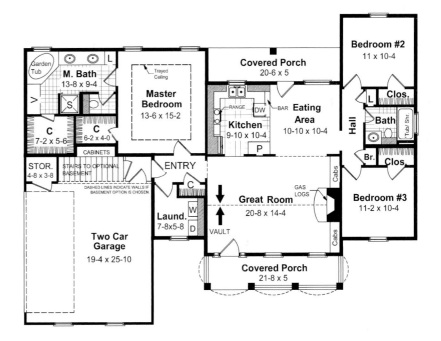

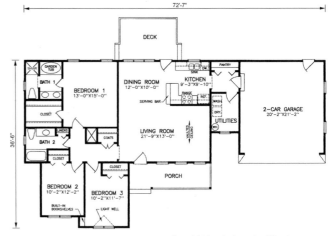

Copyright by designer/architect.

Plan #341071

Dimensions: 72'7" W x 38'6" D
Levels: 1
Heated Square Footage: 1,500
Bedrooms: 3
Bathrooms: 2
Foundation: Crawl space; slab or basement for fee
Materials List Available: Yes
Price Category: C

Images provided by designer/architect.

CAD FILE AVAILABLE

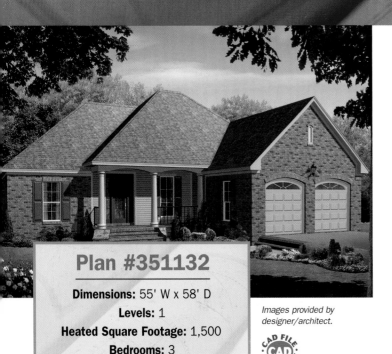

Plan #351132

Dimensions: 55' W x 58' D
Levels: 1
Heated Square Footage: 1,500
Bedrooms: 3
Bathrooms: 2
Foundation: Crawl space or slab
Material List Available: Yes
Price Category: E

Images provided by designer/architect.

CAD FILE AVAILABLE

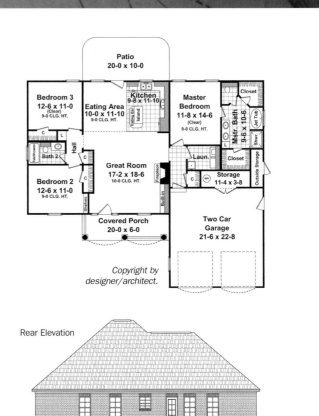

Copyright by designer/architect.

Rear Elevation

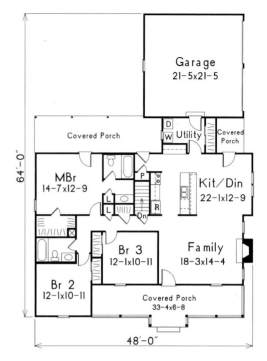

Plan #321015

Dimensions: 48' W x 64' D

Levels: 1

Heated Square Footage: 1,501

Bedrooms: 3

Bathrooms: 2

Foundation: Crawl space, slab, or basement

Materials List Available: Yes

Price Category: C

Images provided by designer/architect.

CAD FILE AVAILABLE

Copyright by designer/architect.

Garage 21-5x21-5
Covered Porch
Utility
Covered Porch
MBr 14-7x12-9
Kit/Din 22-1x12-9
Br 3 12-1x10-11
Family 18-3x14-4
Br 2 12-1x10-11
Covered Porch 33-4x6-8
64'-0"
48'-0"

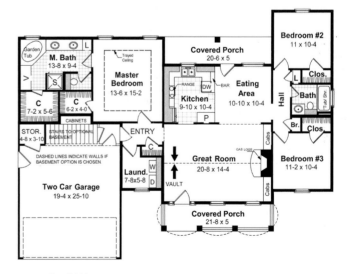

Plan #351005

Dimensions: 61' W x 47'4" D

Levels: 1

Heated Square Footage: 1,501

Bedrooms: 3

Bathrooms: 2

Foundation: Crawl space, slab, or basement

Materials List Available: Yes

Price Category: E

Images provided by designer/architect.

CAD FILE AVAILABLE

Copyright by designer/architect.

Garden Tub
M. Bath 13-8 x 9-4
Trayed Ceiling
Master Bedroom 13-6 x 15-2
Covered Porch 20-6 x 5
Bedroom #2 11 x 10-4
Clos.
Bath
Eating Area 10-10 x 10-4
Kitchen 9-10 x 10-4
RANGE DW BAR
Hall
C 7-2 x 5-6
C 6-2 x 4-0
CABINETS
STOR. 4-8 x 3-10
STAIRS TO OPTIONAL BASEMENT
ENTRY
DASHED LINES INDICATE WALLS IF BASEMENT OPTION IS CHOSEN
Laund. 7-8x5-8
Great Room 20-8 x 14-4
GAS LOGS
Bedroom #3 11-2 x 10-4
Clos.
Two Car Garage 19-4 x 25-10
VAULT
Covered Porch 21-8 x 5

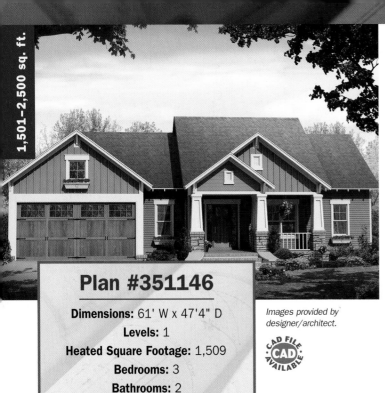

1,501-2,500 sq. ft.

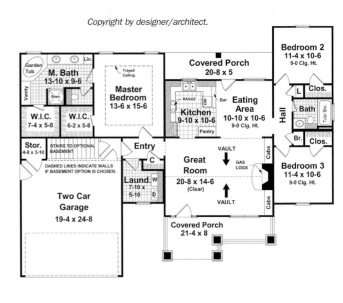

Garden Tub

M. Bath
13-10 x 9-6

Trayed Ceiling

Master Bedroom
13-6 x 15-6

Covered Porch
20-8 x 5

Bedroom 2
11-4 x 10-6
9-0 Clg. Ht.

Vanity

Shwr

RANGE

Bar

DW

Eating Area
10-10 x 10-6
9-0 Clg. Ht.

Clos.

W.I.C.
7-4 x 5-8

W.I.C.
6-2 x 5-8

Kitchen
9-10 x 10-6

Pantry

Hall

Bath

Tub/ Shr

Stor.
4-8 x 3-10

STAIRS TO OPTIONAL BASEMENT

Entry

C

VAULT

GAS LOGS

Br.

Clos.

DASHED LINES INDICATE WALLS IF BASEMENT OPTION IS CHOSEN.

Great Room
20-8 x 14-6
(Clear)

Cabs

Bedroom 3
11-4 x 10-6
9-0 Clg. Ht.

Laund.
7-10 x 5-10

W

D

VAULT

Cabs

Two Car Garage
19-4 x 24-8

Covered Porch
21-4 x 8

CAD FILE AVAILABLE

Plan #351146

Dimensions: 61' W x 47'4" D

Levels: 1

Heated Square Footage: 1,509

Bedrooms: 3

Bathrooms: 2

Foundation: Crawl space, slab or basement

Material List Available: Yes

Price Category: C

Rear View

Plan #151169

Dimensions: 51'6" W x 49'10" D

Levels: 1

Heated Square Footage: 1,525

Bedrooms: 3

Bathrooms: 2

Foundation: Crawl space, slab, basement, or daylight basement

CompleteCost List Available: Yes

Price Category: C

CAD FILE AVAILABLE

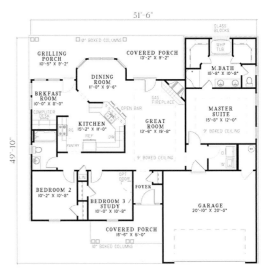

51'-6"

GLASS BLOCKS

GRILLING PORCH
10'-5" X 9'-2"

10" BOXED COLUMNS

COVERED PORCH
13'-2" X 9'-2"

WHP TUB

M.BATH
15'-8" X 10'-8"

DINING ROOM
11'-0" X 9'-6"

BRKFAST ROOM
10'-0" X 8'-0"

GAS FIREPLACE

OPEN BAR

MASTER SUITE
15'-8" X 12'-0"

9' BOXED CEILING

49'-10"

COMPUTER DESK

KITCHEN
15'-2" X 11'-0"

REF

GREAT ROOM
13'-6" X 19'-8"

PANTRY

9' BOXED CEILING

BEDROOM 2
10'-2" X 10'-8"

OPT. DOOR

FOYER

GARAGE
20'-10" X 20'-0"

BEDROOM 3 / STUDY
10'-0" X 10'-8"

COVERED PORCH
18'-6" X 5'-0"

10" BOXED COLUMNS

Rear Elevation

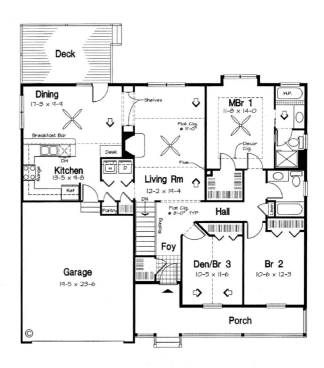

Plan #391039

Dimensions: 50' W x 45'4" D

Levels: 1

Heated Square Footage: 1,539

Bedrooms: 3

Bathrooms: 2

Foundation: Crawl space, basement, slab

Materials List Available: Yes

Price Category: C

Images provided by designer/architect.

Copyright by designer/architect.

Plan #251004

Dimensions: 50'9" W x 42'1" D

Levels: 1

Heated Square Footage: 1,550

Bedrooms: 3

Bathrooms: 2

Foundation: Crawl space, slab

Materials List Available: Yes

Price Category: C

Images provided by designer/architect.

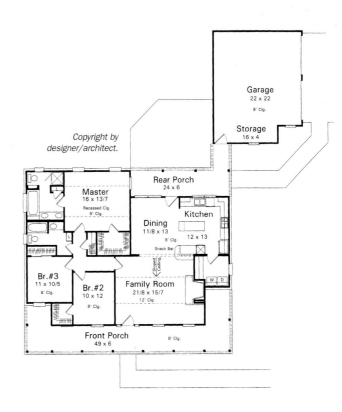

Copyright by designer/architect.

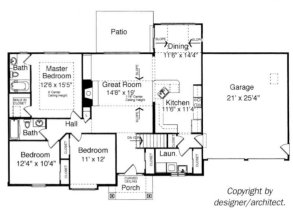

Copyright by designer/architect.

Images provided by designer/architect.

Rear Elevation

Plan #161090

Dimensions: 69'4" W x 42'4" D

Levels: 1

Heated Square Footage: 1,563

Bedrooms: 3

Bathrooms: 2

Foundation: Basement

Materials List Available: Yes

Price Category: C

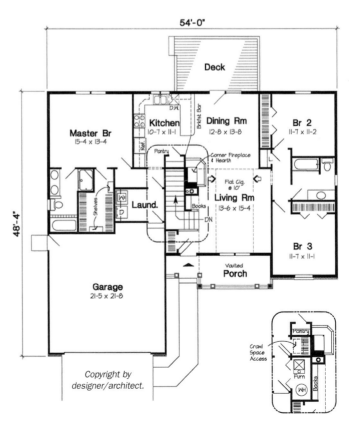

Copyright by designer/architect.

Images provided by designer/architect.

Plan #391021

Dimensions: 54' W x 48'4" D

Levels: 1

Heated Square Footage: 1,568

Bedrooms: 3

Bathrooms: 2

Foundation: Crawl space, basement, slab

Materials List Available: Yes

Price Category: C

Copyright by designer/architect.

Master Bedroom 15'3" x 12 (9' ceiling height)

Dining 12'4" x 12

Porch 11'4" x 10'9"

Great Room 18'2" x 17

Kitchen 17'4" x 9'6"

Storage 7' x 14'8"

pantry

Bath

walk-in closet

Hall

Bath

Foyer

Laun.

Two-car Garage 20' x 22'

Bedroom 11' x 10'2"

Bedroom 10'6" x 11'

Porch

slope ceiling   slope ceiling

60'

48'10"

Images provided by designer/architect.

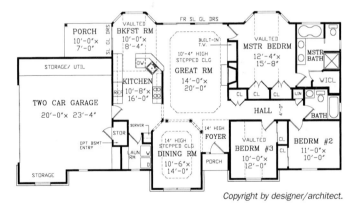

Rear Elevation

Plan #161005

Dimensions: 60' W x 48'10" D
Levels: 1
Heated Square Footage: 1,593
Bedrooms: 3
Bathrooms: 2
Foundation: Basement
Materials List Available: Yes
Price Category: C

Plan #131005

Dimensions: 70' W x 37'4" D
Levels: 1
Heated Square Footage: 1,595
Bedrooms: 3
Bathrooms: 2
Foundation: Crawl space, slab, or basement
Materials List Available: Yes
Price Category: D

Images provided by designer/architect.

PORCH 10'-0" x 7'-0"

VAULTED BKFST RM 10'-0" x 8'-4"

FR SL GL DRS

BUILT-IN T.V.

VAULTED MSTR BEDRM 12'-4" x 15'-8"

MSTR BATH

STORAGE/ UTIL

10'-4" HIGH STEPPED CLG

GREAT RM 14'-0" x 20'-0"

WICL

TWO CAR GARAGE 20'-0" x 23'-4"

KITCHEN 10'-8" x 16'-0"

CL   CL   CL   LIN

HALL

BATH

SERVER

STOR

OPT BSMT ENTRY

LAUN RM

14' HIGH STEPPED CLG

DINING RM 10'-6" x 14'-0"

14' HIGH STEPPED CLG

FOYER

PORCH

VAULTED BEDRM #3 10'-0" x 12'-0"

BEDRM #2 11'-0" x 10'-0"

STORAGE

Copyright by designer/architect.

SMARTtip

Create a Courtyard

Create a private walled-garden retreat with fences covered by climbing vines. Add height with trellises, and divide spaces with clipped boxwood hedges. Include an (almost) instant patio by digging away an area of sod and then covering it with a layer of sand and landscaping mesh to discourage weeds. Then cover it with pea gravel, and add a garden bench, statuary, and perhaps an antique or two. The result? European ambiance for even the most nondescript suburban yard.

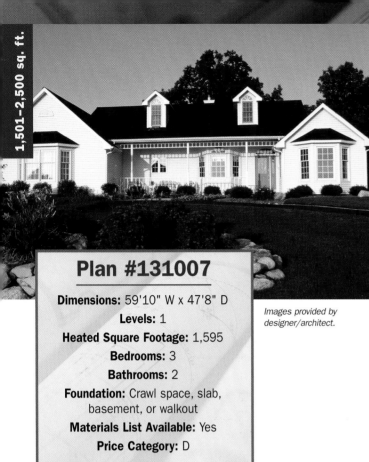

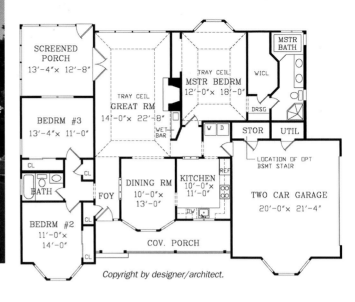

Copyright by designer/architect.

Plan #131007

Dimensions: 59'10" W x 47'8" D

Levels: 1

Heated Square Footage: 1,595

Bedrooms: 3

Bathrooms: 2

Foundation: Crawl space, slab, basement, or walkout

Materials List Available: Yes

Price Category: D

Images provided by designer/architect.

Rear Elevation

SMARTtip

Brackets in Window Treatments

Although it is rarely noticed, a bracket plays an important role in supporting rods and poles. If a treatment rubs against a window frame, an extension bracket solves the problem. It projects from the wall at an adjustable length, providing enough clearance. A hold-down bracket anchors a cellular shade or a blind to the bottom of a door, preventing the treatment from moving when the door is opened or closed.

Plan #211030

Dimensions: 75' W x 37' D

Levels: 1

Heated Square Footage: 1,600

Bedrooms: 3

Bathrooms: 2

Foundation: Slab

Materials List Available: Yes

Price Category: C

Images provided by designer/architect.

Copyright by designer/architect.

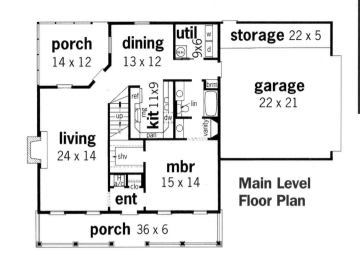

porch 14 x 12

dining 13 x 12

util 9 x 6

storage 22 x 5

garage 22 x 21

living 24 x 14

kit 11 x 9

ref

up

mbr 15 x 14

ent

porch 36 x 6

Main Level Floor Plan

Images provided by designer/architect.

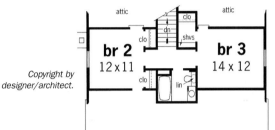

CAD FILE AVAILABLE

Plan #211069

Dimensions: 58' W x 42' D

Levels: 1½

Heated Square Footage: 1,600

Main Level Sq. Ft.: 1,136

Upper Level Sq. Ft.: 464

Bedrooms: 3

Bathrooms: 2

Foundation: Crawl space

Materials List Available: Yes

Price Category: C

Copyright by designer/architect.

attic | attic

br 2 12 x 11

br 3 14 x 12

Upper Level Floor Plan

Plan #161007

Dimensions: 66'4" W x 43'10" D

Levels: 1

Heated Square Footage: 1,611

Bedrooms: 3

Bathrooms: 2

Foundation: Basement; crawl space option for fee

Materials List Available: Yes

Price Category: C

Images provided by designer/architect.

CAD FILE AVAILABLE

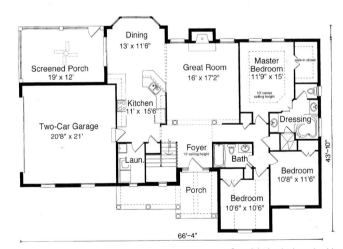

Screened Porch 19' x 12'

Dining 13' x 11'6"

Great Room 16' x 17'2"

Master Bedroom 11'9" x 15'

walk-in closet

Kitchen 11' x 15'6"

Two-Car Garage 20'8" x 21'

Dressing

Foyer 10' ceiling height

Laun.

Bath

Porch

Bedroom 10'8" x 11'6"

Bedroom 10'6" x 10'6"

66'-4"

43'-10"

Copyright by designer/architect.

Rear Elevation

Plan #281022

Dimensions: 48' W x 58' D
Levels: 1
Heated Square Footage: 1,506
Bedrooms: 3
Bathrooms: 2
Foundation: Basement
Material List Available: Yes
Price Category: C

Images provided by designer/architect.

Rear View

You'll spend hours enjoying the sunshine on this home's wraparound porch and gazebo.

CAD FILE AVAILABLE

Features:

- **Porch:** Stretching from the front to the back of the house, this porch has a gazebo on one corner and becomes a covered deck at the back.

- **Great Room:** This beautiful great room includes a three-sided fireplace and French doors that open out onto the porch by the gazebo.

- **Kitchen:** Divided from the dining room and great room by an island with a raised snack bar, this kitchen also has French doors nearby that open out to the covered deck, a wonderful location for outdoor meals.

- **Master Suite:** Close to the secondary bedrooms, this master suite includes a spacious walk-in closet, a whirlpool tub, and a dual-sink vanity.

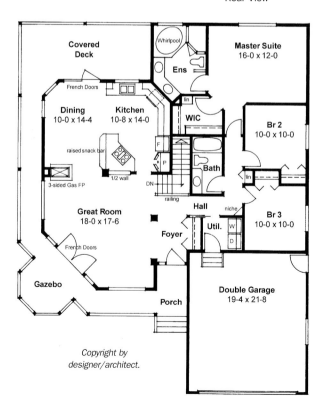

Copyright by designer/architect.

Plan #441003

Dimensions: 50' W x 48' D
Levels: 1
Heated Square Footage: 1,580
Bedrooms: 3
Bathrooms: 2½
Foundation: Crawl space;
slab or basement available for fee
Materials List Available: No
Price Category: C

Images provided by designer/architect.

Craftsman styling with modern floor planning—that's the advantage of this cozy design. Covered porches at front and back enhance both the look and the livability of the plan.

Features:

- **Great Room:** This vaulted entertaining area boasts a corner fireplace and a built-in media center. The area is open to the kitchen and the dining area.

- **Kitchen:** This large, open island kitchen will please the chef in the family. The raised bar is open to the dining area and the great room.

- **Master Suite:** Look for luxurious amenities such as double sinks and a separate tub and shower in the master bath. The master bedroom has a vaulted ceiling and a walk-in closet with built-in shelves.

- **Bedrooms:** Two secondary bedrooms are located away from the master suite. Each has a large closet and access to a common bathroom.

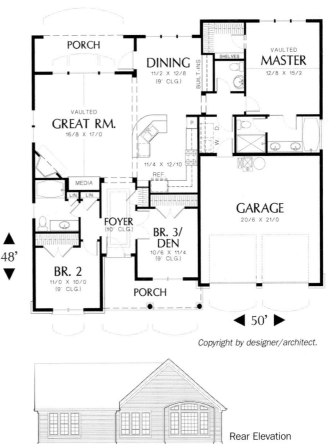

Copyright by designer/architect.

Rear Elevation

Plan #131001

Dimensions: 72'4" W x 32'4" D

Levels: 1

Heated Square Footage: 1,615

Bedrooms: 3

Bathrooms: 2

Foundation: Crawl space, slab, basement, or walkout

Materials List Available: Yes

Price Category: D

Images provided by designer/architect.

Copyright by designer/architect.

Plan #181128

Dimensions: 36' W x 36' D

Levels: 2

Heated Square Footage: 1,634

Main Level Sq. Ft.: 1,087

Second Level Sq. Ft.: 547

Bedrooms: 3

Bathrooms: 2

Foundation: Basement, or daylight basement

Materials List Available: Yes

Price Category: D

Images provided by designer/architect.

CAD FILE AVAILABLE

Upper Level Floor Plan

Main Level Floor Plan

Copyright by designer/architect.

Plan #151043

Dimensions: 53' W x 59'10" D

Levels: 1

Heated Square Footage: 1,636

Bedrooms: 3

Bathrooms: 2

Foundation: Crawl space, slab; basement option for fee

CompleteCost List Available: Yes

Price Category: C

Images provided by designer/architect.

Copyright by designer/architect.

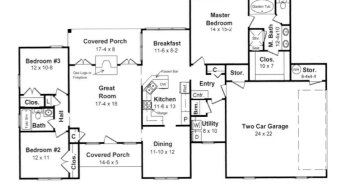

Plan #351006

Dimensions: 64' W x 39' D

Levels: 1

Heated Square Footage: 1,638

Bedrooms: 3

Bathrooms: 2

Foundation: Crawl space, slab, or basement

Materials List Available: Yes

Price Category: D

Images provided by designer/architect.

Stair Location for Basement Option

Copyright by designer/architect.

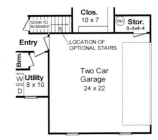

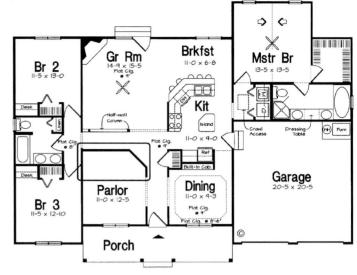

Images provided by designer/architect.

CAD FILE AVAILABLE

Plan #391038

Dimensions: 59' W x 44' D

Levels: 1

Heated Square Footage: 1,642

Bedrooms: 3

Bathrooms: 2

Foundation: Crawl space, slab, and basement

Materials List Available: Yes

Price Category: C

Copyright by designer/architect.

Optional Basement Stairs

Images provided by designer/architect.

Copyright by designer/architect.

Plan #161009

Dimensions: 60'9" W x 49' D

Levels: 1

Heated Square Footage: 1,651

Bedrooms: 3

Bathrooms: 2

Foundation: Basement

Materials List Available: No

Price Category: C

Rear Elevation

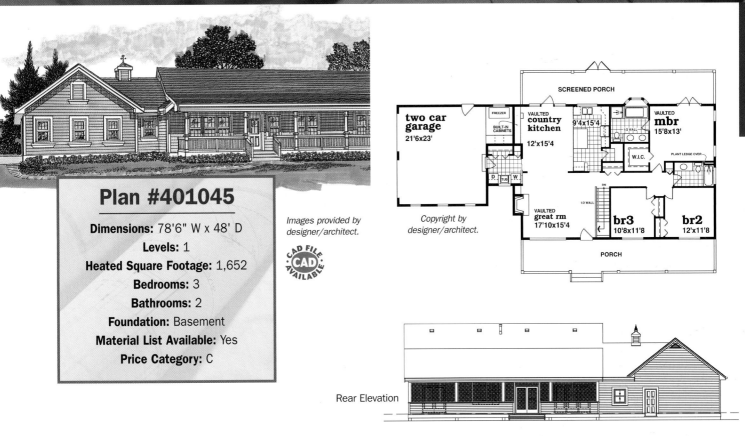

Plan #401045

Dimensions: 78'6" W x 48' D

Levels: 1

Heated Square Footage: 1,652

Bedrooms: 3

Bathrooms: 2

Foundation: Basement

Material List Available: Yes

Price Category: C

Images provided by designer/architect.

Copyright by designer/architect.

Rear Elevation

Plan #351098

Dimensions: 51'8" W x 60' D

Levels: 1

Heated Square Footage: 1,655

Bedrooms: 3

Bathrooms: 2

Foundation: Crawl space or slab

Material List Available: Yes

Price Category: E

Images provided by designer/architect.

Copyright by designer/architect.

Plan #351033

Dimensions: 64' W x 39' D

Levels: 1

Heated Square Footage: 1,654

Bedrooms: 3

Bathrooms: 2

Foundation: Crawl space, slab, or basement

Materials List Available: Yes

Price Category: E

This gorgeous three-bedroom brick home would be the perfect place to raise your family.

Features:

- Great Room: This terrific room has a gas fireplace with built-in cabinets on either side.

- Kitchen: This island kitchen with breakfast area is open to the great room.

- Master Suite: This private room features a vaulted ceiling and a large walk-in closet. The bath area has a walk-in closet, jetted tub, and double vanities.

- Bedrooms: The two additional bedrooms share a bathroom located in the hall.

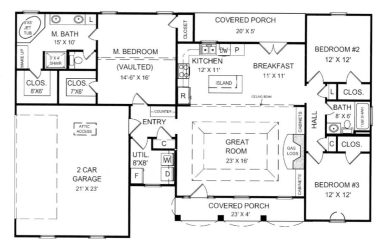

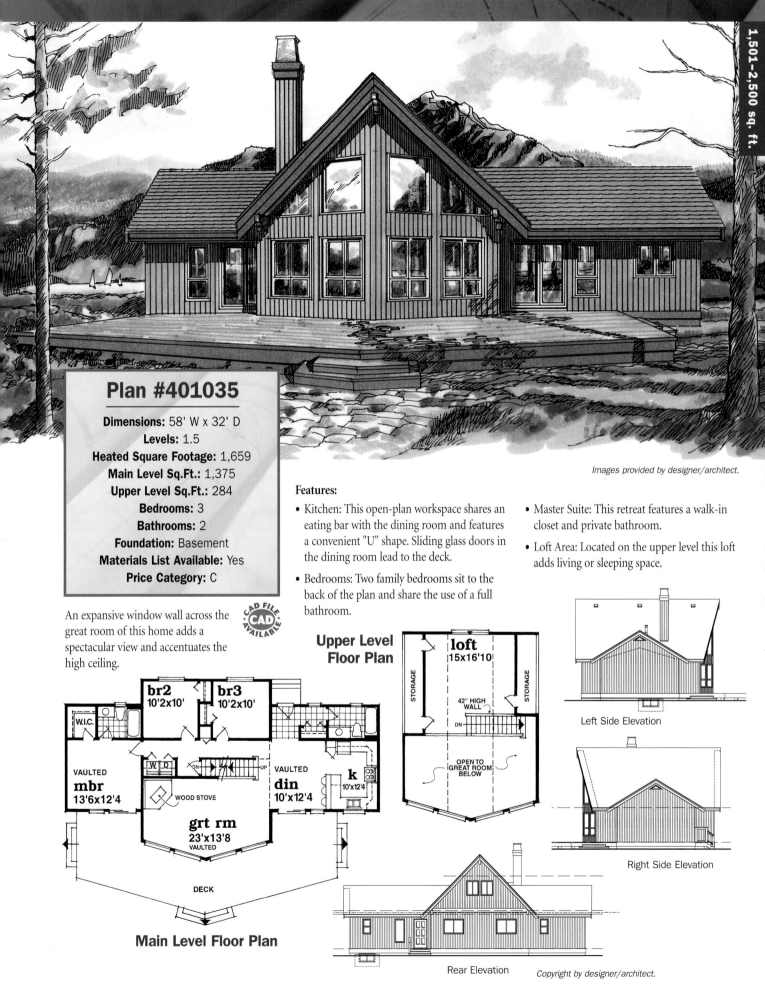

Plan #401035

Dimensions: 58' W x 32' D

Levels: 1.5

Heated Square Footage: 1,659

Main Level Sq.Ft.: 1,375

Upper Level Sq.Ft.: 284

Bedrooms: 3

Bathrooms: 2

Foundation: Basement

Materials List Available: Yes

Price Category: C

Images provided by designer/architect.

Features:

- **Kitchen:** This open-plan workspace shares an eating bar with the dining room and features a convenient "U" shape. Sliding glass doors in the dining room lead to the deck.

- **Bedrooms:** Two family bedrooms sit to the back of the plan and share the use of a full bathroom.

- **Master Suite:** This retreat features a walk-in closet and private bathroom.

- **Loft Area:** Located on the upper level this loft adds living or sleeping space.

An expansive window wall across the great room of this home adds a spectacular view and accentuates the high ceiling.

CAD FILE AVAILABLE

Upper Level Floor Plan

loft 15x16'10

STORAGE STORAGE

42" HIGH WALL

DN

OPEN TO GREAT ROOM BELOW

Main Level Floor Plan

W.I.C.

br2 10'2x10'

br3 10'2x10'

VAULTED mbr 13'6x12'4

W D WOOD STOVE

DN UP

VAULTED din 10'x12'4

k 10'x12'4

grt rm 23'x13'8 VAULTED

DECK

Left Side Elevation

Right Side Elevation

Rear Elevation

Copyright by designer/architect.

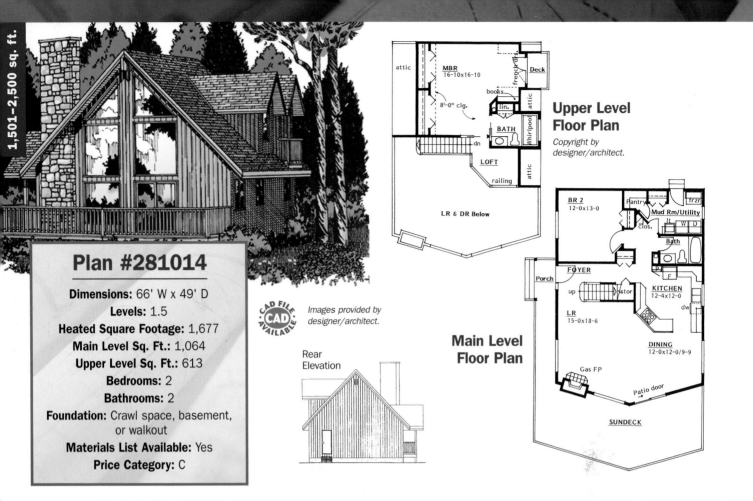

Upper Level Floor Plan

Copyright by designer/architect.

Main Level Floor Plan

attic
MBR 16-10x16-10
Deck
books
8'-0" clg.
lin.
BATH
Whirlpool
LOFT
dn
railing
attic
LR & DR Below

BR 2 12-0x13-0
Pantry
Mud Rm/Utility
W D
Clos.
Bath
FOYER
Porch
up
stor
KITCHEN 12-4x12-0
LR 15-0x18-6
dw
DINING 12-0x12-0/9-9
Gas FP
Patio door
SUNDECK

Plan #281014

Dimensions: 66' W x 49' D
Levels: 1.5
Heated Square Footage: 1,677
Main Level Sq. Ft.: 1,064
Upper Level Sq. Ft.: 613
Bedrooms: 2
Bathrooms: 2
Foundation: Crawl space, basement, or walkout
Materials List Available: Yes
Price Category: C

Images provided by designer/architect.

Rear Elevation

1,501-2,500 sq. ft.

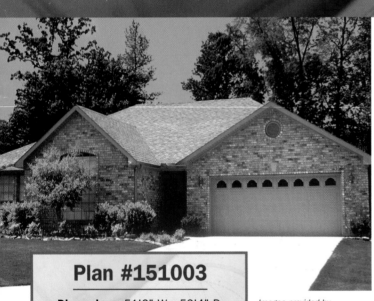

Plan #151003

Dimensions: 51'6" W x 52'4" D
Levels: 1
Heated Square Footage: 1,680
Bedrooms: 3
Bathrooms: 2
Foundation: Crawl space, slab, basement, or walkout
CompleteCost List Available: Yes
Price Category: C

Images provided by designer/architect.

This home, as shown in the photograph, may differ from the actual blueprints. For more detailed information, please check the floor plans carefully.

51'-6"
52'-4"
MASTER SUITE 20'-10" X 13'-0" 9' PAN CEILING
BEDROOM 2 12'-4" X 10'-0"
GREAT ROOM 17'-0" X 20'-0" 9' PAN CEILING
LAU.
M.B. 7'-6" X 10'-0"
STRG.
BATH
GARAGE 20'-10" X 20'-0"
BEDROOM 3 12'-4" X 11'-8"
KITCHEN 12'-0" X 12'-0"
FOYER
DINING 12'-0" X 10'-0"
VAULTED CEILING
PRCH

Copyright by designer/architect.

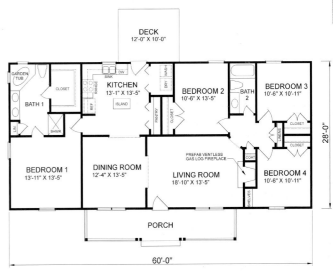

DECK
12'-0" X 10'-0"

GARDEN TUB

CLOSET

BATH 1

LIN

SHWR

KITCHEN
13'-1" X 13'-5"

SINK DW

RANGE

REF

ISLAND

DRY WASH

PANTRY

CLOSET

BEDROOM 2
10'-6" X 13'-5"

BATH 2

BEDROOM 3
10'-6" X 10'-11"

28'-0"

BEDROOM 1
13'-11" X 13'-5"

DINING ROOM
12'-4" X 13'-5"

PREFAB VENTLESS GAS LOG FIREPLACE

LIVING ROOM
18'-10" X 13'-5"

COAT

SHELVES

LINENS

CLOSET

CLOSET

BEDROOM 4
10'-6" X 10'-11"

PORCH

60'-0"

Images provided by designer/architect.

CAD FILE AVAILABLE

Copyright by designer/architect.

Plan #341035

Dimensions: 60' W x 28' D

Levels: 1

Heated Square Footage: 1,680

Bedrooms: 4

Bathrooms: 2

Foundation: Crawl space, slab; basement option for fee

Materials List Available: Yes

Price Category: C

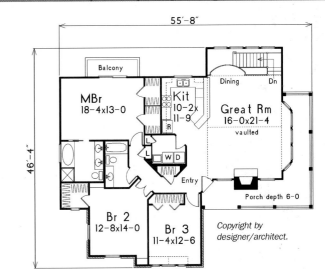

55'-8"

Balcony

MBr
18-4x13-0

Kit
10-2x 11-9

Dining

Dn

Great Rm
16-0x21-4
vaulted

46'-4"

L

L

R

L

W D

Entry

Porch depth 6-0

Br 2
12-8x14-0

Br 3
11-4x12-6

Copyright by designer/architect.

Optional Basement Level Floor Plan

Up

Garage
22-4x26-8

Family
15-6x20-8

Plan #321009

Dimensions: 55'8" W x 46'4" D

Levels: 1

Heated Square Footage: 1,684

Bedrooms: 3

Bathrooms: 2

Foundation: Walkout

Materials List Available: Yes

Price Category: E

CAD FILE AVAILABLE

Images provided by designer/architect.

Rear View

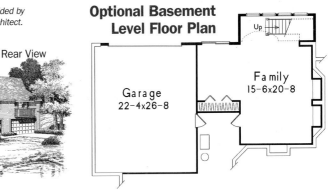

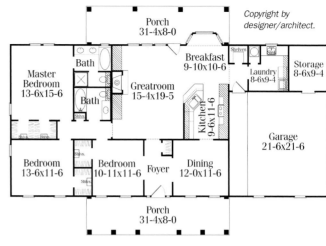

Porch
31-4x8-0

Master
Bedroom
13-6x15-6

Bath

Bath

Greatroom
15-4x19-5

Breakfast
9-10x10-6

Shelves

Laundry
8-6x9-4

Storage
8-6x9-4

Kitchen
9-6x11-6

Garage
21-6x21-6

Bedroom
13-6x11-6

Bedroom
10-11x11-6

Foyer

Dining
12-0x11-6

Porch
31-4x8-0

Plan #311008

Dimensions: 70'1" W x 48' D

Levels: 1

Heated Square Footage: 1,688

Bedrooms: 3

Bathrooms: 2

Foundation: Basement, crawl space, or slab

Materials List Available: Yes

Price Category: C

Images provided by designer/architect.

Rear View

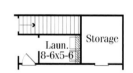

Laun.
8-6x5-6

Storage

Basement Stair Option

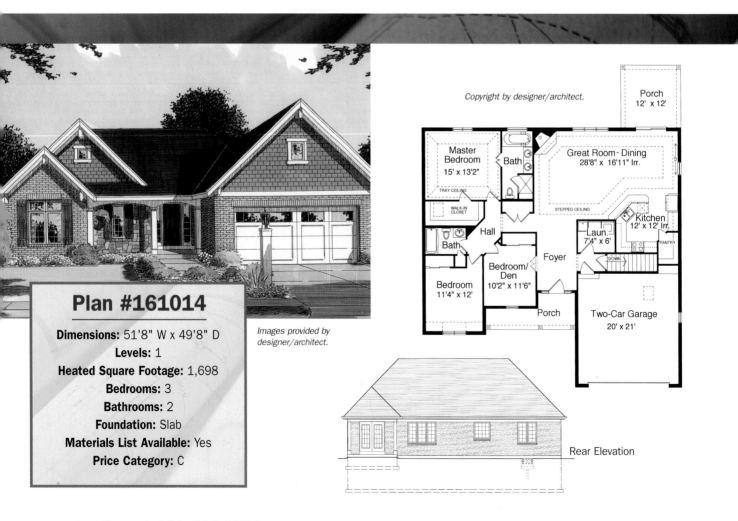

Porch
12' x 12'

Master
Bedroom
15' x 13'2"
TRAY CEILING

Bath

Great Room- Dining
28'8" x 16'11" Irr.

STEPPED CEILING

WALK-IN
CLOSET

Kitchen
12' x 12' Irr.

Hall

Laun.
7'4" x 6'

PANTRY

Bath

Bedroom/
Den
10'2" x 11'6"

Foyer

DOWN

Bedroom
11'4" x 12'

Porch

Two-Car Garage
20' x 21'

Plan #161014

Dimensions: 51'8" W x 49'8" D

Levels: 1

Heated Square Footage: 1,698

Bedrooms: 3

Bathrooms: 2

Foundation: Slab

Materials List Available: Yes

Price Category: C

Images provided by designer/architect.

Rear Elevation

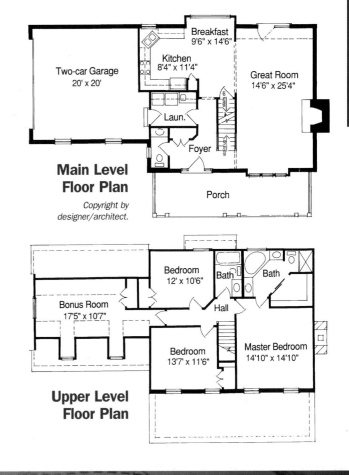

**Main Level
Floor Plan**

*Copyright by
designer/architect.*

- Breakfast 9'6" x 14'6"
- Kitchen 8'4" x 11'4"
- Two-car Garage 20' x 20'
- Great Room 14'6" x 25'4"
- Laun.
- Foyer
- Porch

Plan #161024

Dimensions: 54'4" W x 26'8" D
Levels: 2
Heated Square Footage: 1,698
Main Level Sq. Ft.: 868
Upper Level Sq. Ft.: 830
Bonus Space Sq. Ft.: 269
Bedrooms: 3
Bathrooms: 2½
Foundation: Basement
Materials List Available: No
Price Category: C

*Images provided by
designer/architect.*

*This home, as shown
in the photograph, may
differ from the actual
blueprints. For more
detailed information,
please check the floor
plans carefully.*

**Upper Level
Floor Plan**

- Bedroom 12' x 10'6"
- Bath
- Bath
- Bonus Room 17'5" x 10'7"
- Hall
- Bedroom 13'7" x 11'6"
- Master Bedroom 14'10" x 14'10"

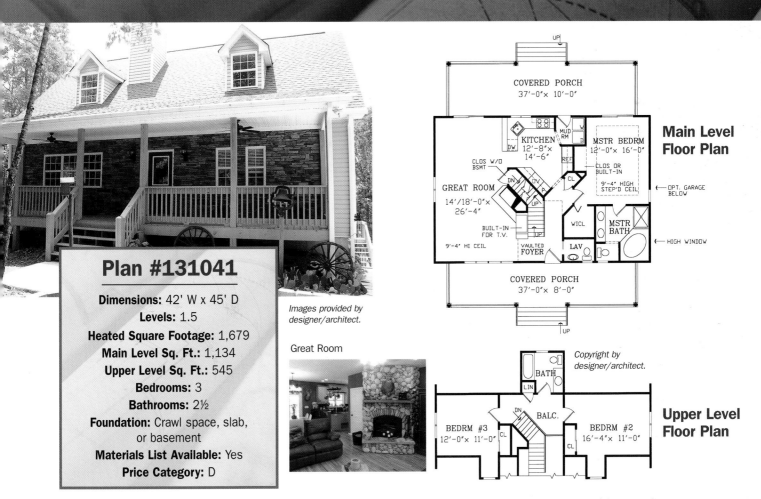

Plan #131041

Dimensions: 42' W x 45' D
Levels: 1.5
Heated Square Footage: 1,679
Main Level Sq. Ft.: 1,134
Upper Level Sq. Ft.: 545
Bedrooms: 3
Bathrooms: 2½
Foundation: Crawl space, slab,
or basement
Materials List Available: Yes
Price Category: D

*Images provided by
designer/architect.*

Great Room

**Main Level
Floor Plan**

- COVERED PORCH 37'-0" x 10'-0"
- KITCHEN 12'-8" x 14'-6"
- MUD RM
- MSTR BEDRM 12'-0" x 16'-0"
- CLOS W/O BSMT
- GREAT ROOM 14'/18'-0" x 26'-4"
- BUILT-IN FOR T.V.
- 9'-4" HI CEIL
- VAULTED FOYER
- WICL
- MSTR BATH
- LAV
- CLOS OR BUILT-IN
- 9'-4" HIGH STEP'D CEIL
- OPT. GARAGE BELOW
- HIGH WINDOW
- COVERED PORCH 37'-0" x 8'-0"

*Copyright by
designer/architect.*

**Upper Level
Floor Plan**

- BATH
- LIN
- BALC.
- BEDRM #3 12'-0" x 11'-0"
- BEDRM #2 16'-4" x 11'-0"

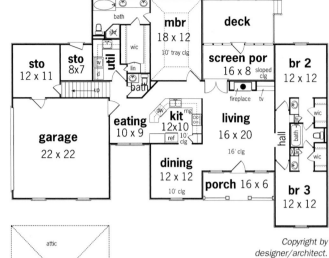

Images provided by designer/architect.

Copyright by designer/architect.

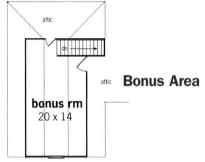

Bonus Area

Plan #211086

Dimensions: 71' W x 50' D

Levels: 1

Heated Square Footage: 1,704

Bedrooms: 3

Bathrooms: 2½

Foundation: Crawl space

Materials List Available: Yes

Price Category: C

CAD FILE AVAILABLE

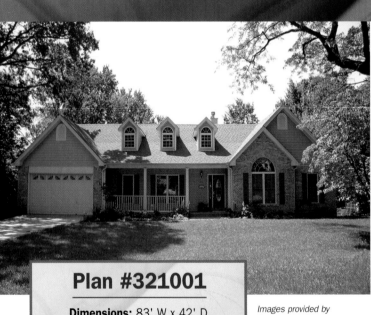

Plan #321001

Dimensions: 83' W x 42' D

Levels: 1

Heated Square Footage: 1,721

Bedrooms: 3

Bathrooms: 2

Foundation: Crawl space, slab, or basement

Materials List Available: Yes

Price Category: E

CAD FILE AVAILABLE

Images provided by designer/architect.

This home, as shown in the photograph, may differ from actual blueprints. For more detailed information, please check the floor plans carefully.

Copyright by designer/architect.

Rear View

Main Level Floor Plan

Copyright by designer/architect.

Upper Level Floor Plan

Images provided by designer/architect.

Kitchen

Plan #181224

Dimensions: 36' W x 39'8" D

Levels: 2

Heated Square Footage: 1,727

Main Level Sq. Ft.: 837

Upper Level Sq. Ft.: 890

Bedrooms: 3

Bathrooms: 2

Foundation: Basement

Material List Available: Yes

Price Category: C

Plan #441004

Dimensions: 55' W x 48' D

Levels: 1

Heated Square Footage: 1,728

Bedrooms: 2

Bathrooms: 2

Foundation: Crawl space; slab or basement available for fee

Materials List Available: No

Price Category: C

Images provided by designer/architect.

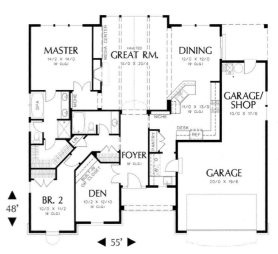

Copyright by designer/architect.

Rear Elevation

Plan #131002

Dimensions: 70'1" W x 60'7" D

Levels: 1

Heated Square Footage: 1,709

Bedrooms: 3

Bathrooms: 2½

Foundation: Crawl space, slab, or basement

Materials List Available: Yes

Price Category: D

Images provided by designer/architect.

COV. PORCH
30'-5" x 8'-0"

FRENCH DR

BUILT IN

DINING RM
14'-0" x 10'-0"

SNACK BAR

KITCHEN
14'-8" x 9'-4"

MSTR BEDRM
12'-0" x 18'-4"

TRAY CEIL

WICL

DRSG AREA

VAULTED CEIL.

MSTR BATH

LOCATION OF OPT. BSMT STAIR

STDR

UTIL

PAN.

CL

LAUN RM

LAV.

TWO CAR GARAGE
20'-0" x 21'-0"

10' HIGH STEPPED CLG

GREAT RM
14'-0" x 22'-8"

BUILT IN

FOYER

T.V.

CL

BEDRM #2
10'-0" x 12'-8"

LIN

BATH

CL

COV. PORCH

BEDRM #3
12'-4" x 12'-0"

Copyright by designer/architect.

Rear View

You'll love the way this angled ranch brings out the best in a corner lot or on a slope.

Features:

- **Ceiling Height:** 8 ft.

- **Front Porch:** Hang baskets of plants from the roof of this porch, which is just the right size for a couple of rockers and a side table.

- **Dining Room:** Well-placed windows flood this room with sunlight during the day and a built-in cabinet gives ample storage space for all your china, linens, and collectables.

- **Foyer:** Open to the great room, the foyer gives a lovely area to greet your visitors.

- **Great Room:** A built-in media center surrounds the fireplace where friends and family are sure to gather.

- **Master Suite:** You'll love the privacy of this somewhat isolated but easily accessed room. Decorate to show off the large bay window and tray ceiling, and enjoy the luxury of a separate toilet room.

Living Room

Images provided by designer/architect.

Plan #341029

Dimensions: 49' W x 57' D

Levels: 1

Heated Square Footage: 1,737

Bedrooms: 3

Bathrooms: 2

Foundation: Crawl space; slab or basement for fee

Material List Available: Yes

Price Category: C

You'll love going to this vacation home with its generous deck space and artful window array.

Features:

- **Deck:** The front and side of this home are graced with an open deck, which is attached to a screened-in porch, wonderful for enjoying the great outdoors rain or shine.

- **Great Room:** This great room's open layout, vaulted ceiling, fireplace, and large windows create a spacious feeling and a connection with the outdoors.

- **Kitchen:** The open kitchen area features a work island/serving counter and connects to the screened-in porch for outdoor dining.

- **Master Suite:** This master suite features a walk-in closet and large bedroom area.

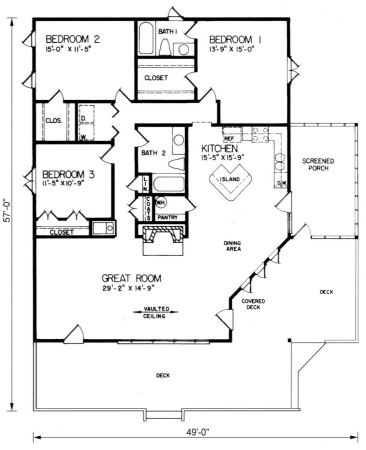

Copyright by designer/architect.

1,501–2,500 sq. ft.

Plan #121006

Dimensions: 46' W x 58' D
Levels: 1
Heated Square Footage: 1,762
Bedrooms: 3
Bathrooms: 2
Foundation: Slab;
crawl space or basement for fee
Materials List Available: Yes
Price Category: C

Images provided by designer/architect.

The entry has a trio of arched openings that leads you to other areas of this amenity-packed home.

Features:

- Ceiling Height: 8 ft. except as noted.

- Eating Bar: Conveniently located between the kitchen and family room, this is sure to be a favorite spot for informal entertaining and family gatherings.

- Family room: A wall of windows, a fireplace, and a vaulted ceiling stretching to 11 ft. work together to make this a bright and warm room.

- Kitchen: There's no shortage of counter space in this well-planned kitchen that features a center island in addition to the eating bar.

- Master Suite: Luxuriate at the end of the day in this large bedroom with its decorative tray ceiling and walk-in closet. Enjoy the pampering bath with its sunlit corner whirlpool flanked by vanities.

- Garage: Two bays provide room for cars and plenty of storage as well.

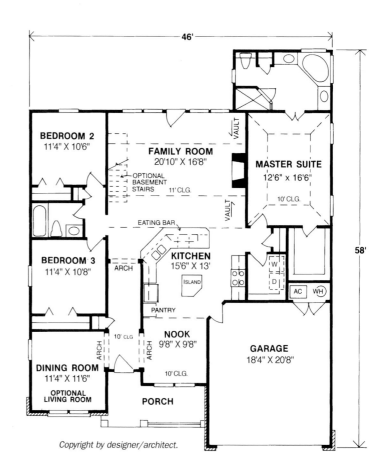

Copyright by designer/architect.

Plan #151548

Dimensions: 55'10" W x 52' D

Levels: 1

Heated Square Footage: 1,763

Bedrooms: 3

Bathrooms: 2

Foundation: Crawl space or slab

CompleteCost List Available: Yes

Price Category: C

Round-top windows and a sleek roofline provide a sense of elegance in this plan.

Features:

- **Entertaining:** A spacious great room with a fireplace and a backyard view blends with the kitchen and breakfast room, which has access to the grilling porch, creating the perfect area for entertaining.

- **Master Suite:** Indulge yourself in this private suite. The bath has a relaxing whirlpool tub, with a privacy glass-block window above, as well as a walk-in closet and split vanities.

- **Garage:** This front-loading two-car garage has extra storage space.

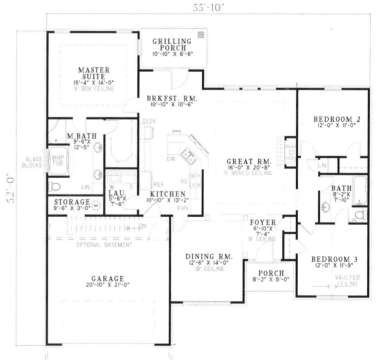

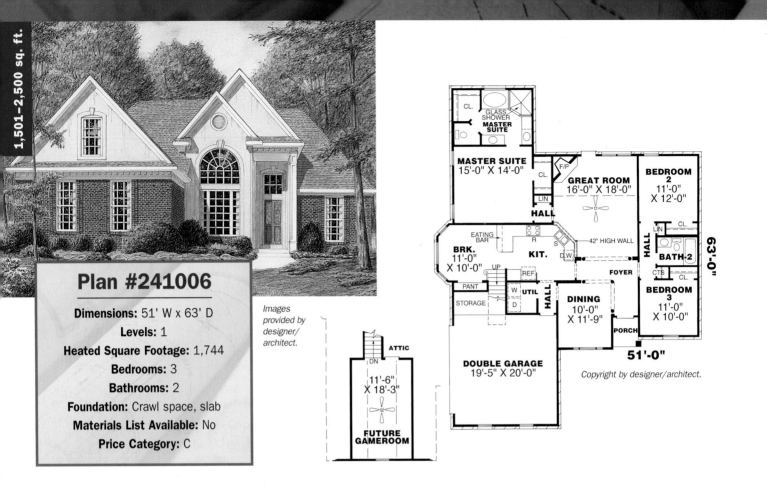

Plan #241006

Dimensions: 51' W x 63' D

Levels: 1

Heated Square Footage: 1,744

Bedrooms: 3

Bathrooms: 2

Foundation: Crawl space, slab

Materials List Available: No

Price Category: C

Images provided by designer/architect.

Copyright by designer/architect.

Plan #151007

Dimensions: 54'2" W x 56'2" D

Levels: 1

Heated Square Footage: 1,787

Bedrooms: 3

Bathrooms: 2

Foundation: Crawl space, slab, basement, or walkout

CompleteCost List Available: Yes

Price Category: C

Images provided by designer/architect.

This home, as shown in the photograph, may differ from the actual blueprints. For more detailed information, please check the floor plans carefully.

CAD FILE AVAILABLE

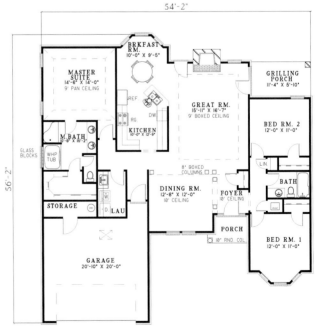

Copyright by designer/architect.

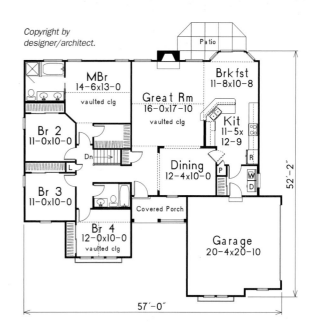

Copyright by designer/architect.

Images provided by designer/architect.

Plan #321008

Dimensions: 57' W x 52'2" D

Levels: 1

Heated Square Footage: 1,761

Bedrooms: 4

Bathrooms: 2

Foundation: Basement

Materials List Available: Yes

Price Category: C

CAD FILE AVAILABLE

SMARTtip
Hanging Wallpaper
Use liner paper to smooth out a damaged wall and to provide uniform support for expensive paper.

Plan #221004

Dimensions: 67'8" W x 43' D

Levels: 1

Heated Square Footage: 1,763

Bedrooms: 3

Bathrooms: 2

Foundation: Basement

Materials List Available: No

Price Category: C

CAD FILE AVAILABLE

Images provided by designer/architect.

Copyright by designer/architect.

Rear Elevation

Plan #351002

Dimensions: 64' W x 45'10" D
Levels: 1
Heated Square Footage: 1,751
Bedrooms: 3
Bathrooms: 2
Foundation: Crawl space, slab, or basement
Materials List Available: Yes
Price Category: E

Images provided by designer/architect.

This is a beautiful classic traditional home with a European touch.

Features:

- **Great Room:** This gathering area has a gas log fireplace that is flanked by two built-in cabinets. The area has a 10-ft.-tall tray ceiling.

- **Kitchen:** This L-shaped island kitchen has a raised bar and is open to the eating area and great room. The three open spaces work together as one large room.

- **Master Suite:** Located on the opposite side of the home from the secondary bedrooms, this suite has a vaulted ceiling. The master bath has dual vanities and a garden tub.

- **Bedrooms:** The two secondary bedrooms share a hall bathroom and have ample closet space.

Great Room

Kitchen

Master Bathroom

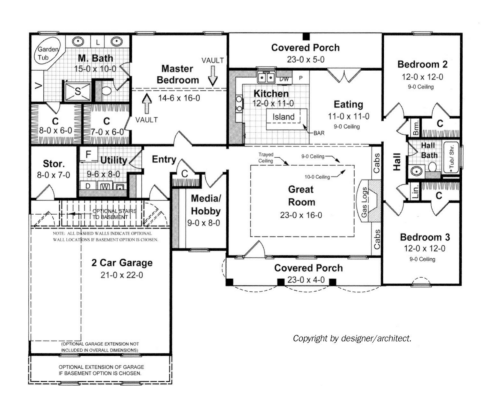

Copyright by designer/architect.

Hardscaping Your Yard

Landscape designs often benefit from vertical elements such as walls, fences, arches, arbors, pergolas, and decorative freestanding plant supports. Walls and fences help define boundaries while enclosing special spaces. Properly positioned, an arbor or arch is an eye-catching accent, adding visual drama to the scene and providing an attractive focal point or point of passage between two parts of the garden. A pergola transforms an ordinary path into a special, shaded, and sheltered passageway, while a freestanding plant support is like an exclamation point, drawing attention to itself and creating a pleasant focus.

As an added bonus, any one of these features provides an opportunity to grow and enjoy the wide range of climbing plants such as clematis, wisteria, climbing roses, honeysuckle, trumpet vine, and jasmine. These vertical plants add a sense of lushness to the garden as they scramble up walls and over trellised arches or droop heavy panicles of flowers through the open fretwork ceiling of a pergola. Here are some ideas for hardscaping your front yard with these elements.

Fences, opposite, not only serve as boundary markers, they are a design element in their own right. There are so many styles from which to choose that you should have no trouble finding one that is both functional and decorative. The posts on this classic style are topped with decorative finials.

The brick wall, above, that encloses this garden complements the brick pathway. Both have weathered to the point where they look as though they have always been part of the setting.

Consider installing a fence, below, as a backdrop to a group of lush plantings. This simple rail fence defines the garden path and separates the front yard from the side yard, but it also seems to support the flowering plants.

A traditional picket fence, right, serves as a backdrop for a group of border plants. In addition to their utilitarian functions, vertical elements such as fences and walls add texture and visual interest to a landscape.

The classic picket fence, below, can be used with a variety of house styles. A purely decorative section of fence spans an opening in a hedge that borders the front yard of this house.

Fence posts, bottom right, especially posts that mark an entry, can become focal points if you add special cap treatments or adorn one with fresh flowers.

Designing a Fence

Erecting a fence is the quickest and generally easiest way to define the boundary of your property. To be a successful part of a landscape design, a fence should be planned to complement the architecture of your house, possibly even echoing a distinctive design feature. Also bear in mind the character of your neighborhood and region. Your fence may be beautiful in and of itself but look out of place in the neighborhood where you live. In addition to style, other considerations for making a fence harmonious with its surroundings include height, color, and material.

With that in mind, the possibilities for fence designs are limitless. Traditional options include wrought iron, wooden pickets (or palings), stockade, split-rail, double- and triple-bar ranch fences, and even chain-link fences. Within those basic styles are many variations. For example, iron can be wrought in fanciful designs from modern clean-cut to the fancy curlicues of the Romanesque style. Picket points can take the form of arrows, fleurs-de-lis, or any other design. The pickets can be spaced in a variety of ways. Stockade fences can be closed- or open-board, or have angled paling boards. To add extra charm and interest, a solid wooden fence can be topped with lattice. The main components of a

board fence are pickets, horizontal rails, a top rail to protect the end grain of the pickets from moisture, the kickboard, and the support post.

Fence Anatomy

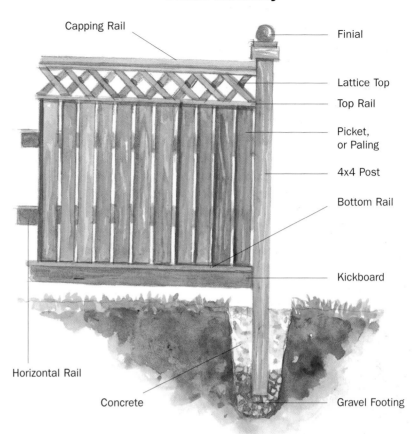

Capping Rail
Finial
Lattice Top
Top Rail
Picket, or Paling
4x4 Post
Bottom Rail
Kickboard
Horizontal Rail
Concrete
Gravel Footing

Building Fences on Slopes

A slope presents a special challenge for fence design as fence sections are generally straight and parallel with the ground. Three possible solutions include stepping the fence down the slope, allowing gaps to occur as the slope progresses downward; building the fence to follow the hillside so that the top of the fence is angled at the same degree as the slope; and custom-building the fence so each paling touches the ground, creating a wavy line across the fence top and bottom.

Stepped Fencing

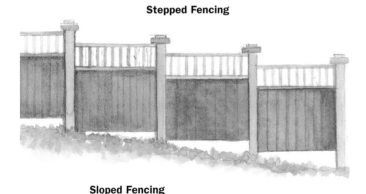

Sloped Fencing

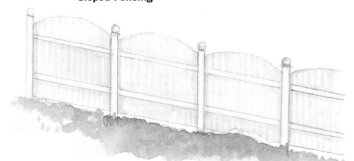

Contour Fencing

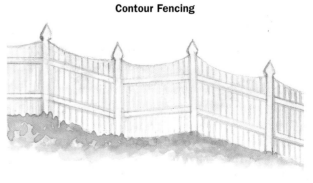

Designing a Gate

The garden gate meets many needs, from practical to aesthetic to psychological. It is a place of romance—where else would an ardent suitor steal a kiss or wait for a late-night romantic tryst but by the garden gate?

On the purely practical side, a gate allows passage to and between a front and back garden. This functional aspect is closely tied to a gate's symbolic meaning. A locked, solid gate set in a high wall or fence provides a sense of privacy, enclosure, and security. A gate with an open design, even when set into a solid wall, has a welcoming air about it.

An open gate beckons; a tall, solid gate adds mystery, suggesting the entrance to a secret garden. It can guide the eye to a focal point or add charm, intimacy, drama, or panache.

Gates, even short ones that stand only 3 feet high, serve as important transition points from the garden to the outside world or from one part of the garden to another. They define boundaries while linking the two areas together. For that reason, gates and pathways tend to go together in a landscape design.

Don't confine your gates to the perime-

Formal front yards, above, require a distinctive-looking entrance. The metalwork shown here works well with the formal brick wall and posts topped with decorative urns.

ter of your property. Use them within your garden as well, to divide space visually and to mark the boundaries between different areas or garden rooms.

Gates come in a seemingly endless variety of styles and sizes. Massive wrought-iron gates mark the entrances to many large Victorian parks and private estates. Painted, slatted gates set in white picket fences tend to belong with small, intimate

cottages or traditional country homes. The gate to a vegetable plot at the bottom of the garden might be rough-hewn, in keeping with an untreated wooden fence designed to keep out foraging wildlife. Japanese moon gates have cutout circles symbolic of the full moon. These circles may be open or filled in with a fretted design of wood or iron to add visual interest and increase security.

Hanging a Gate

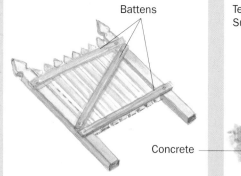

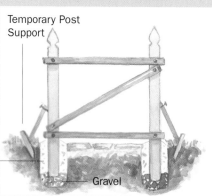

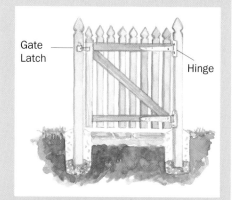

Step One: Space the Posts. Lay the gate on the ground, and position the posts on each side, allowing enough space for the hinges and latch. Make sure the tops and bottoms of the posts are even. Nail temporary battens onto the posts as shown. (The bottom batten should be at the bottom of the gate.)

Step Two: Set the Posts. Dig postholes. Set the posts on a gravel bed, making sure the bottom batten is 3 inches off the ground and that the posts are plumb and level. Secure the posts temporarily with braces and stakes, and then fill the holes with concrete. Check again for plumb and level before the concrete sets.

Step Three: Hang the Gate. When the concrete has completely cured, remove the braces and battens, attach the hinges (with the gate attached) to the post, and then attach the latch. The job is easier if one person holds the gate in position while the other person drills the screw holes and attaches the hardware.

Choose your gates to fit the style of your garden, but don't be afraid to have fun. For example, use a terra-cotta color to blend with a Spanish-style house, or set a light-colored gate set against a dark backdrop of heavy foliage.

Informal designs, above, put visitors at ease. This type of fence and gate is a good way to welcome visitors to a rear or side yard. It also helps support tall plants.

This distinctive gate, far left, is attached to a house of similar style. Look to the facade of the house and the landscaping style of the front yard when selecting a fence and gate style.

Gates, left, don't always need a fence. Here a decorative metal gate forms part of an arbor that is set in a hedge. This gate opens to a field beyond the garden.

The simple lattice design, above, of this fence is both appealing and practical. It not only encloses the garden but also serves as a trellis for climbing plants. A fence builder can create a custom design for you, or you can buy sections of fencing at home centers and fence speciality retailers.

This arbor and trellis, left, can serve as a destination in a large garden. You might find this type of structure in a front yard, but only in a very informal garden setting. Many large arbors contain a bench as part of the design. For interest, try placing a tall arbor in a rear or side yard that can be seen from the street.

Designing a Trellis

Trellises were a key element in Renaissance gardens and continued in popularity through the eighteenth century. Trellises enjoyed a resurgence of popularity in the late-nineteenth century, but never to the extent of earlier times. Trellises can lend an air of magic and mystery to a garden. Generally, we think of trellises in terms of the prefabricated sheets of diamond- or square-grid lattice and the fan-shaped supports for training climbers, both of which are readily available at home and garden centers in both wood and plastic. Lacking a pattern book, most gardeners are unaware of the incredible variety of designs, patterns, and optical illusions that can be created with trellises.

A trellis screen is a wonderfully airy way to achieve privacy or to partition off a space. The lath slats of lattice interrupt the view without totally obscuring it, creating the effect of a transparent curtain. Left bare, the pretty design of diamonds or squares makes an attractive effect. Covered in vines or decorated with hanging baskets, a trellis screen is enchanting.

The art of *treillage*, as the French call it, is not limited to screens. You can cover a bare wall or unattractive fence with a trellis pattern. Arrange the trellis pieces to create an optical illusion of an archway in the wall. Paint a realistic mural of the make-believe garden space

Typical Trellis Designs

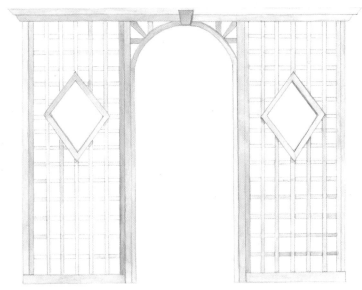

Trellis with Arched Entry

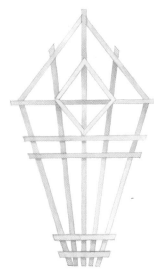

Traditional Wood Trellis

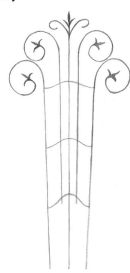

Wire Trellis

beyond. Use a trellis for the walls of a gazebo to provide enclosure without being claustrophobic. Put a trellis screen with a pleasing, intricate pattern at the end of a walkway as a focal point.

Closely spaced horizontal slats, left, topped with decorative beams combine to form a handsome trellis and arbor that forms a border in this garden. The slats on the structure provide some privacy without impeding air flow into the garden. Decorative posts and beams add interest when seen from the street.

Plan #351003

Dimensions: 64' W x 45'10" D

Levels: 1

Heated Square Footage: 1,751

Bedrooms: 3

Bathrooms: 2

Foundation: Crawl space, slab, or basement

Materials List Available: Yes

Price Category: D

Images provided by designer/architect.

This beautiful three-bedroom brick house with a covered porch is perfect for today's family.

Features:

- **Great Room:** This gathering room features a tray ceiling, a gas fireplace, and built-in cabinets.

- **Kitchen:** This island kitchen with a raised bar is open to the great room and eating area.

- **Master Suite:** This primary bedroom features a vaulted ceiling and large walk-in closet. The private bath boasts a double vanity, corner tub, and walk-in closet.

- **Bedrooms:** Two additional bedrooms are located on the other side of the home from the master suite and share a common bathroom.

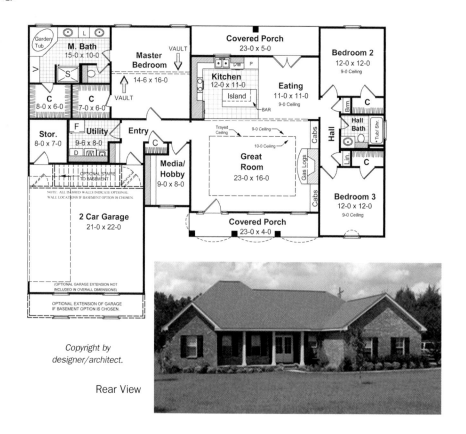

Copyright by designer/architect.

Rear View

Dining Room

Kitchen

Great Room

Rear View

Master Bathroom

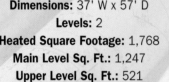

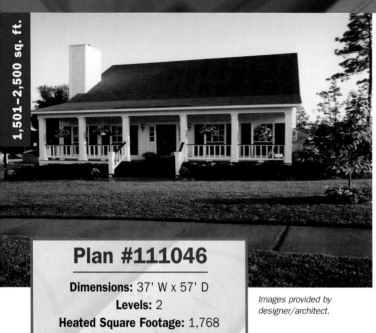

Main Level Floor Plan

Wood Deck 12'6"x 8'
Covered Porch 12'2"x 10'
Ext. Storage
Master Bath
WIC
Breakfast 11'10"x 9'6"
Utility
Master Bedroom 12'6"x 15'6"
1/2 Ba.
Kitchen 10'x 11'6"
Living 14'4"x 17'6"
Dining 13'x 12'
Porch 32'x 5'

Images provided by designer/architect.

Upper Level Floor Plan

Bedroom 10'6"x 13'2"
Balcony
Bedroom 12'6"x 14'

Copyright by designer/architect.

Plan #111046

Dimensions: 37' W x 57' D
Levels: 2
Heated Square Footage: 1,768
Main Level Sq. Ft.: 1,247
Upper Level Sq. Ft.: 521
Bedrooms: 3
Bathrooms: 2½
Foundation: Crawl space
Materials List Available: No
Price Category: C

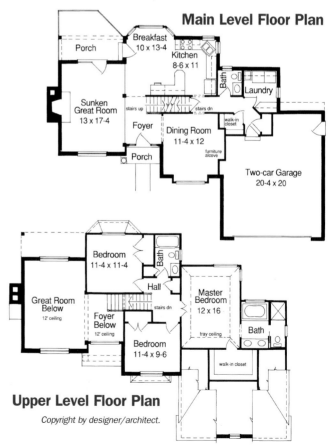

Main Level Floor Plan

Porch
Breakfast 10 x 13-4
Kitchen 8-6 x 11
Bath
Laundry
Sunken Great Room 13 x 17-4
stairs up
stairs dn
walk-in closet
Foyer
Dining Room 11-4 x 12
Porch
furniture alcove
Two-car Garage 20-4 x 20

Images provided by designer/architect.

Bedroom 11-4 x 11-4
Bath
Great Room Below 12' ceiling
Hall
Foyer Below 12' ceiling
stairs dn
Master Bedroom 12 x 16
tray ceiling
Bath
Bedroom 11-4 x 9-6
walk-in closet

Upper Level Floor Plan

Copyright by designer/architect.

Plan #161015

Dimensions: 55'4" W x 40'4" D
Levels: 2
Heated Square Footage: 1,768
Main Level Sq. Ft.: 960
Upper Level Sq. Ft.: 808
Bedrooms: 3
Bathrooms: 2½
Foundation: Basement
Materials List Available: Yes
Price Category: C

1,501–2,500 sq. ft.

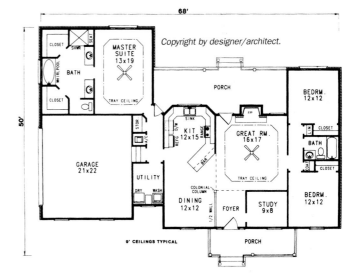

1,501-2,500 sq. ft.

Copyright by designer/architect.

Plan #171009

Dimensions: 68' W x 50' D

Levels: 1

Heated Square Footage: 1,771

Bedrooms: 3

Bathrooms: 2

Foundation: Crawl space, slab

Materials List Available: Yes

Price Category: C

Images provided by designer/architect.

SMARTtip

Deck Awnings

Awnings come in bright colors. As light filters through, it will cast a hue to anything under the deck. Warm colors, such as red or pink, will create a rosy glow; cool colors, such blues or greens, will enhance the shade.

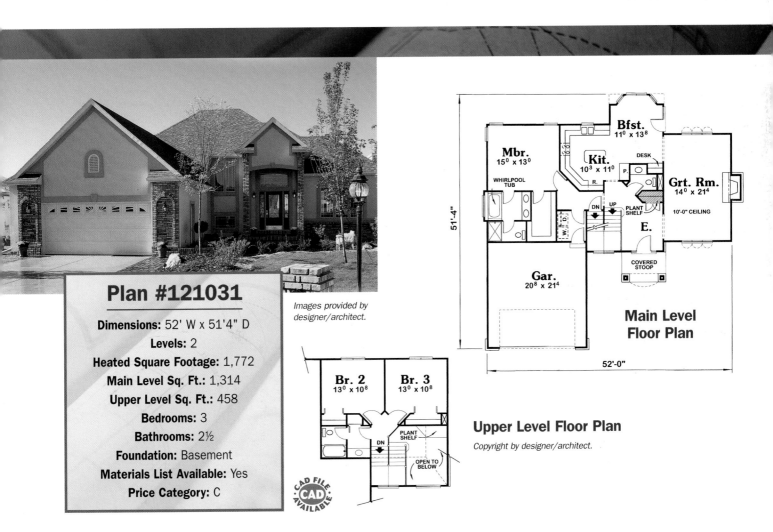

Plan #121031

Dimensions: 52' W x 51'4" D

Levels: 2

Heated Square Footage: 1,772

Main Level Sq. Ft.: 1,314

Upper Level Sq. Ft.: 458

Bedrooms: 3

Bathrooms: 2½

Foundation: Basement

Materials List Available: Yes

Price Category: C

Images provided by designer/architect.

Main Level Floor Plan

Upper Level Floor Plan

Copyright by designer/architect.

CAD FILE AVAILABLE

Copyright by designer/architect.

Rear Elevation

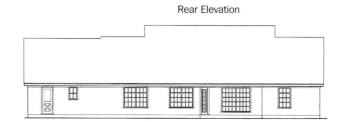

Plan #371072

Dimensions: 75'10" W x 38'8" D

Levels: 1

Heated Square Footage: 1,772

Bedrooms: 3

Bathrooms: 2

Foundation: Crawl space, slab

Materials List Available: No

Price Category: C

Images provided by designer/architect.

CAD FILE AVAILABLE

Copyright by designer/architect.

Plan #161164

Dimensions: 65'3" W x 49' D

Levels: 1

Heated Square Footage: 1,776

Bedrooms: 3

Bathrooms: 2

Foundation: Basement or walkout; crawl space or slab for fee

Material List Available: Yes

Price Category: C

Images provided by designer/architect.

CAD FILE AVAILABLE

Rear Elevation

Plan #271125

Dimensions: 45' W x 34'8" D
Levels: 1
Heated Square Footage: 1,776
Main Level Sq. Ft.: 1,329
Lower Level Sq. Ft.: 447
Bedrooms: 3
Bathrooms: 2½
Foundation: Walkout
Material List Available: No
Price Category: C

Images provided by designer/architect.

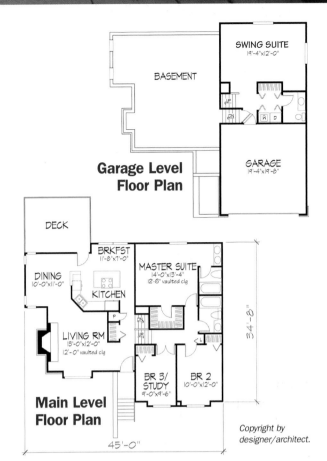

Garage Level Floor Plan

Main Level Floor Plan

Copyright by designer/architect.

Plan #391052

Dimensions: 68' W x 34'10" D
Levels: 2
Heated Square Footage: 1,778
Main Level Sq. Ft.: 1,306
Upper Level Sq. Ft.: 472
Bedrooms: 3
Bathrooms: 2
Foundation: Crawl space, slab, or basement
Material List Available: Yes
Price Category: C

Images provided by designer/architect.

This home, as shown in the photograph, may differ from the actual blueprints. For more detailed information, please check the floor plans carefully.

Upper Level Floor Plan

Copyright by designer/architect.

Main Level Floor Plan

Plan #151016

Dimensions: 60'2" W x 39'10" D
Levels: 2
Heated Square Footage: 1,783; 2,107 with bonus
Main Level Sq. Ft.: 1,124
Upper Level Sq. Ft.: 659
Bonus Room Sq. Ft.: 324
Bedrooms: 3
Bathrooms: 2½
Foundation: Crawl space, slab, or basement
CompleteCost List Available: Yes
Price Category: C

Images provided by designer/architect.

Main Level Floor Plan

Bonus Room Above Garage

Upper Level Floor Plan

Copyright by designer/architect.

Plan #321010

Dimensions: 59' W x 37'8" D
Levels: 1
Heated Square Footage: 1,787
Bedrooms: 3
Bathrooms: 2
Foundation: Basement, or walkout
Materials List Available: Yes
Price Category: C

Images provided by designer/architect.

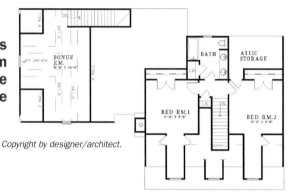

Copyright by designer/architect.

SMARTtip
Country Décor in Your Bathroom

Collections are often part of a country decor, even in the bathroom. All you need is three or more of anything that have size, shape, or color in common. You can mass them on walls, on shelves, on the windowsills, or even along the edge of the tub.

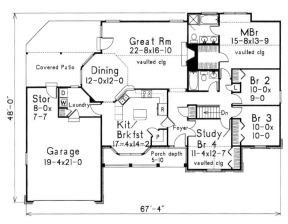

Copyright by designer/architect.

Plan #321003

Dimensions: 67'4" W x 48' D
Levels: 1
Heated Square Footage: 1,791
Bedrooms: 4
Bathrooms: 2
Foundation: Basement
Material List Available: Yes
Price Category: C

Images provided by designer/architect.

CAD FILE AVAILABLE

SMARTtip

Bay& Bow Windows

Occasionally too little room exists between the window frame (if there is one) and the ceiling. In this situation you might be able to use ceiling-mounted hardware. Alternatively, a cornice across the top and a rod mounted inside the cornice will give you the dual benefit of visually lowering the top of the window and concealing the hardware.

Plan #211002

Dimensions: 68' W x 62' D
Levels: 1
Heated Square Footage: 1,792
Bedrooms: 3
Bathrooms: 2
Foundation: Crawl space
Materials List Available: Yes
Price Category: C

Images provided by designer/architect.

CAD FILE AVAILABLE

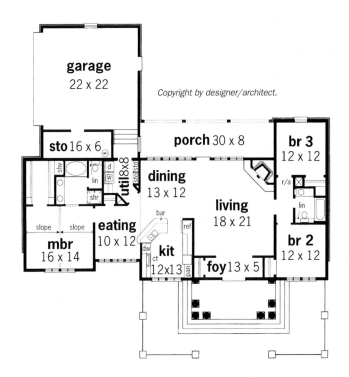

Copyright by designer/architect.

Plan #101004

Dimensions: 55'8" W x 56'6" D

Levels: 1

Heated Square Footage: 1,787

Bedrooms: 3

Bathrooms: 2

Foundation: Crawl space, slab, or basement

Materials List Available: Yes

Price Category: D

This carefully designed ranch provides the feel and features of a much larger home.

Features:

- **Ceiling Height:** 9 ft. unless otherwise noted.

- **Entry:** Guests will step up onto the inviting front porch and into this entry, with its impressive 11-ft. ceiling.

- **Dining Room:** Open to the entry and to its left is this elegant dining room, perfect for entertaining or informal family gatherings.

- **Family Room:** This family gathering place features an 11-ft. ceiling to enhance its sense of spaciousness.

- **Kitchen:** This intelligently designed kitchen has an open plan. A breakfast bar and a serving bar are features that add to its convenience.

- **Master Suite:** This suite is loaded with amenities, including a double-step tray ceiling, direct access to the screened porch, a sitting room, deluxe bath, and his and her walk-in closets.

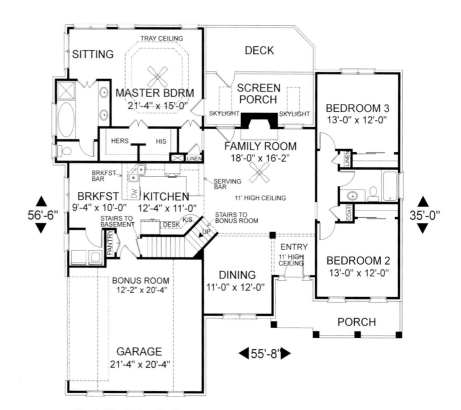

Copyright by designer/architect.

Kitchen

Family Room

Dining Room

Master Bath

Bedroom

Master Bedroom

Plan #391019

Dimensions: 56' W x 32' D
Levels: 1
Heated Square Footage: 1,792
Bedrooms: 3
Bathrooms: 2
Foundation: Basement
Materials List Available: Yes
Price Category: C

This southern-style cottage with sociable porch fits in almost anywhere, from a leafy lane to hillside or curbside and renders a lot of living space and hospitality.

Images provided by designer/architect.

Features:

• **Family Room:** This room features a central stone fireplace, plus two walls of windows to usher in the light. Sloping ceilings and decorative beams boost its rustic charm. An enormously generous space, it opens wide to the corner kitchen.

• **Dining Room:** This room has its own level of sophistication, including entry outside to the deck.

• **Utility Areas:** The family-sized pantry and laundry area are set off by themselves to avoid interference with everyday living.

• **Master Suite:** A leisurely hall leads to the master bedroom and private full bath, wide walk-in closets, and a trio of windows.

• **Bedrooms:** Across the hall the two secondary bedrooms share a roomy bath and a view of the front porch.

Front View

Side/Rear View

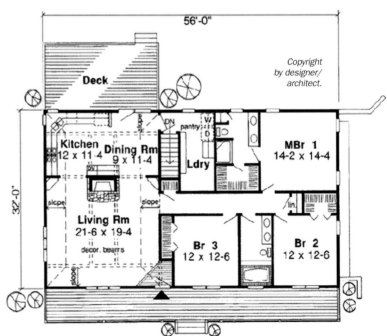

Copyright by designer/ architect.

56'-0"

32'-0"

Deck

Kitchen 12 x 11-4

Dining Rm 9 x 11-4

pantry

Ldry

MBr 1 14-2 x 14-4

Living Rm 21-6 x 19-4
decor. beams

slope

slope

Br 3 12 x 12-6

Br 2 12 x 12-6

Plan #151196

Dimensions: 89' W x 49'4" D
Levels: 1
Heated Square Footage: 1,800
Bedrooms: 3
Bathrooms: 2
Foundation: Crawl space, slab
CompleteCost List Available: Yes
Price Category: C

This charming home, with its wide front porch, is perfect on a little piece of land or a quiet suburban street.

Features:

- **Screened Porch:** This screened-in porch creates extra living space where you can enjoy warm summer breezes in a bug-free atmosphere.

- **Great Room:** Make a "great" first impression by welcoming guests into this spacious, fire-light-illuminated great room.

- **Kitchen:** This efficient area is surrounded on all sides by workspace and storage. A snack bar, adjacent dining room, and attached grilling porch create plenty of mealtime options.

- **Master Suite:** This master suite creates a stress-free environment with its, large walk-in closet, whirlpool tub, standing shower, and his and her vanities.

Images provided by designer/architect.

Plan #131047

Dimensions: 69'10" W x 51'8" D

Levels: 1

Heated Square Footage: 1,793

Bedrooms: 3

Bathrooms: 2

Foundation: Crawl space, slab, or basement

Materials List Available: Yes

Price Category: D

Family Room

This beautiful home will be a welcome addition to any neighborhood.

Features:

• Family Room: Conveniently located at the center of the home, this spacious family room provides a wonderful space to entertain guests or relax with the family.

• Kitchen: This gourmet kitchen provides plenty of cooking and storage space for the home chef. An eating bar is a versatile spot for grabbing a quick lunch, entertaining guests, or an after-school snack.

• Den: This well-situated room can be used in a variety of ways. Depending on your family's needs, it can be an additional bedroom, a home office, or study.

• Master Suite: You'll love this large master suite with his and her sinks and walk-in closet. Direct access to the covered patio in the rear of the house is perfect for relaxing at night or waking up to see the sunrise.

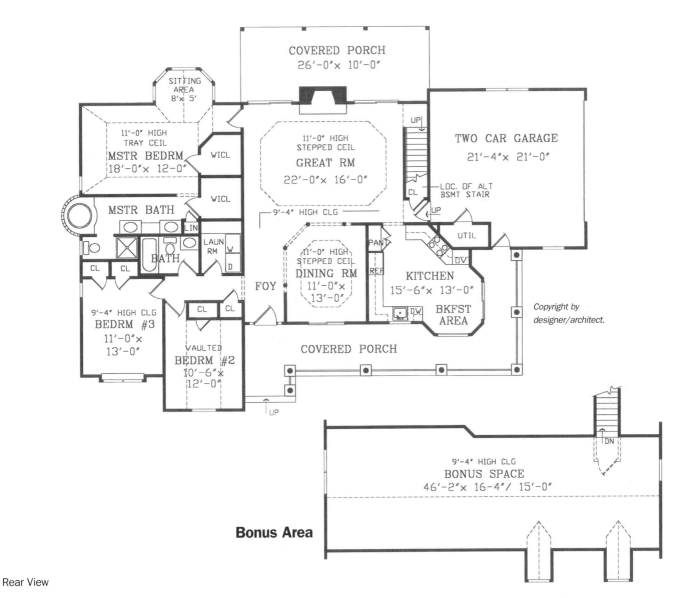

COVERED PORCH
26'-0" x 10'-0"

SITTING AREA
8'x 5'

11'-0" HIGH TRAY CEIL
MSTR BEDRM
18'-0"x 12'-0"

WICL

TWO CAR GARAGE
21'-4"x 21'-0"

UP

11'-0" HIGH STEPPED CEIL
GREAT RM
22'-0"x 16'-0"

9'-4" HIGH CLG

LOC. OF ALT BSMT STAIR

CL

UP

MSTR BATH

WICL

UTIL

LIN

LAUN RM

BATH

W   D

PANT

REF

DV

CL   CL

9'-4" HIGH CLG
BEDRM #3
11'-0"x 13'-0"

CL   CL

FOY

11'-0" HIGH STEPPED CEIL
DINING RM
11'-0"x 13'-0"

KITCHEN
15'-6"x 13'-0"

DW

BKFST AREA

Copyright by designer/architect.

VAULTED
BEDRM #2
10'-6"x 12'-0"

COVERED PORCH

UP

9'-4" HIGH CLG
BONUS SPACE
46'-2"x 16-4"/ 15'-0"

DN

Bonus Area

Rear View

58'8"

TERRACE

9' CEILING
DINING
11' X 10'

BEDROOM 2
12' X 11'

9' CEILING

KITCHEN
13'4" X 10'2"

GREAT ROOM
24'4" X 17'6"

16'3" CLG

9' CEILING
BEDROOM 1
15' X 14'

CL

BATH

WALK IN CLOS

WALK IN CLOS

BEDROOM 3
12'4" X 12'

9' CEILING

COAT CLOS

LAV

FRONT PORCH
18'9" X 10'8"

MASTER BATH

62'

STOR CLOS

DN

2-CAR GARAGE
24'7" X 21'4"

Copyright by designer/architect.

Images provided by designer/architect.

Plan #431001

Dimensions: 58'8" W x 62' D

Levels: 1

Heated Square Footage: 1,792

Bedrooms: 3

Bathrooms: 2½

Foundation: Crawl space or basement

Material List Available: Yes

Price Category: C

Rear
Elevation

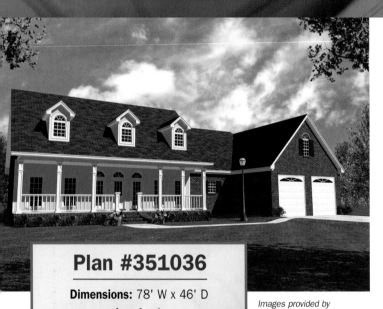

Plan #351036

Dimensions: 78' W x 46' D

Levels: 1

Heated Square Footage: 1,799

Bedrooms: 3

Bathrooms: 2½

Foundation: Crawl space or slab

Materials List Available: Yes

Price Category: E

Images provided by designer/architect.

CAD FILE AVAILABLE

Bedroom 2
12-2 x 11-10
9-0 Ceiling

Covered or
Screened-in Porch
16-2 x 8-0

Dining
12-0 x 17-4
9-0 Ceiling

Jet Tub

Master
Bedroom
14-4 x 17-6
9-0 Ceiling

Optional
Office, Shop,
Bonus, Porch, or
Storage
11-4 x 12-6

Hall

Bath

Great Room
16-0 x 26-0

VAULT

Raised Bar

M. Bath

Shr.

Stairs Option

Storage
11-4 x 5-0

Bedroom 3
12-0 x 11-4
9-0 Ceiling

VAULT

Foyer

Kitchen
13-4 x 12-8

Hall

Utility

2 or 3-Car Garage
24-0 x 24-0

Optional Side
Entrance
Garage

Covered Porch
41-6 x 6-0

Bonus Area Floor Plan

Copyright by designer/architect.

Full Bath

Bonus
Room
14-8 x 19-6

Sloped Clg.

Sloped Clg.

Rear View

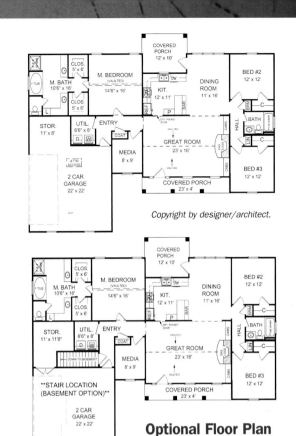

Copyright by designer/architect.

Images provided by designer/architect.

CAD FILE AVAILABLE

Plan #351043

Dimensions: 65' W x 50'10" D

Levels: 1

Heated Square Footage: 1,802

Bedrooms: 3

Bathrooms: 2

Foundation: Crawl space, slab, or basement

Materials List Available: Yes

Price Category: E

Optional Floor Plan

Plan #441005

Dimensions: 50' W x 59' D

Levels: 1

Heated Square Footage: 1,800

Bedrooms: 3

Bathrooms: 2

Foundation: Crawl space; slab or basement for fee

Materials List Available: No

Price Category: D

Images provided by designer/architect.

CAD FILE AVAILABLE

Copyright by designer/architect.

59'

50'

Rear Elevation

Plan #351082

Dimensions: 65' W x 56'8" D

Levels: 1

Heated Square Footage: 1,800

Bedrooms: 3

Bathrooms: 2

Foundation: Crawl space, slab or basement

Material List Available: Yes

Price Category: E

This inviting home combines country style with upscale features.

Features:

- **Porches:** Located in the front and the rear, covered porches add usable outdoor living space.

- **Great Room:** This vaulted great room includes built-in cabinets and a fireplace. It also connects to the covered porch at the back of the house.

- **Kitchen:** This spacious kitchen features an island complete with an eating bar. The attached breakfast area is wonderful for enjoying a meal by the window.

- **Master Suite:** This master suite has a raised ceiling and opens into the well-equipped bath that contains a dual-sink vanity, a corner whirlpool tub, and a walk-in closet.

Images provided by designer/architect.

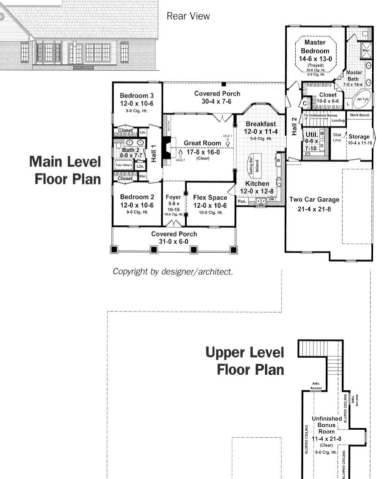

Rear View

Main Level Floor Plan

Copyright by designer/architect.

Upper Level Floor Plan

100   order direct: 1-800-523-6789

Plan #171014

Dimensions: 47' W x 52' D
Levels: 2
Heated Square Footage: 1,815
Main Level Sq. Ft.: 1,257
Upper Level Sq. Ft.: 558
Bedrooms: 3
Bathrooms: 2½
Foundation: Crawl space or slab
Material List Available: Yes
Price Category: D

Images provided by designer/architect.

The spacious and open areas of this home make it wonderful for entertaining friends or relaxing with family.

Features:

- **Great Room:** With its vaulted two-story ceiling, this great room is open to both the kitchen and dining rooms, so you and your guests can move about with ease.

- **Kitchen:** The corner location of this kitchen ensures that you will always be close to the action. An eating bar makes it easy to chat while preparing food or to grab a quick snack.

- **Master Suite:** Two closets, a master bath with a whirlpool tub, two vanities, and a separate shower, border a large bedroom.

- **Secondary Bedrooms:** Upstairs, two secondary bedrooms share a sitting area and a bath.

Main Level Floor Plan

Upper Level Floor Plan

Copyright by designer/architect.

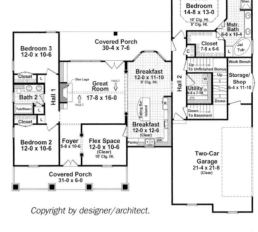

Plan #351108

Dimensions: 65' W x 60'8" D

Levels: 1

Heated Square Footage: 1,816

Bedrooms: 3

Bathrooms: 2

Foundation: Crawl space, slab or basement

Material List Available: Yes

Price Category: E

Images provided by designer/architect.

Copyright by designer/architect.

CAD FILE AVAILABLE

Bedroom 3
12-0 x 10-6

Covered Porch
30-4 x 7-6

Master Bedroom
14-8 x 13-0
10' Clg. Ht.
9' Clg. Ht.

Mstr. Bath
6-6 x 16-4

Closet

Bath 2

Hall 1

Gas Logs

Great Room
17-8 x 16-0

Breakfast
12-0 x 11-10
9' Clg. Ht.

Hall 2

Closet
7-8 x 6-6

Work Bench

Up To Unfinished Bonus

Up

Storage/Shop
6-4 x 11-10

Jet Tub

Utility
6-4 x 7-10

Closet

Bedroom 2
12-0 x 10-6

Foyer
5-8 x 10-6

Flex Space
12-0 x 10-6
(Clear)
10' Clg. Ht.

Breakfast
12-0 x 12-6
(Clear)

Pantry

Down To Basement

Two-Car Garage
21-4 x 21-8
(Clear)

Covered Porch
31-0 x 6-0

Rear Elevation

Bonus Area

Down

Bonus Rm.
11-4 x 25-8
8' Clg. Ht.

Sloped Clg

Plan #651089

Dimensions: 23' W x 49' D

Levels: 2

Heated Square Footage: 1,824

Main Level Sq. Ft.: 888

Upper Level Sq. Ft.: 936

Bedrooms: 3

Bathrooms: 2½

Foundation: Slab

Material List Available: No

Price Category: D

Images provided by designer/architect.

CAD FILE AVAILABLE

STO.
8 x 5

UTIL.
6 x 5

PORCH
8 x 6

P.

KITCHEN
8 x 13

BREAKFAST/GATHERING
11 x 13

1/2 BATH

DINING ROOM
14 x 10

CTS.

FAMILY ROOM
14 x 11

FOYER
7 x 5

UP

PORCH
23 x 6

49'

23'

Main Level Floor Plan

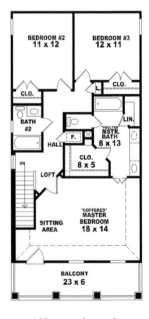

BEDROOM #2
11 x 12

BEDROOM #3
12 x 11

CLO.

CLO.

L

BATH #2

"VAULTED" MSTR. BATH
8 x 13

LIN.

F.

HALL

CLO.
8 x 5

LOFT

DN

SITTING AREA

"COFFERED" MASTER BEDROOM
18 x 14

BALCONY
23 x 6

Upper Level Floor Plan

Copyright by designer/architect.

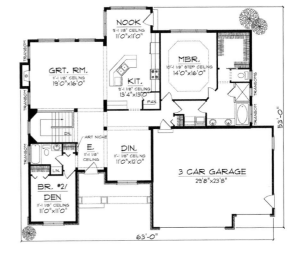

Copyright by designer/architect.

Rear Elevation

Plan #221099

Dimensions: 63' W x 53' D

Levels: 1

Heated Square Footage: 1,829

Bedrooms: 2

Bathrooms: 2

Foundation: Basement

Material List Available: No

Price Category: D

Images provided by designer/architect.

CAD FILE AVAILABLE **CAD**

Main Level Floor Plan

Copyright by designer/architect.

Plan #181133

Dimensions: 38'3" W x 40' D

Levels: 2

Heated Square Footage: 1,832

Main Level Sq. Ft.: 1,212

Upper Level Sq. Ft.: 620

Bedrooms: 3

Bathrooms: 2

Foundation: Basement

Material List Available: Yes

Price Category: D

Images provided by designer/architect.

CAD FILE AVAILABLE **CAD**

Upper Level Floor Plan

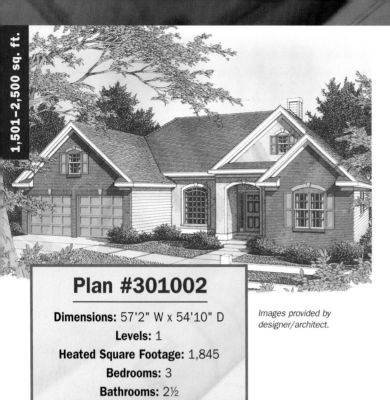

Images provided by designer/architect.

Plan #301002

Dimensions: 57'2" W x 54'10" D

Levels: 1

Heated Square Footage: 1,845

Bedrooms: 3

Bathrooms: 2½

Foundation: Crawl space, slab

Materials List Available: Yes

Price Category: D

Copyright by designer/architect.

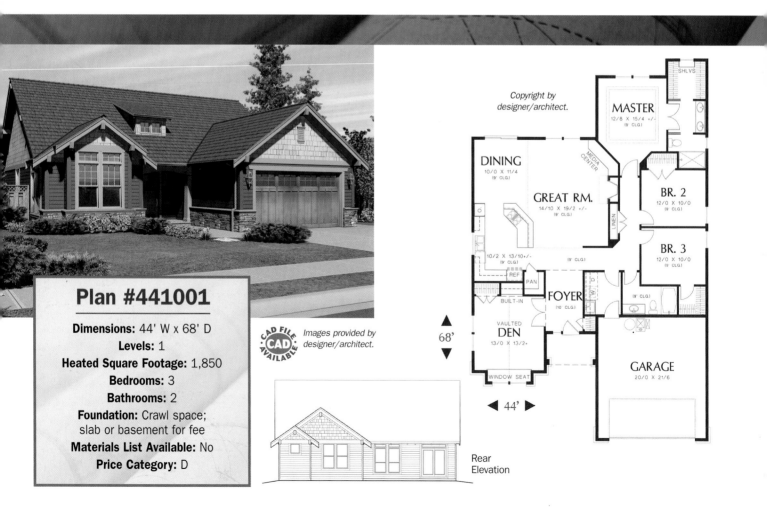

Plan #441001

Dimensions: 44' W x 68' D

Levels: 1

Heated Square Footage: 1,850

Bedrooms: 3

Bathrooms: 2

Foundation: Crawl space; slab or basement for fee

Materials List Available: No

Price Category: D

Images provided by designer/architect.

Rear Elevation

Images provided by designer/architect.

Copyright by designer/architect.

66'-0"

74'-0"

Screened Porch 11'5" x 11'7"

Breakfast 10'9" x 11'8"

Great Room 17'6" x 17'

Master Bedroom 15' x 13'

Bath

SLOPED CEILING

WALK IN CLOSET

Kitchen 14'3" x 12'3"

Dining Room 10'8" x 8'7"

Hall

LINEN

Bath

Foyer

CLOSET

Laun.

PANTRY

CLOSET

Bedroom 11' x 12'6"

Bedroom 12'6" x 11'4"

Porch

Garage 22'4" x 26'4"

Rear Elevation

Plan #161121

Dimensions: 66' W x 74' D

Levels: 1

Square Footage: 1,824

Bedrooms: 3

Bathrooms: 2

Foundation: Basement

Material List Available: Yes

Price Category: D

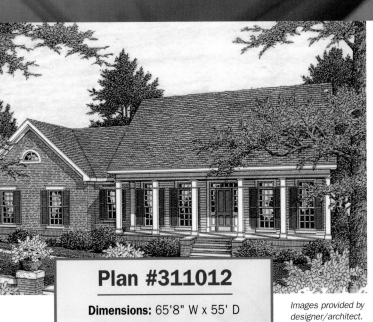

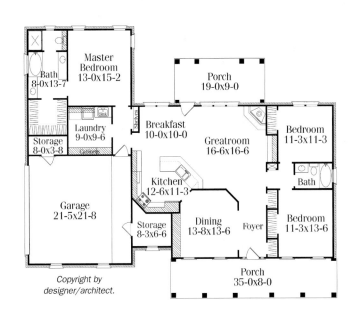

Images provided by designer/architect.

Copyright by designer/architect.

Bath 8-0x13-7

Master Bedroom 13-0x15-2

Porch 19-0x9-0

Storage 8-0x3-8

Laundry 9-0x9-6

Shelves

Breakfast 10-0x10-0

Greatroom 16-6x16-6

Bedroom 11-3x11-3

Kitchen 12-6x11-3

Bath

Garage 21-5x21-8

Storage 8-3x6-6

Dining 13-8x13-6

Foyer

Bedroom 11-3x13-6

Porch 35-0x8-0

Plan #311012

Dimensions: 65'8" W x 55' D

Levels: 1

Heated Square Footage: 1,836

Bedrooms: 3

Bathrooms: 2

Foundation: Basement, crawl space, or slab

Materials List Available: Yes

Price Category: D

Basement Stair Location

Laundry 9-0x5-8

Stor. 4-8x3-6

Plan #121064

Dimensions: 44' W x 40' D
Levels: 2
Heated Square Footage: 1,846
Main Level Sq. Ft.: 919
Upper Level Sq. Ft.: 927
Bedrooms: 4
Bathrooms: 2½
Foundation: Basement;
crawl space or slab for fee
Materials List Available: Yes
Price Category: D

This home, as shown in the photograph, may differ from the actual blueprints. For more detailed information, please check the floor plans carefully.

Images provided by designer/architect.

You'll love the features and design in this compact but amenity-filled home.

Features:

• **Entry:** A balcony overlooks this two-story entry, where a plant shelf tops the coat closet.

• **Great Room:** A trio of tall windows points up the large dimensions of this room, which is sure to be the hub of your home. Arrange the

furniture to create a cozy space around the fireplace, or leave it open to the room.

• **Kitchen:** You'll love to work in this well-designed kitchen area.

• **Master Suite:** On the second floor, this master suite features a tiered ceiling and two walk-in closets. In the bath, you'll find a double vanity, whirlpool tub, and separate shower.

Upper Level Floor Plan

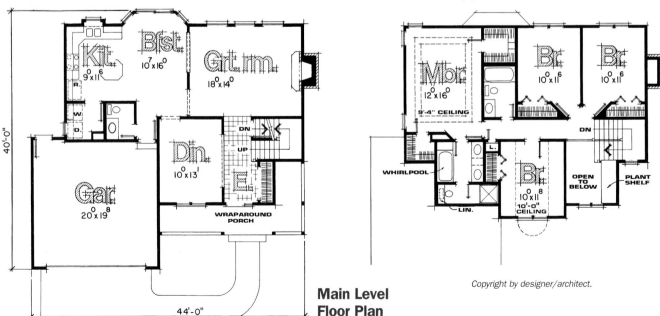

Copyright by designer/architect.

Plan #351004

Dimensions: 78' W x 49'6" D
Levels: 1
Heated Square Footage: 1,852
Bedrooms: 3
Bathrooms: 2½
Foundation: Crawl space, slab, or basement
Materials List Available: Yes
Price Category: E

CAD FILE AVAILABLE

Images provided by designer/architect.

You'll love this design if you've been looking for a one-story home large enough for both a busy family life and lots of entertaining.

Features:

- **Great Room:** A vaulted ceiling, substantial corner fireplace, and door to the rear porch give character to this sizable, airy room.

- **Dining Room:** This well-positioned room, lit by a wall of windows, can comfortably hold a crowd.

- **Kitchen:** The center island and deep pantry add efficiency to this well-planned kitchen, which also features a raised snack bar.

- **Master Suite:** Two walk-in closets and a bath with jet tub and separate shower complement the spacious bedroom here.

- **Garage Storage:** Barn doors make it easy to store yard equipment and tools here. Finish the optional area at the rear of the garage or overhead for a home office or media room.

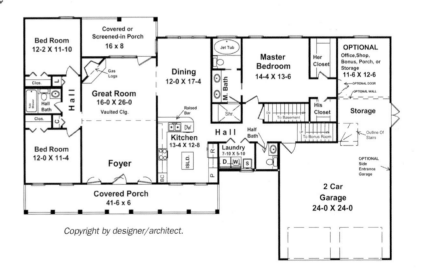

Copyright by designer/architect.

Rear Elevation

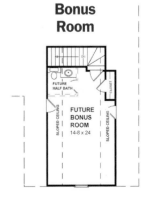

Bonus Room

Images provided by designer/architect.

Plan #441002

Dimensions: 70' W x 51' D
Levels: 1
Heated Square Footage: 1,873
Bedrooms: 3
Bathrooms: 2
Foundation: Crawl space
Materials List Available: No
Price Category: D

CAD FILE AVAILABLE

Shutters flank tall windows to adorn the front of this charming home. A high roofline gives presence to the façade and allows vaulted ceilings in all the right places inside.

Features:

- **Great Room:** The entry hall overlooks this room, where a fireplace warms gatherings on chilly evenings and built-in shelves, to the right of the fireplace, add space that might be used as an entertainment center. A large three-panel window wall allows for a rear-yard view.

- **Dining Room:** This area is connected directly to the great room and features double doors to a covered porch.

- **Kitchen:** This open work area contains ample counter space with an island cooktop and large pantry.

- **Bedrooms:** The bedrooms are split, with the master suite in the back and additional bedrooms at the front.

- **Master Suite:** This suite boasts a 9-ft.-high ceiling and is graced by a luxurious bathroom and a walk-in closet.

Copyright by designer/architect.

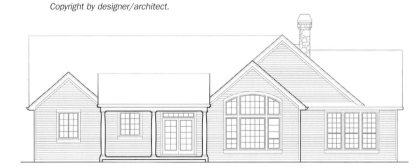

Plan #161002

Dimensions: 64'2" W x 44'2" D
Levels: 1
Heated Square Footage: 1,860
Bedrooms: 3
Bathrooms: 2
Foundation: Basement
Materials List Available: Yes
Price Category: D

Images provided by designer/architect.

Great Room/Foyer

Rear Elevation

The brick, stone, and cedar shake facade provides color and texture to the exterior, while the unique nooks and angles inside this delightful one-level home give it character.

Features:

- **Great Room/Dining Room:** This spacious great room is furnished with a wood-burning fireplace, a high ceiling, and French doors. Wide entrances to the breakfast room and dining room expand its space to comfortably hold large gatherings.

- **Kitchen:** The breakfast bar offers additional seating. The covered porch lets you enjoy a view of the landscape and is conveniently located for outdoor meals off this kitchen and breakfast area.

- **Master Suite:** The master suite is a private retreat. An alcove creates a comfortable sitting area, and an angled entry leads to the bath with whirlpool and a double-bowl vanity.

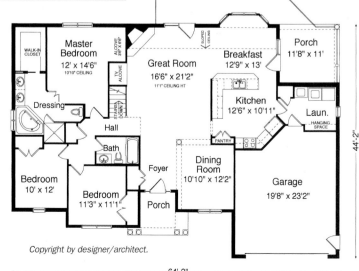

Copyright by designer/architect.

Plan #351001

Dimensions: 72'8" W x 51' D

Levels: 1

Heated Square Footage: 1,855

Bedrooms: 3

Bathrooms: 2½

Foundation: Crawl space, slab, or basement

Materials List Available: Yes

Price Category: E

CAD FILE AVAILABLE

From the lovely arched windows on the front to the front and back covered porches, this home is as comfortable as it is beautiful.

Features:

- **Great Room:** Come into this room with 12-ft. ceilings, and you're sure to admire the corner gas fireplace and three windows overlooking the porch.

- **Dining Room:** Set off from the open design, this room is designed to be used formally or not.

- **Kitchen:** You'll love the practical walk-in pantry, broom closet, and angled snack bar here.

- **Breakfast Room:** Brightly lit and leading to the covered porch, this room will be a favorite spot.

- **Bonus Room:** Develop a playroom or study in this area.

- **Master Suite:** The large bedroom is complemented by the private bath with garden tub, separate shower, double vanity, and spacious walk-in closet.

Copyright by designer/architect.

Master Bedroom 14-0 x 17-0 9-0 Ceiling

Garden Tub / Shwr.

M. Bath 10-0 x 13-6

Closet 10-0 x 8-0

Stor. 8-4 x 4-4

Covered Porch 17 x 8

Breakfast 12-0 x 11-0 9-0 Ceiling

Entry

Stor. or Stairs

Outline of Stairs

Optional Stairs To Basement

Bedroom 3 12-0 x 12-0 9-0 Ceiling

Clos.

Gas Logs

Clos.

Bath

Great Room 17-0 x 22-0 12-0 Ceiling

Kitchen 12-0 x 15-0

Bar

DW

HVAC

Utility 8-0 x 9-0

W D

Two Car Garage 24-0 x 22-0

Hall

Bath

Bedroom 2 12-0 x 12-0 9-0 Ceiling

Clos.

Covered Porch 14-4 x 5

Br

Dining 12-0 x 12-0 9-0 Ceiling

P

EXTENSION OF GARAGE IF BASEMENT FOUNDATION IS CHOSEN.

Master Bath

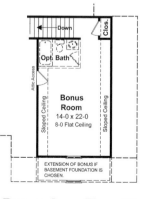

Down

Clos.

Opt. Bath

Attic Access

Sloped Ceiling

Bonus Room 14-0 x 22-0 8-0 Flat Ceiling

Sloped Ceiling

EXTENSION OF BONUS IF BASEMENT FOUNDATION IS CHOSEN.

Bonus Area Floor Plan

Great Room

Kitchen

Great Room

Dining Room

Great Room

Breakfast Area

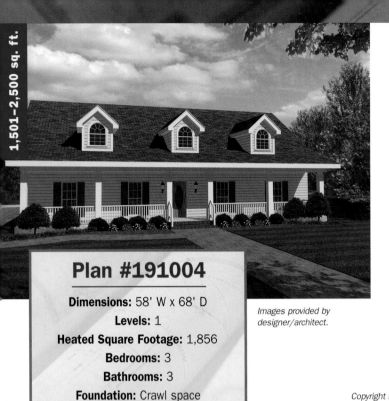

Plan #191004

Dimensions: 58' W x 68' D

Levels: 1

Heated Square Footage: 1,856

Bedrooms: 3

Bathrooms: 3

Foundation: Crawl space

Material List Available: No

Price Category: D

Images provided by designer/architect.

Kitchen

Copyright by designer/architect.

Plan #131015

Dimensions: 57'4" W x 56'10" D

Levels: 1

Heated Square Footage: 1,860

Bedrooms: 3

Bathrooms: 2

Foundation: Crawl space, slab, or basement

Materials List Available: Yes

Price Category: E

Images provided by designer/architect.

This home, as shown in the photograph, may differ from the actual blueprints. For more detailed information, please check the floor plans carefully.

Copyright by designer/architect.

Rear Elevation

Great Room

Plan #351101

Dimensions: 64' W x 53'10" D

Levels: 1

Heated Square Footage: 1,865

Bedrooms: 3

Bathrooms: 2

Foundation: Crawl space or slab

Material List Available: Yes

Price Category: E

Images provided by designer/architect.

CAD FILE AVAILABLE

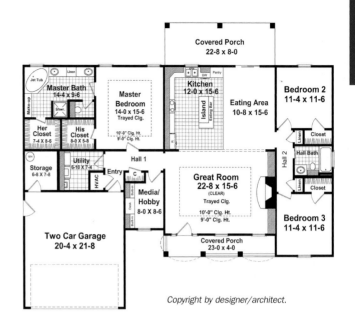

Copyright by designer/architect.

Plan #151490

Dimensions: 52' W x 69'6" D

Levels: 1

Heated Square Footage: 1,869

Bedrooms: 3

Bathrooms: 2

Foundation: Crawl space or slab

CompleteCost List Available: Yes

Price Category: D

Images provided by designer/architect.

CAD FILE AVAILABLE

Bonus Area Floor Plan

Copyright by designer/architect.

Images provided by designer/architect.

Plan #121001

Dimensions: 56' W x 58' D

Levels: 1

Heated Square Footage: 1,911

Bedrooms: 3

Bathrooms: 2

Foundation: Basement

Materials List Available: Yes

Price Category: D

Detailed, soaring ceilings and top-notch amenities set this distinctive home apart.

Features:

- Ceiling Height: 8 ft. except as noted.

- Formal Dining Room: The entry enjoys a pleasing view of this dining room's detailed 12-ft. ceiling and picture window.

- Great Room: At the back of the home, a see-through fireplace in this great room is joined by a built-in entertainment center.

- Hearth Room: This bayed room shares the see-through fireplace with the great room.

- Master Suite: Enjoy the stars and the sun in the private bath's whirlpool and separate shower. The bath features the same decorative ceiling as the dining room.

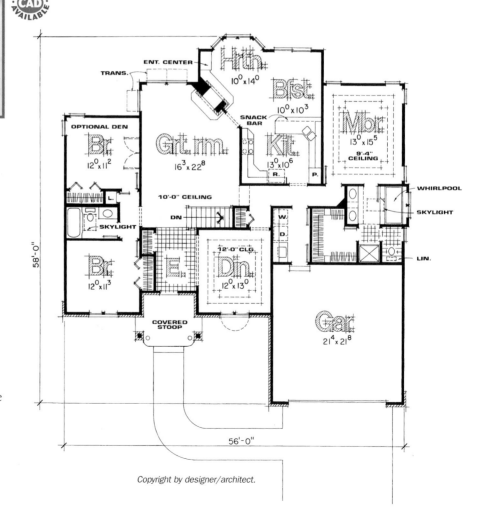

Copyright by designer/architect.

Images provided by designer/architect.

Plan #131011

Dimensions: 75'2" W x 60'9" D
Levels: 1
Heated Square Footage: 1,897
Bedrooms: 4
Bathrooms: 2
Foundation: Crawl space, slab, or basement
Materials List Available: Yes
Price Category: E

You'll love this home if you're looking for a plan for a sloping lot or flat one or if you want to orient the rear porch to face into or away from the sun.

Features:

• Ceiling Height: 8 ft.

• Living Area: The whole family will find it easy to congregate in this lovely room.

• Kitchen: The angle of this home makes the kitchen especially convenient while also giving it an unusual amount of character.

• Study: Located near the front door, this room can serve as a home office or fourth bedroom as easily as it does a private study.

• Master Suite: Located at the opposite end of the home from the other two bedrooms, this master suite offers privacy and quiet.

• Additional Bedrooms: These two bedrooms share a distinctive hall bathroom.

Copyright by designer/architect.

Rear View

Plan #571078

Dimensions: 30' W x 32' D

Levels: 2

Heated Square Footage: 1,870

Main Level Sq. Ft.: 935

Upper Level Sq. Ft.: 935

Bedrooms: 3

Bathrooms: 2½

Foundation: Basement

Material List Available: Yes

Price Category: D

Images provided by designer/architect.

Main Level Floor Plan

Upper Level Floor Plan

Copyright by designer/architect.

Plan #151068

Dimensions: 57' W x 61'8" D

Levels: 1

Heated Square Footage: 1,880

Bedrooms: 4

Bathrooms: 2

Foundation: Crawl space, slab, or basement

CompleteCost List Available: Yes

Price Category: D

Images provided by designer/architect.

CAD FILE AVAILABLE

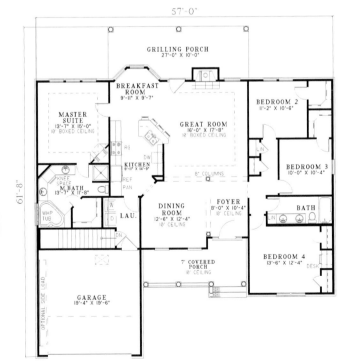

Copyright by designer/architect.

Copyright by designer/architect.

GARAGE
19/0 X 21/6

ALT GARAGE DR LOC

MASTER
14/0 X 15/0
(9' CLG.)

DINING
12/0 X 16/0
(9' CLG.)

HUTCH RECESS.

12/8x13/2 +/-
(9' CLG.)

PAN

REF.

NICHE

LINEN

OFFICE
/BR. 3
10/0 X 10/2
(9' CLG.)

GREAT RM.
17/0 X 17/0 +
(9' CLG.)

MEDIA

BR. 2
14/0 X 12/0
(9' CLG.)

PORCH

Images provided by designer/architect.

CAD FILE AVAILABLE CAD

Rear Elevation

64'

48'

Plan #441006

Dimensions: 48' W x 64' D

Levels: 1

Heated Square Footage: 1,891

Bedrooms: 3

Bathrooms: 2

Foundation: Crawl space; slab or basement for fee

Materials List Available: No

Price Category: D

SL GL DRS

BEDRM #2
12'-0"x 11'-0"

10'-5" HIGH STEPPED CLG
GREAT RM
FIREPLACE
18'-0"x 21'-4"
BUILT-INS

BKFST RM
10'-0"x 12'-0"

10'-5" HIGH TRAY CEIL
MSTR BEDRM
13'-0"x 17'-0"
+ BAY

SEAT

WICL

LIN

MSTR BATH

WICL

BATH

CL

LIN

CL

KIT
10'-0"x 11'-0"

REF

NICHE

UP TO OPT BONUS RM

LOCATION OF OPT BSMT STAIR

BEDRM #3
12'-0"x 11'-0"

HIGH CEIL
FOY

10'-5" HIGH STEPPED CLG
DINING RM
13'-0"x 11'-0"

LAV

LAUN

TWO CAR GARAGE
20'-0"x 20'-4"/ 24'-0"
+ BAY

COV. PORCH

SEAT

Images provided by designer/architect.

Rear Elevation

Bonus Area

Copyright by designer/architect.

DN

8'-1" HIGH VAULTED CLG
BONUS RM
10'-6"x 23'-0"

Plan #131035

Dimensions: 65'4" W x 45'10" D

Levels: 1

Heated Square Footage: 1,892

Bedrooms: 3

Bathrooms: 2½

Foundation: Basement, crawl space, or slab

Materials List Available: Yes

Price Category: E

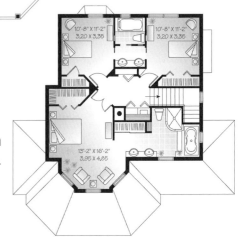

**Main Level
Floor Plan**

*Images provided by
designer/architect.*

Upper Level Floor Plan

Copyright by designer/architect.

Plan #181291

Dimensions: 32' W x 34' D

Levels: 2

Heated Square Footage: 1,898

Main Level Sq. Ft.: 949

Upper Level Sq. Ft.: 949

Bedrooms: 3

Bathrooms: 2½

Foundation: Basement

Materials List Available: Yes

Price Category: D

*Illustration provided by
designer/architect.*

Copyright by designer/architect.

Plan #151075

Dimensions: 56' W x 64'4" D

Levels: 1

Heated Square Footage: 1,909

Bedrooms: 3

Bathrooms: 2

Foundation: Crawl space, slab
(basement option for fee)

Materials List Available: Yes

Price Category: D

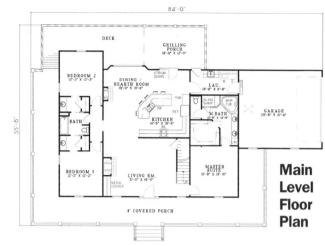

Main Level Floor Plan

Copyright by designer/architect.

Images provided by designer/architect.

Plan #151542

Dimensions: 84' W x 55'6" D

Levels: 1.5

Heated Square Footage: 1,921

Bedrooms: 3

Bathrooms: 3

Foundation: Crawl space, slab, basement, or walkout

CompleteCost List Available: Yes

Price Category: D

Upper Level Floor Plan

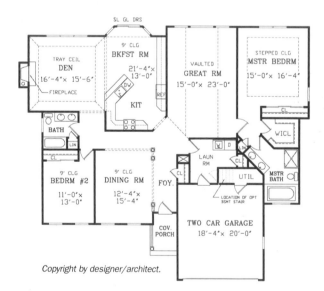

Copyright by designer/architect.

Images provided by designer/architect.

Plan #131006

Dimensions: 61' W x 53'6" D

Levels: 1

Heated Square Footage: 2,193

Bedrooms: 3

Bathrooms: 2

Foundation: Crawl space, slab, or basement

Materials List Available: Yes

Price Category: E

Alternate Floor Plan

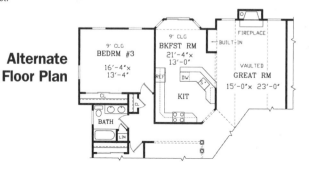

Plan #441035

Dimensions: 50' W x 56' D

Levels: 2

Heated Square Footage: 2,196

Main Level Sq. Ft.: 1,658

Upper Level Sq. Ft.: 538

Bedrooms: 4

Bathrooms: 2½

Foundation: Crawl space; slab or basement available for fee

Materials List Available: No

Price Category: D

Images provided by designer/architect.

This home's stone-and-cedar-shingle facade is delightfully complemented by French Country detailing, dormer windows, and shutters at the large arched window and its second-story sister.

Features:

- Great Room: Containing a fireplace and double doors to the rear yard, this large room is further enhanced by a vaulted ceiling.

- Kitchen: This cooking center has an attached nook with corner windows overlooking the backyard.

- Master Suite: This suite is well designed with a vaulted ceiling and Palladian window. Its bath sports a spa tub.

- Bonus Space: This huge space, located on the second level, provides for a future bedroom, game room, or home office. Two dormer windows grace it.

- Garage: A service hall, with laundry alcove, opens to this garage. There is space enough here for three cars or two and a workshop.

Rear Elevation

Main Level Floor Plan

Upper Level Floor Plan

Copyright by designer/architect.

Plan #151089

Dimensions: 84" W x 55'6" D
Levels: 1
Heated Square Footage: 1,921
Bedrooms: 3
Bathrooms: 3
Foundation: Crawl space, slab, or basement
CompleteCost List Available: Yes
Price Category: D

If your family loves to combine indoor and outdoor living, this home's fabulous porches and deck space make it perfect.

Features:

- **Porches:** A huge wraparound front porch, sizable rear porch, and deck that joins them give you space for entertaining or simply lounging.

- **Living Room:** A fireplace and built-in media center could be the focal points in this large room.

- **Hearth Room:** Open to both the living room and kitchen, this hearth room also features a fireplace.

- **Kitchen:** This step-saving kitchen includes ample storage and work space, as well as an angled bar it shares with the hearth room. Atrium doors lead to the rear porch.

- **Bonus Upper Level:** A large game room and a full bath make this area a favorite with the children.

Images provided by designer/architect.

Copyright by designer/architect.

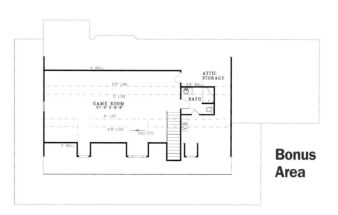

Bonus Area

Custom Flooring

Floors are rarely the focal point of a room. However, this need not be the case. Flooring can steal the show. One way is to design your own custom floor. Many flooring materials lend themselves to customization. Another approach is to enhance an otherwise plain floor with decorative accents, such as medallions and borders. You can design your own or buy them ready-made. Painted designs on floor cloths, carpet, or wood can also grab attention. Even concrete and stone flooring can be etched or sandblasted with the textures, patterns, or images you desire.

design ideas for CREATIVE HOMEOWNER®
Flooring
| products | | inspiration | | materials |

Joseph R. Provey

The following article was reprinted from *Design Ideas for Flooring* (Creative Homeowner 2006).

This painted compass, opposite, looks like an inlay of marble, wood, and metal. The artist muted the wood grain and coloring of the surrounding floor to heighten the contrast.

This detail shows an elaborate border, right, based upon a classic pattern popular in the Victorian era. Composed of pieces of veneer glued to solid tongue-and-groove planks, it is available by the foot.

For a more contemporary feeling, a border (bottom left) is fashioned by alternating light and dark segments of solid-wood planking.

Ready-made borders, bottom middle, are available for vinyl flooring that's made to look like wood.

Borders, bottom right, can also be very simple. In this sunroom, two tones of wood plank are used to create a subtle border.

Borders

Borders are another way to bring attention to your floors. They work in much the same way as a frame around a picture. Use them with just about any kind of flooring, including wood, stone, ceramic, vinyl, cork, and linoleum. Opt for ready-made patterns that range from floral to geometric designs, or compose your own. Border modules include straight sections and 90-degree turns for corners. Wood borders are available prefinished or unfinished, so you can match the stain and finish to your site-finished floor. When selecting borders, keep scale in mind. A wide, elaborate border may overpower a small room. If you are going to fill the room with furniture, you may be wise to skip the borders because you won't see much of them and they are costly—$10 to $70 per lineal foot (before installation), depending on design complexity. Save them for a large space or entry.

Medallions and Accents

Medallions make dramatic focal points, best suited to large floor areas where they can be seen. They are typically round or oval, but they're also available in octagonals, stars, and squares. They are created from exotic woods, marble, granite, limestone, onyx, and ceramics. Brass or aluminum inlay can be used to set off the shapes. Sizes usually range from 2 to 6 feet in diameter.

Wood medallions can be set into either solid or engineered wood floors. Computerized cutting machines make a wide variety of designs possible. Even small wood medallions can cost over $1,000. Check with the manufacturer about how the medallion finish will wear in traffic before you install one in your foyer.

Stone medallions are best suited to stone and ceramic floors. They typically come preassembled on mesh backings, allowing the joints to be grouted on site. Water jet technology, where water and an abrasive are shot through small nozzles at high pressure to create the desired cuts, have made such works of art more economically feasible—but they are still expensive. A 30-inch-diameter marble-and-granite medallion, for example, can easily cost $2,000. Labor to install it will add to the cost. Medallions can be created with other materials as well, including ceramic and glass tile or linoleum.

Decorative accents are a more subtle way to bring attention to your floors. They are smaller, often only a few inches square, and usually used in repetitive patterns. Otherwise, they are made using the same methods as medallions.

Most stone medallions are custom-made—not stock items—so homeowners can select materials that coordinate with their floor, left.

Variations, left, on compass and rose motifs are popular for medallions in both stone and wood.

This wood medallion, bottom left, was site-finished to match the finish on the rest of the room's flooring.

Decorative wood accents, below top, are available in stock patterns, including this rose motif.

Decorative accents, below center, such as this one, are fabricated using water-jet technology.

Etched slate tiles, bottom right, are available in a variety of patterns and sizes. Custom designs are also an option.

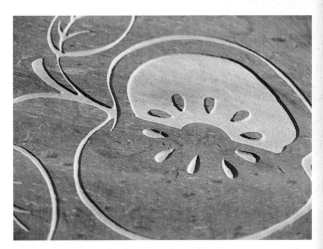

Mosaics

Mosaic floors are composed of small pieces of colored stone, glass, tile, and other materials. They may be used to create interesting textures, patterns, or pictures. An ancient craft first popularized by the Greeks using pebbles and later by Romans using small tiles, mosaic floors often have a classical look. They can, however, be used in traditional, eclectic, and contemporary decorating schemes as well. Mosaics can be used to create borders, inlay strips (between larger field tiles), inserts (to replace larger tiles), and medallions. Pictorial subjects may include historical reproductions and a vast array of floral, animal, and celestial motifs. Mosaic tiles are sold individually or in preassembled motifs; set them with either mortar or adhesive. Some manufacturers allow you to design your own pattern, tile by tile. Then they ship it to you preassembled on a mesh backing or held together with a paper top sheet.

Versatile ceramic mosaics, left, can be used to create free-form patterns, as in this contemporary bath.

Patterns, inset, can be generated with computer design software and then preassembled in sections for easier installation.

The mosaics in this shower, opposite, have a baked-on finish that makes them resistant to lime deposits, dirt, and mold.

order direct: 1-800-523-6789

Pictorial mosaics, opposite, make interesting decorative accents in floors, especially when they are placed along a border.

Translucent glass mosaics sparkle against the opaque matte-finished field tiles in this foyer floor, left.

Traditional white hexagonal mosaics, with borders and accents, above, evoke the turn of the last century in this kitchen.

Inexpensive accents in stone and ceramic, below, transform a plain tile floor.

Plan #101005

Dimensions: 63' W x 57'2" D

Levels: 1

Heated Square Footage: 1,992

Bedrooms: 3

Bathrooms: 2½

Foundation: Crawl space, slab, or basement

Materials List Available: Yes

Price Category: D

Images provided by designer/architect.

Rear View

This midsized ranch is accented with Palladian windows and inviting front porch.

Features:

- Ceiling Height: 9 ft. unless otherwise noted.

- Special Ceilings: Tray or vaulted ceilings adorn the living room, family room, dining room, and master suite.

- Kitchen: This bright and airy kitchen is designed to be a pleasure in which to work. It shares a big bay window with the contiguous breakfast room.

- Breakfast Room: The light streaming in from the bay window makes this the perfect place to linger with coffee and the Sunday paper.

- Master Suite: This lovely suite is exceptional, with its sitting area and direct access to the deck, as well as a full-featured bath, and spacious walk-in closet.

- Secondary Bedrooms: The other bedrooms each measure about 13 ft. x 11 ft. They have walk-in closets and share a "Jack-and-Jill" bath.

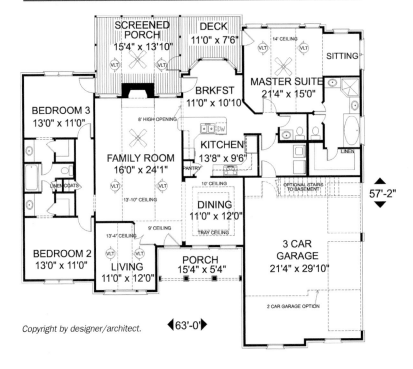

Copyright by designer/architect.

Kitchen

Living Room

Dining Room

Family Room

Master Bedroom

Master Bath

Rear Elevation

Plan #221015

Dimensions: 69'8" W x 46' D

Levels: 1

Heated Square Footage: 1,926

Bedrooms: 3

Bathrooms: 2½

Foundation: Basement; walkout basement for fee

Materials List Available: No

Price Category: D

Images provided by designer/architect.

CAD FILE AVAILABLE

Copyright by designer/architect.

Plan #351205

Dimensions: 70'8" W x 60' D

Levels: 1

Heated Square Footage: 1,934

Bedrooms: 3

Bathrooms: 2

Foundation: Crawl space or slab

Material List Available: Yes

Price Category: D

Images provided by designer/architect.

CAD FILE AVAILABLE

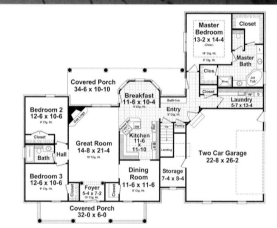

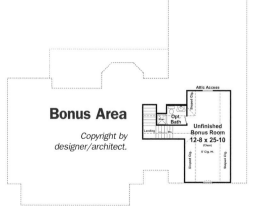

Bonus Area

Copyright by designer/architect.

Rear Elevation

Plan #151838

Dimensions: 47' W x 75' D

Levels: 1

Heated Square Footage: 1,943

Bedrooms: 3

Bathrooms: 2

Foundation: Crawl space or slab; basement or walkout for fee

CompleteCost List Available: Yes

Price Category: D

Images provided by designer/architect.

Copyright by designer/architect.

Plan #441032

Dimensions: 45' W x 55' D

Levels: 2

Heated Square Footage: 1,944

Main Level Sq. Ft.: 1,514

Upper Level Sq. Ft.: 430

Bedrooms: 3

Bathrooms: 2½

Foundation: Crawl space; slab or basement available for fee

Materials List Available: Yes

Price Category: D

Images provided by designer/architect.

Main Level Floor Plan

Upper Level Floor Plan

Copyright by designer/architect.

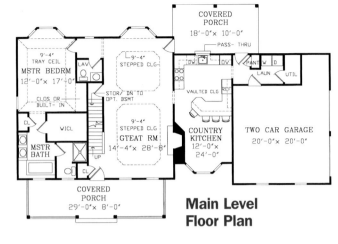

Main Level Floor Plan

Images provided by designer/architect.

Upper Level Floor Plan

Copyright by designer/architect.

Plan #131043

Dimensions: 65'8" W x 43'10" D

Levels: 1.5

Heated Square Footage: 1,945

Main Level Sq. Ft.: 1,375

Upper Level Sq. Ft.: 570

Bedrooms: 3

Bathrooms: 2½

Foundation: Crawl space, slab, or basement

Materials List Available: Yes

Price Category: E

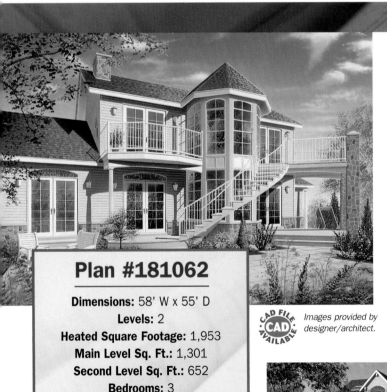

Plan #181062

Dimensions: 58' W x 55' D

Levels: 2

Heated Square Footage: 1,953

Main Level Sq. Ft.: 1,301

Second Level Sq. Ft.: 652

Bedrooms: 3

Bathrooms: 2½

Foundation: Half crawl space, half basement

Materials List Available: Yes

Price Category: D

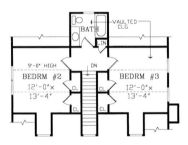

Rear View

Main Level Floor Plan

Upper Level Floor Plan

Copyright by designer/architect.

Images provided by designer/architect.

CAD FILE AVAILABLE

1,501–2,500 sq. ft.

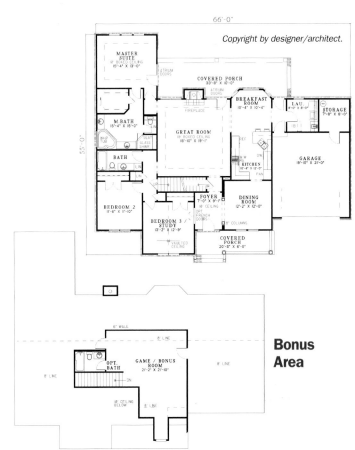

Copyright by designer/architect.

Bonus Area

Plan #151117

Images provided by designer/architect.

CAD FILE AVAILABLE

Dimensions: 66' W x 55' D
Levels: 1
Heated Square Footage: 1,957
Bedrooms: 3
Bathrooms: 3
Foundation: Crawl space, slab, or basement
CompleteCost List Available: Yes
Price Category: D

Main Level Floor Plan

Upper Level Floor Plan

Copyright by designer/architect.

Plan #661062

Images provided by designer/architect.

CAD FILE AVAILABLE

Dimensions: 59'4" W x 45' D
Levels: 2
Heated Square Footage: 1,962
Main Level Sq. Ft.: 1,482
Upper Level Sq. Ft.: 480
Bedrooms: 3
Bathrooms: 2½
Foundation: Slab
Material List Available: No
Price Category: D

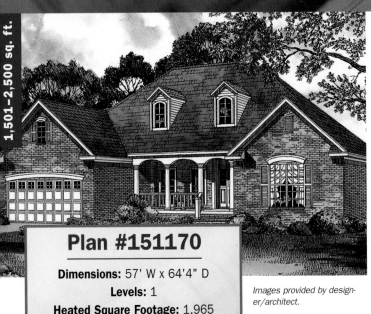

Plan #151170

Dimensions: 57' W x 64'4" D

Levels: 1

Heated Square Footage: 1,965

Bedrooms: 4

Bathrooms: 2

Foundation: Crawl space, slab
(basement or walkout basement
option for fee)

CompleteCost List Available: No

Price Category: E

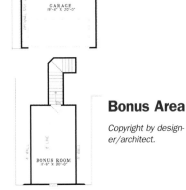

Images provided by design-er/architect.

Bonus Area

Copyright by design-er/architect.

Plan #321006

Dimensions: 76' W x 45' D

Levels: 1, optional lower

Heated Square Footage: 1,977

**Optional Basement Level
Sq. Ft.:** 1,416

Bedrooms: 4

Bathrooms: 2½

Foundation: Basement

Materials List Available: No

Price Category: E

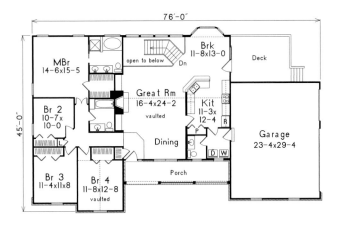

Images provided by design-er/architect.

**Optional
Basement Level
Floor Plan**

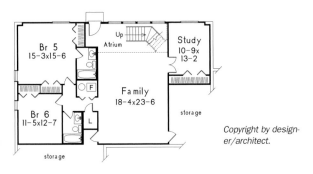

Copyright by design-er/architect.

Plan #101006

Dimensions: 63' W x 58' D

Levels: 1

Heated Square Footage: 1,982

Bedrooms: 3

Bathrooms: 2½

Foundation: Crawl space, slab, basement, or walkout

Materials List Available: Yes

Price Category: D

Images provided by designer/architect.

Copyright by designer/architect.

SMARTtip

Art in Pools

The tiled walls and floor of a pool make great canvases for art, so incorporate a serious or whimsical design. Also, make the stairs wide and shallow to form a wading area for kids.

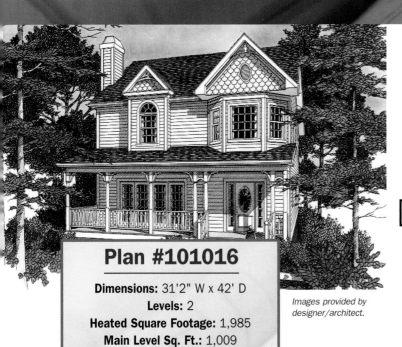

Plan #101016

Dimensions: 31'2" W x 42' D

Levels: 2

Heated Square Footage: 1,985

Main Level Sq. Ft.: 1,009

Upper Level Sq. Ft.: 976

Bedrooms: 3

Bathrooms: 2½

Foundation: Slab, crawl space, or basement

Materials List Available: No

Price Category: D

Images provided by designer/architect.

Main Level Floor Plan

Upper Level Floor Plan

Copyright by designer/architect.

Images provided by designer/architect.

Plan #311017

Dimensions: 72' W x 55'2" D

Levels: 1

Heated Square Footage: 1,974

Bedrooms: 3

Bathrooms: 2½

Foundation: Crawl space, slab or basement

Material List Available: No

Price Category: D

This charming home features an efficient design that allows for large rooms contained in a modest footprint.

Features:

• Great Room: There's plenty of room for all kinds of family activities in this large room that features a soaring cathedral ceiling. The fireplace adds character and warmth to this gathering area.

• Kitchen: The family chef will have plenty of space to work in this large kitchen. An abundance of cabinets and counter space makes this room a dream come true.

• Master Suite: Separated from the secondary bedrooms for privacy, this oasis will help you relax after a busy day. The master bath and large walk-in closet are just the right size.

• Secondary Bedrooms: Two large bedrooms are close to the main full bathroom. One bedroom has direct access to the rear patio.

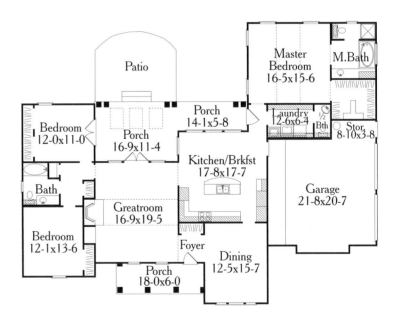

Copyright by designer/architect.

Images provided by designer/architect.

Plan #321053

Dimensions: 35' W x 56' D
Levels: 2
Heated Square Footage: 1,985
Main Level Sq. Ft.: 1,114
Upper Level Sq. Ft.: 871
Bedrooms: 4
Bathrooms: 3½
Foundation: Crawl space, slab or basement
Materials List Available: Yes
Price Category: D

CAD FILE AVAILABLE

This charming design is perfect for a narrow lot.

Features:

- **Entry:** The great room and the dining room are conveniently located near the entry. A coat closet is close at hand, making it easy to receive guests into your home.

- **Great Room:** This dramatic sunken great room features a vaulted ceiling, large double-hung windows, and patio doors. The large fireplace flanked by windows adds charm to this gathering area.

- **Kitchen:** This large peninsula kitchen provides plenty of storage and cooking space for the home chef. Being open to the dining room makes the space feel larger than it really is.

- **Master Suite:** This grand master suite includes a double-door entry, a large closet, an elegant bath and patio access. Its location on the main level separates it from the secondary bedrooms.

- **Upper Level:** Three bedrooms and two full bathrooms occupy this upper level. A view down into the great room gives an open and airy feeling to the home.

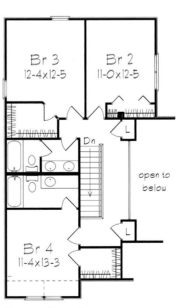

Upper Level Floor Plan

Br 3
12-4x12-5

Br 2
11-0x12-5

open to below

Br 4
11-4x13-3

Copyright by designer/architect.

35'-0"

MBr
17-0x13-10

Deck

56'-0"

Kitchen
11-4x12-0

Great Rm
13-7x18-8
Sunken
vaulted

Dining
11-4x12-0

Garage
18-4x21-4

Main Level Floor Plan

Plan #101022

Dimensions: 66'2" W x 62' D

Levels: 1

Heated Square Footage: 1,992

Bedrooms: 3

Bathrooms: 3

Foundation: Crawl space, slab, or basement

Materials List Available: Yes

Price Category: D

The exterior of this lovely home is traditional, but the unusually shaped rooms and amenities are contemporary.

Features:

- **Foyer:** This two-story foyer is open to the family room, but columns divide it from the dining room.

- **Family Room:** A gas fireplace and TV niche, flanked by doors to the covered porch, sit at the rear of this seven-sided, spacious room.

- **Breakfast Room:** Set off from the family room by columns, this area shares a snack bar with the kitchen and has windows looking over the porch.

- **Bedroom 3:** Use this room as a living room if you wish, and transform the guest room to a media room or a family bedroom.

- **Master Suite:** The bedroom features a tray ceiling, has his and her dressing areas, and opens to the porch. The bath has a large corner tub, separate shower, linen closet, and two vanities.

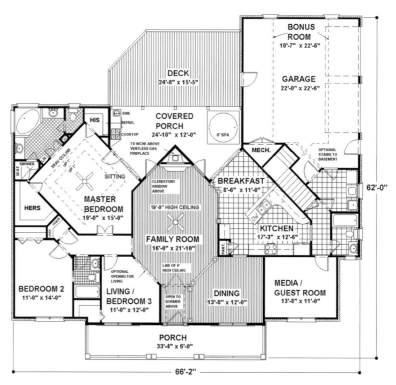

Images provided by designer/architect.

Plan #441008

Dimensions: 60' W x 50' D
Levels: 1
Heated Square Footage: 2,001
Bedrooms: 3
Bathrooms: 2
Foundation: Crawl space;
slab or basement available for fee
Materials List Available: No
Price Category: D

CAD FILE AVAILABLE

A fine design for a country setting, this one-story plan offers a quaint covered porch at the entry, cedar shingles in the gables, and stonework at the foundation line.

Features:

- **Entry:** The pretty package on the outside is prelude to the fine floor plan on the inside. It begins at this entry foyer, which opens on the right to a den with a 9-ft.-high ceiling and space for a desk or closet.

- **Great Room:** This entertaining area is vaulted and contains a fireplace and optional media center. The rear windows allow a view onto the rear deck.

- **Kitchen:** Open to the dining room and great room to form one large space, this kitchen boasts a raised bar and a built-in desk.

- **Master Suite:** The vaulted ceiling in this master suite adds an elegant touch. The master bath features a dual vanities and a spa tub.

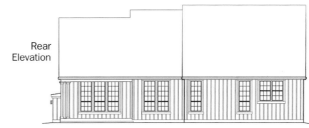

Rear Elevation

Copyright by designer/architect.

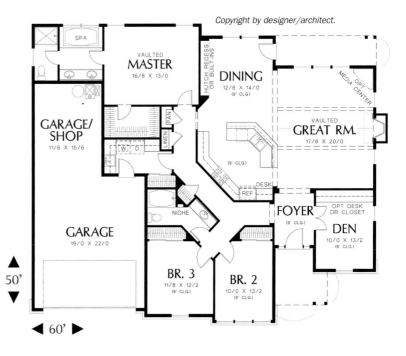

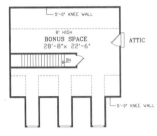

57'-6" OVERALL
(77'-10" W/ OPT. GARAGE)

ALT. LOCATION OF GAR. DRS.

OPTIONAL
TWO CAR GARAGE
20'-0" x 20'-0"

ALT. LOCATION OF GAR. DRS.

COVERED PORCH

Plan #131044

Dimensions: 57'6" W x 42'4" D

Levels: 1

Heated Square Footage: 1,994

Bedrooms: 4

Bathrooms: 2

Foundation: Crawl space, slab, or basement

Materials List Available: Yes

Price Category: E

Images provided by designer/architect.

Rear Elevation

Bonus Area

5'-0" KNEE WALL

8' HIGH
BONUS SPACE
28'-8" x 22'-6"

ATTIC

5'-0" KNEE WALL

Copyright by designer/architect.

Plan #121050

Dimensions: 64' W x 50' D

Levels: 1

Heated Square Footage: 1,996

Bedrooms: 2

Bathrooms: 2

Foundation: Basement; crawl space for fee

Materials List Available: Yes

Price Category: D

Images provided by designer/architect.

Copyright by designer/architect.

Plan #121086

Dimensions: 55'4" W x 37'8" D
Levels: 2
Heated Square Footage: 1,998
Main Level Sq. Ft.: 1,093
Upper Level Sq. Ft.: 905
Bedrooms: 3
Bathrooms: 2½
Foundation: Basement
Materials List Available: Yes
Price Category: D

Images provided by designer/architect.

CAD FILE AVAILABLE

Main Level Floor Plan

Upper Level Floor Plan

Copyright by designer/architect.

Plan #211005

Dimensions: 68' W x 64' D
Levels: 1
Heated Square Footage: 2,000
Bedrooms: 3
Bathrooms: 2
Foundation: Crawl space or slab
Materials List Available: No
Price Category: D

Images provided by designer/architect.

CAD FILE AVAILABLE

Copyright by designer/architect.

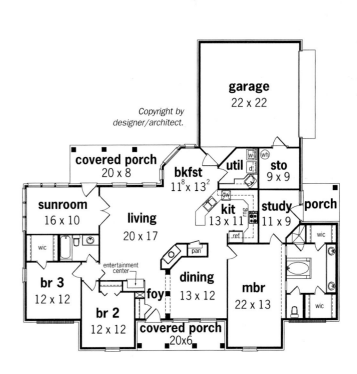

Images provided by designer/architect.

Plan #351105

Dimensions: 69' W x 59'10" D
Levels: 1
Square Footage: 2,000
Bedrooms: 3
Bathrooms: 2½
Foundation: Crawl space, slab or basement
Material List Available: Yes
Price Category: F

This inviting home has rustic styling with upscale features.

CAD FILE · AVAILABLE · CAD

Features:

• Outdoor Living: The front and rear covered porches add plenty of usable outdoor living space and include that much-requested outdoor kitchen.

• Great Room: This expansive great room includes a beautiful trayed ceiling and features built-in cabinets and a gas fireplace.

• Kitchen: This spacious kitchen features an oversize island with a large eating bar and breakfast area.

• Master Suite: The master bedroom has a raised ceiling and opens into the well-equipped bath that includes dual sinks, oversize corner jet tub, and large his and her walk-in closets.

• Flex Space: There is a storage area off of the garage for projects and storage. The media/hobby space could be used as a home office, dining room, or playroom.

Kitchen

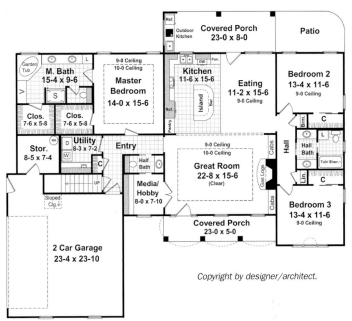

Copyright by designer/architect.

**Bonus Area
Floor Plan**

Master Bathroom

Rear View

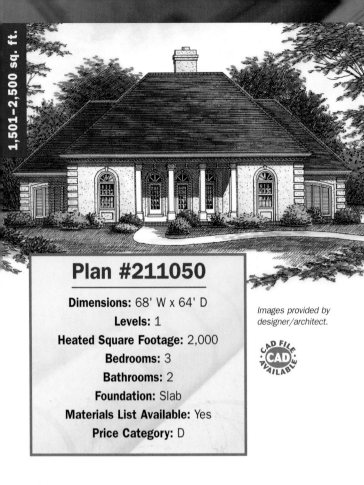

Plan #211050

Dimensions: 68' W x 64' D

Levels: 1

Heated Square Footage: 2,000

Bedrooms: 3

Bathrooms: 2

Foundation: Slab

Materials List Available: Yes

Price Category: D

Images provided by designer/architect.

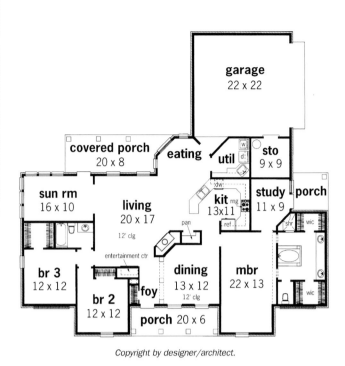

Copyright by designer/architect.

Plan #351102

Dimensions: 67' W x 56' D

Levels: 1

Heated Square Footage: 2,000

Bedrooms: 3

Bathrooms: 2½

Foundation: Crawl space, slab or basement

Material List Available: Yes

Price Category: F

Images provided by designer/architect.

Copyright by designer/architect.

Plan #221018

Dimensions: 67' W x 53' D

Levels: 1

Heated Square Footage: 2,007

Bedrooms: 3

Bathrooms: 2

Foundation: Basement

Materials List Available: No

Price Category: D

Images provided by designer/architect.

Copyright by designer/architect.

Rear Elevation

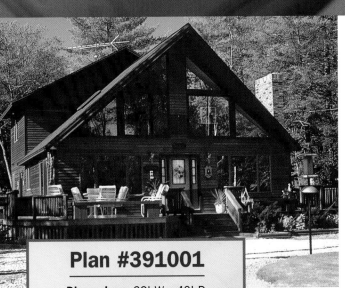

Plan #391001

Dimensions: 32' W x 40' D

Levels: 2

Heated Square Footage: 2,015

Main Level Sq. Ft.: 1,280

Upper Level Sq. Ft.: 735

Bedrooms: 3

Bathrooms: 2½

Foundation: Crawl space

Materials List Available: Yes

Price Category: D

Images provided by designer/architect.

Main Level Floor Plan

Upper Level Floor Plan

Copyright by designer/architect.

Images provided by designer/architect.

Plan #151138

Dimensions: 53' W x 49'4" D
Levels: 1
Heated Square Footage: 1,935
Bedrooms: 3
Bathrooms: 2
Foundation: Basement or walkout
CompleteCost List Available: Yes
Price Category: C

This versatile offering fits anywhere. Its design is as comfortable in the city as it is in the country.

CAD FILE AVAILABLE

Features:

- Porches: Two porches-a covered porch at the front of the home and a grilling porch at the back-are wonderful for entertaining or relaxing.

- Great Room: This beautiful great room is a wonderful, versatile space, with its vaulted ceiling and fireplace.

- Kitchen: In this kitchen, there is space for cooks and diners alike, thanks to the spacious countertop and raised eating bar. For a more formal setting, there is an adjoining dining room.

- Master Suite: Spacious areas define this wonderful master suite, with its large bedroom area and sizable walk-in closet.

Main Level Floor Plan

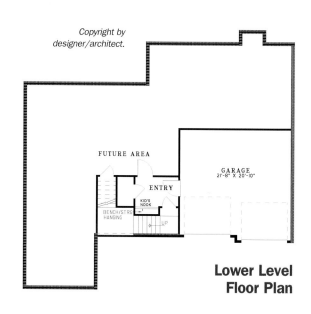

Copyright by designer/architect.

Lower Level Floor Plan

Images provided by designer/architect.

Plan #321030

Dimensions: 61' W x 51' D

Levels: 1

Heated Square Footage: 2,029

Bedrooms: 4

Bathrooms: 2

Foundation: Crawl space, slab, basement, or walkout

Materials List Available: Yes

Price Category: F

Two covered porches and a rear patio make this lovely home fit right into a site with a view.

Features:

- **Great Room:** Boxed entryway columns, a vaulted ceiling, corner fireplace, widowed wall, and door to the patio are highlights in this spacious room.

- **Study:** Tucked into the back of the house for privacy, the study also opens to the rear patio.

- **Dining Area:** The windowed alcove lets natural light flow into this room, which adjoins the kitchen.

- **Kitchen:** A central island, deep pantry, and ample counter area make this room a cook's delight.

- **Master Suite:** You'll love the two walk-in closets, decorative bedroom window, and double doors opening to the private porch. The bath includes a garden tub, a separate shower, and two vanities.

- **Additional Bedrooms:** Both bedrooms have a walk-in closet.

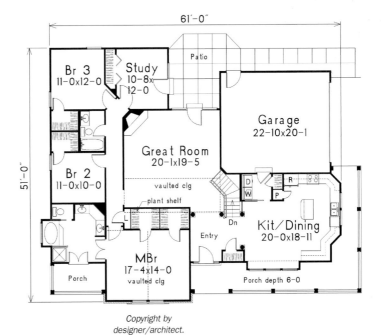

Copyright by designer/architect.

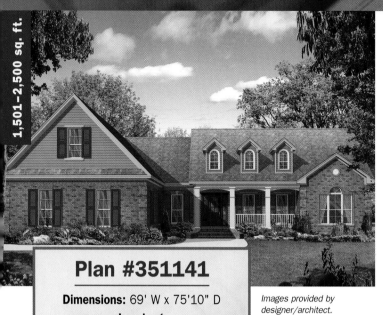

Plan #351141

Dimensions: 69' W x 75'10" D

Levels: 1

Heated Square Footage: 2,021

Bedrooms: 3

Bathrooms: 2½

Foundation: Crawl space, slab or basement

Material List Available: Yes

Price Category: F

Images provided by designer/architect.

CAD FILE AVAILABLE

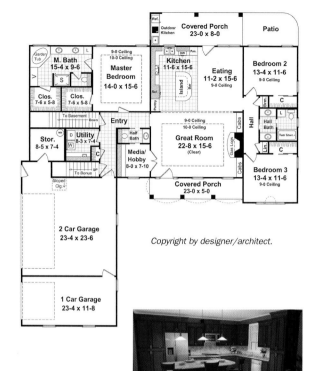

Copyright by designer/architect.

Kitchen

Plan #241007

Dimensions: 58'10" W x 59'1" D

Levels: 1

Heated Square Footage: 2,036

Bedrooms: 3

Bathrooms: 2

Foundation: Crawl space, slab

Materials List Available: No

Price Category: D

Images provided by designer/architect.

Bonus Area Floor Plan

Copyright by designer/architect.

Plan #151105

Dimensions: 60'6" W x 91'4" D

Levels: 1

Heated Square Footage: 2,039

Bedrooms: 4

Bathrooms: 3

Foundation: Crawl space, slab, or optional basement

CompleteCost List Available: Yes

Price Category: D

Images provided by designer/architect.

Bonus Area

Copyright by designer/architect.

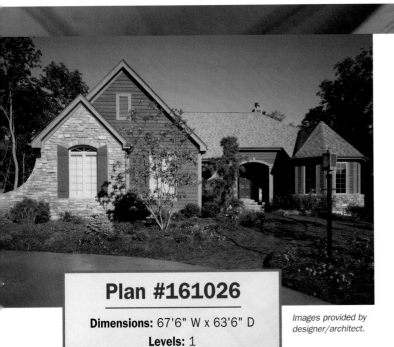

Basement Level Floor Plan

Plan #161026

Dimensions: 67'6" W x 63'6" D

Levels: 1

Heated Square Footage: 2,041

Bedrooms: 3

Bathrooms: 2

Foundation: Basement

Materials List Available: No

Price Category: D

Images provided by designer/architect.

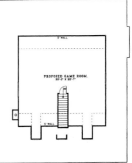

Copyright by designer/architect.

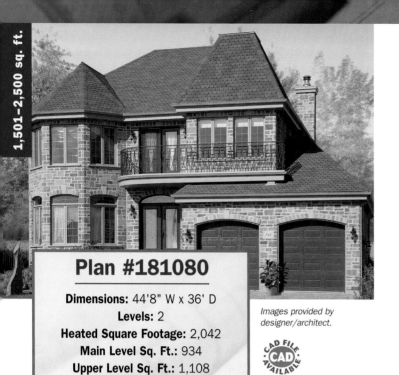

Plan #181080

Dimensions: 44'8" W x 36' D
Levels: 2
Heated Square Footage: 2,042
Main Level Sq. Ft.: 934
Upper Level Sq. Ft.: 1,108
Bedrooms: 3
Bathrooms: 2½
Foundation: Full basement
Materials List Available: Yes
Price Category: E

Images provided by designer/architect.

CAD FILE AVAILABLE

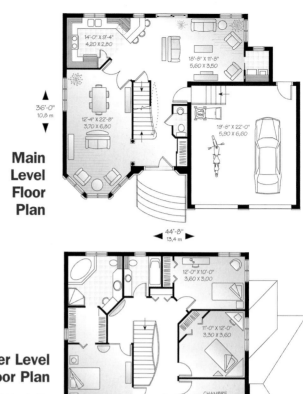

Main Level Floor Plan

36'-0"
10,8 m

44'-8"
13,4 m

Upper Level Floor Plan

Copyright by designer/architect.

CHAMBRE OU BUREAU
10'-0" X 10'-0"
3,00 X 3,00

Plan #171011

Dimensions: 70' W x 58' D
Levels: 1
Heated Square Footage: 2,069
Bedrooms: 3
Bathrooms: 2½
Foundation: Crawl space, slab
Materials List Available: Yes
Price Category: D

Images provided by designer/architect.

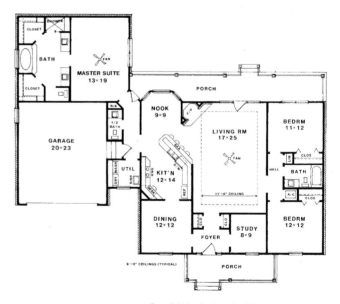

Copyright by designer/architect.

63'-0"

63'-0"

Plan #101030

Dimensions: 63' W x 63' D

Levels: 1

Heated Square Footage: 2,071

Bedrooms: 3

Bathrooms: 2½

Foundation: Crawl space or basement

Materials List Available: Yes

Price Category: E

Images provided by designer/architect.

CAD FILE AVAILABLE

Bonus Area Floor Plan

Copyright by designer/architect.

OPT. BONUS ROOM
11'-4" x 37'-6"
434 Sq. Ft.

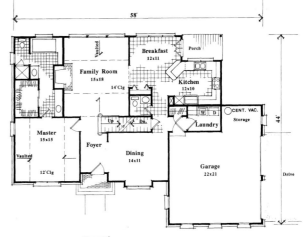

58'

44'

Drive

Main Level Floor Plan

Plan #251013

Dimensions: 58' W x 44' D

Levels: 2

Heated Square Footage: 2,073

Main Level Sq. Ft.: 1,441

Upper Level Sq. Ft.: 632

Bedrooms: 4

Bathrooms: 2½

Foundation: Basement

Materials List Available: Yes

Price Category: D

Images provided by designer/architect.

CAD FILE AVAILABLE

Upper Level Floor Plan

Copyright by designer/architect.

Images provided by designer/architect.

Plan #151850

Dimensions: 66' W x 52' D
Levels: 1
Heated Square Footage: 2,075
Bedrooms: 4
Bathrooms: 3
Foundation: Crawl space, slab; basement or walkout for fee
CompleteCost List Available: Yes
Price Category: D

This European-style home has beautiful details both inside and outside.

Features:

- Courtyard: Upon walking up the path to the entry of this home, you are greeted by a courtyard, where you can plant flowers and set up an area to relax in the sun.

- Great Room: Entertain your friends and family in this great room, which features access to the grilling porch at the rear of the home, a fireplace, and a connection to the kitchen.

- Kitchen: This kitchen was created with many wonderful details, including a pantry, an eating bar, and an attached breakfast room.

- Master Suite: Featuring access to the grilling porch, a spacious walk-in closet, a dual-sink vanity, and a whirlpool tub, this master suite is a great place to relax after a long day.

Copyright by designer/architect.

Plan #161045

Dimensions: 57' W x 49'8" D
Levels: 2
Heated Square Footage: 2,077
Main Level Sq. Ft.: 1,532
Upper Level Sq. Ft.: 545
Bedrooms: 4
Bathrooms: 2½
Foundation: Basement
Materials List Available: No
Price Category: D

Images provided by designer/architect.

Multiple gables, arched windows, and the stone accents that adorn the exterior of this lovely two-story home create a dramatic first impression.

Features:

• Great Room: With multiple windows to light your way, grand openings, varied ceiling treatments, and angled walls let you flow from room to room. Enjoy the warmth of the gas fireplace in both this great room and the dining area.

• Master Suite: Experience the luxurious atmosphere of this master suite, with its coffered ceiling and deluxe bath.

• Additional Bedrooms: Angled stairs lead to a balcony with writing desk and to two additional bedrooms.

• Porch: Exit two sets of French doors to the rear yard and a covered porch, perfect for relaxing in comfortable weather.

Main Level Floor Plan

Copyright by designer/architect.

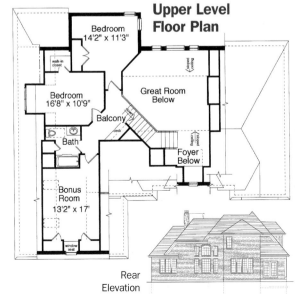

Upper Level Floor Plan

Rear Elevation

Plan #121066

Dimensions: 46' W x 41'5" D

Levels: 2

Heated Square Footage: 2,078

Main Level Sq. Ft.: 1,113

Upper Level Sq. Ft.: 965

Bedrooms: 4

Bathrooms: 2½

Foundation: Basement

Materials List Available: Yes

Price Category: D

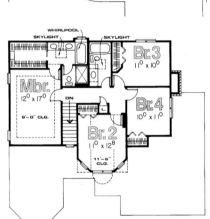

Images provided by designer/architect.

Main Level Floor Plan

Upper Level Floor Plan

Copyright by designer/architect.

Plan #391007

Dimensions: 74' W x 41'6" D

Levels: 2

Heated Square Footage: 2,083

Main Level Sq. Ft.: 1,113

Upper Level Sq. Ft.: 970

Bedrooms: 3

Bathrooms: 2½

Foundation: Crawl space, slab, or basement

Materials List Available: Yes

Price Category: D

Images provided by designer/architect.

Main Level Floor Plan

Upper Level Floor Plan

Copyright by designer/architect.

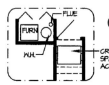

Crawl Space/Slab Option

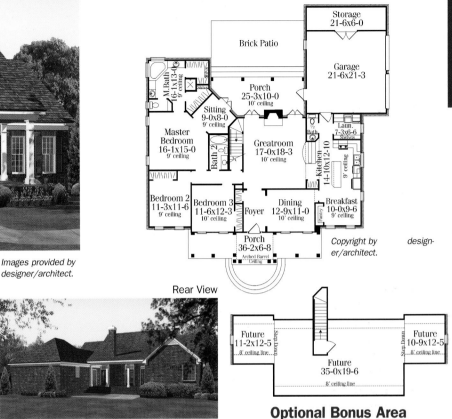

Storage
21-6x6-0

Brick Patio

Garage
21-6x21-3

Porch
25-3x10-0
10' ceiling

M Bath
6-1x13
9' ceiling

Sitting
9-0x8-0
9' ceiling

Master
Bedroom
16-1x15-0
9' ceiling

Bath 2

Greatroom
17-0x18-3
10' ceiling

Laun.
7-3x6-6
Shelves

Bath

Kitchen
14-10x12-10
9' ceiling

Bedroom 2
11-3x11-6
9' ceiling

Bedroom 3
11-6x12-3
10' ceiling

Foyer

Dining
12-9x11-0
10' ceiling

Breakfast
10-0x9-6
9' ceiling

Porch
36-2x6-8
Arched Barrel Ceiling

Copyright by designer/architect.

Images provided by designer/architect.

Rear View

Future
11-2x12-5
8' ceiling line

Future
10-9x12-5
8' ceiling line

Future
35-0x19-6
8' ceiling line

Optional Bonus Area

Plan #311001

Dimensions: 65'11" W x 67'9" D
Levels: 1
Heated Square Footage: 2,085
Bedrooms: 3
Bathrooms: 2½
Foundation: Crawl space, slab, or basement
Materials List Available: No
Price Category: D

Copyright by designer/architect.

DECK

BEDROOM 3
14X11

BRKFST
11X9
11' CEILING

MORNING
PORCH

MASTER
BEDROOM
16X15
11' CEILING

14' CEILING

FAMILY ROOM
17X19

KITCHEN
13X12
11' CEILING

PLANT
SHELF

BEDROOM 2
14X11

LIVING
11X12

FOYER

DINING
13X11
11' CEILING

STORAGE

53

GARAGE
23X20

BONUS ROOM ABOVE

68

Plan #101008

Dimensions: 68' W x 53' D
Levels: 1
Heated Square Footage: 2,088
Bedrooms: 3
Bathrooms: 2½
Foundation: Crawl space, slab, or basement
Materials List Available: Yes
Price Category: E

Images provided by designer/architect.

CAD FILE AVAILABLE

SMARTtip
Accentuating Your Bathroom with Details

No matter how big or small the room, details will pull the style together. Some of the best details that you can include are the smallest—drawer pulls from an antique store or shells in a glass jar or just left on the countertop. Add period flavor with crown molding, or dress up contemporary fixtures with polished stone fittings.

Plan #171015

Dimensions: 79' W x 46' D

Levels: 1

Heated Square Footage: 2,089

Bedrooms: 3

Bathrooms: 2½

Foundation: Crawl space or slab

Materials List Available: Yes

Price Category: D

This lovely three-bedroom country home, with a bonus room above the garage, is a perfect family home.

Features:

- **Dining Room:** This formal room and the great room form a large gathering space with a 12-ft.-high ceiling.

- **Kitchen:** The raised bar defines this kitchen and offers additional seating.

- **Master Suite:** This suite, located on the opposite side of the home from the secondary bedrooms, enjoys a luxurious bath with his and her walk-in closets.

- **Bedrooms:** Two secondary bedrooms have large closets and share a hall bathroom.

Images provided by designer/architect.

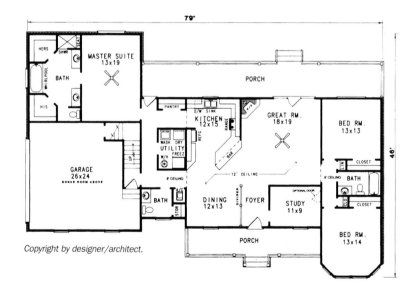

Copyright by designer/architect.

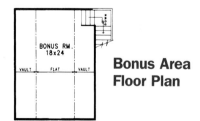

Bonus Area Floor Plan

Plan #191032

Dimensions: 80'4" W x 52' D
Levels: 1
Heated Square Footage: 2,091
Bedrooms: 3
Bathrooms: 2
Foundation: Crawl space or slab
Material List Available: No
Price Category: D

Images provided by designer/architect.

This home has two porches, wonderful for reading a book or watching the sun go down.

Features:

- **Great Room:** Step into this great room from the front porch, and you'll find a spacious area complete with a fireplace.

- **Kitchen/Dining Area:** You'll never have to carry heavy dishes through doors or around walls in this open space. The kitchen area sur rounds an island, perfect for stacking dishes or placing trays before they go to the table.

- **Master Suite:** This master retreat includes a large sleeping area with a fireplace, a spacious walk-in closet, a whirlpool tub, and a dual-sink vanity.

- **Storage Areas:** You'ßll find a variety of uses for these two storage areas. One adjoins the garage, and the other is located off of the laundry/hobby room.

80'-4" WIDE

Copyright by designer/architect.

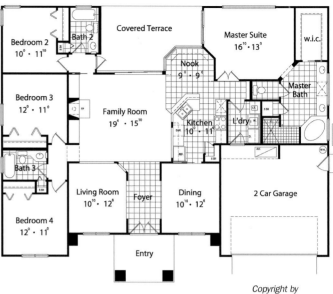

Plan #661002

Dimensions: 61'8" W x 50'4" D
Levels: 2
Heated Square Footage: 2,089
Bedrooms: 4
Bathrooms: 3
Foundation: Slab
Materials List Available: No
Price Category: D

Images provided by designer/architect.

CAD FILE AVAILABLE

Copyright by designer/architect.

Bedroom 2
10⁰ · 11¹⁰

Bath 2

Covered Terrace

Master Suite
16¹⁰ · 13⁰

w.i.c.

Bedroom 3
12⁰ · 11¹⁰

Nook
9⁰ · 9⁰

Family Room
19⁴ · 15¹⁰

Kitchen
10⁰ · 11

Master Bath

L'dry

Bath 3

Living Room
10¹⁰ · 12⁸

Foyer

Dining
10¹⁰ · 12⁸

2 Car Garage

Bedroom 4
12⁰ · 11¹⁰

Entry

Plan #131022

Dimensions: 54'8" W x 43' D
Levels: 2
Heated Square Footage: 2,092
Main Level Sq. Ft.: 1,152
Upper Level Sq. Ft.: 940
Bedrooms: 4
Bathrooms: 2½
Foundation: Crawl space, slab, or basement
Materials List Available: Yes
Price Category: E

Images provided by designer/architect.

This home, as shown in the photograph, may differ from the actual blueprints. For more detailed information, please check the floor plans carefully.

Copyright by designer/architect.

INFORMAL DINING
10'-0"x17'-4"
9' CEILING

KIT

STORAGE

FR. SL. DR.
LOW WALL

FAMILY RM
15'-4"x15'-2"
9' CEILING

FP

DESK OR HUTCH
8'-0"x13'-4"

TWO CAR GARAGE
20'-0"x24'-0"

STAIR TO OPT. BSMT

UTIL

PANTRY

LAUN

LIVING RM
12'-0"x15'-2"
9' CEILING

LAV

CL

DN

UP

FOY

DINING/ OFFICE
12'-0"x13'-0"
9' CEILING

COVERED PORCH

Main Level Floor Plan

WIC

MASTER BATH

LIN

BATH

LIN

BEDRM 3
12'-0"x11'-4"

UNFINISHED EXPANSION LOFT
PLAYRM/BR#4

DN

RAILING

DN

MASTER BEDRM
12'-0"x17'-0"
9'6 HIGH STEPPED CEILING

UPPER FOYER

BEDRM 2
12'-0"x15'-2"

Upper Level Floor Plan

Plan #191012

Dimensions: 60' W x 76' D

Levels: 1

Heated Square Footage: 2,123

Bedrooms: 3

Bathrooms: 2½

Foundation: Crawl space or slab

Materials List Available: No

Price Category: D

Images provided by designer/architect.

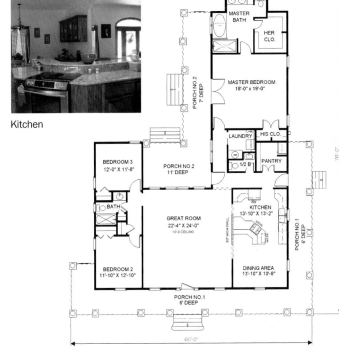

Kitchen

Copyright by designer/architect.

Plan #441049

Dimensions: 50' W x 47'6" D

Levels: 2

Heated Square Footage: 2,124

Main Level Sq. Ft.: 1,157

Upper Level Sq. Ft.: 967

Bedrooms: 3

Bathrooms: 2½

Foundation: Crawl space; slab or basement for fee

Materials List Available: Yes

Price Category: D

Images provided by designer/architect.

CAD FILE AVAILABLE • CAD

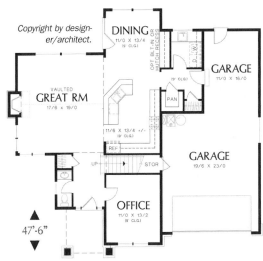

Copyright by designer/architect.

Main Level Floor Plan

Upper Level Floor Plan

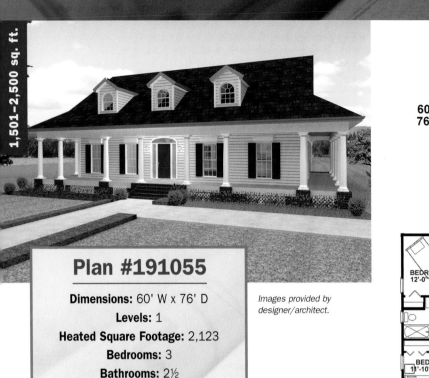

Plan #191055

Dimensions: 60' W x 76' D

Levels: 1

Heated Square Footage: 2,123

Bedrooms: 3

Bathrooms: 2½

Foundation: Crawl space or slab

Material List Available: No

Price Category: D

Images provided by designer/architect.

60'-0" WIDE
76'-0" DEEP

Copyright by designer/architect.

M. BATH

CLOSET
8'-5" X 10'-0"

MASTER BEDROOM
19'-0" X 18'-0"

PORCH 2
7' DEEP

LAUNDRY
7'-0" X 10'-2"

PANTRY
8'-0" X 7'-2"

PORCH 2
11' DEEP

BEDROOM 3
12'-0" X 11'-8"

GREAT ROOM
22'-4" X 16'-0"

KITCHEN
13'-10" X 11'-10"

BEDROOM 2
11'-10" X 12'-10"

SITTING
7'-8" X 8'-0"

FOYER

1/2 B

DINING AREA
13'-10" X 12'-0"

PORCH 1
6' DEEP

Plan #311032

Dimensions: 69' W x 67'4" D

Levels: 1

Heated Square Footage: 2,127

Bedrooms: 3

Bathrooms: 2½

Foundation: Crawl space, slab or basement

Material List Available: Yes

Price Category: D

Images provided by designer/architect.

Copyright by designer/architect.

Storage
4-11x12-6

Garage
21-7x21-5

Porch
9-0x21-6

Bath

Desk

Laun.
5-5x6-0

Master Bedroom
14-3x15-11

Greatroom
18-7x15-11

Breakfast
12-7x10-1

Bedroom
13-3x11-0

Optional Stair

Kitchen
12-7x11-3

Bath

M. Bath

Study/Guest
12-7x12-7

Foyer

Dining
12-7x11-2

Bedroom
13-3x10-2

Porch
32-8x6-0

Future
16-9x14-11

Future
20-2x7-6

Future
22-6x14-11

Future
31-5x9-2

Bonus Area

Rear Elevation

1,501–2,500 sq. ft.

Plan #151171

Dimensions: 63'10" W x 72'2" D

Levels: 1

Heated Square Footage: 2,131

Bedrooms: 3

Bathrooms: 2½

Foundation: Crawl space, slab (basement or daylight basement option for fee)

CompleteCost List Available: Yes

Price Category: D

Images provided by designer/architect.

CAD FILE AVAILABLE

Copyright by designer/architect.

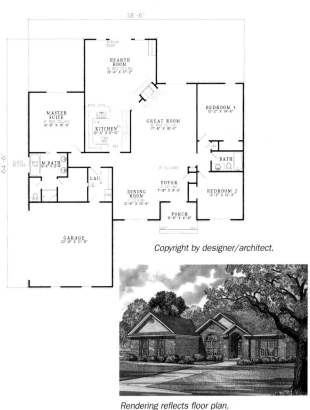

Plan #151034

Dimensions: 58'6" W x 64'6" D

Levels: 1

Heated Square Footage: 2,133

Bedrooms: 3

Bathrooms: 2

Foundation: Crawl space, slab, or basement

CompleteCost List Available: Yes

Price Category: D

Images provided by designer/architect.

This home, as shown in the photograph, may differ from actual blueprints. For more detailed information, please check the floor plans carefully.

CAD FILE AVAILABLE

Copyright by designer/architect.

Rendering reflects floor plan.

Plan #101009

Dimensions: 70'2" W x 59' D
Levels: 1
Heated Square Footage: 2,097
Bedrooms: 3
Bathrooms: 3
Foundation: Crawl space, slab, or basement
Materials List Available: Yes
Price Category: E

Round columns enhance this country porch design, which will nestle into any neighborhood.

Features:

- **Ceiling Height:** 9 ft. unless otherwise noted.

- **Family Room:** This large family room seems even more spacious, thanks to the vaulted ceiling. It's the perfect spot for all kinds of family activities.

- **Dining Room:** This elegant dining room is adorned with a decorative round column and a tray ceiling.

- **Kitchen:** You'll love the convenience of this enormous 14-ft.-3-in. x 22-ft.-6-in. country kitchen, which is open to the family room.

- **Screened Porch:** A French door leads to this breezy porch, with its vaulted ceiling.

- **Master Suite:** This sumptuous suite includes a double tray ceiling, a sitting area, a large walk-in closet, and a luxurious bath.

- **Patio or Deck:** This area is accessible from both the screened porch and master suite.

Images provided by designer/architect.

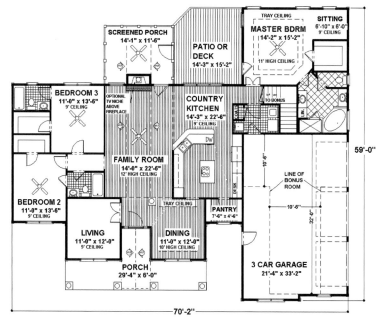

Copyright by designer/architect.

SMARTtip

Single-Level Decks

A single-level deck can use a strong vertical element, such as a pergola or a gazebo, to make it interesting. A simple and less-expensive option is a potted conical shrub or a clematis growing on a trellis.

Plan #151004

Dimensions: 64'8" W x 62'1" D
Levels: 1
Heated Square Footage: 2,107
Bedrooms: 4
Bathrooms: 2½
Foundation: Crawl space, slab, or basement
CompleteCost List Available: Yes
Price Category: E

Images provided by designer/architect.

You'll love the spacious feeling in this comfortable home designed for a family.

Features:

• **Foyer:** A 10-ft. ceiling greets you in this home.

• **Great Room:** A 10-ft. ceiling complements this large room, with its fireplace, built-in cabinets, and easy access to the rear covered porch.

• **Dining Room:** The 9-ft. boxed ceiling in this large room helps to create a beautiful formal feeling.

• **Kitchen:** The island in this kitchen is open to the breakfast room for true convenience.

• **Breakfast Room:** Morning light will stream through the bay window here.

• **Master Suite:** A 9-ft. pan ceiling adds a distinctive note to this room with access to the rear porch. In the bath, you'll find a whirlpool tub, separate shower, double vanities, and two walk-in closets.

Copyright by designer/architect.

Images provided by designer/architect.

Plan #151050

Dimensions: 69'2" W x 74'10" D
Levels: 1
Heated Square Footage: 2,096
Bedrooms: 3
Bathrooms: 2½
Foundation: Crawl space, slab, basement or walkout
CompleteCost List Available: Yes
Price Category: F

CAD FILE AVAILABLE

You'll love this spacious home for both its elegance and its convenient design.

Features:

- Ceiling Height: 8 ft.

- Great Room: A 9-ft. boxed ceiling complements this large room, which sits just beyond the front gallery. A fireplace and door to the rear porch make it a natural gathering spot.

- Kitchen: This well-designed kitchen includes a central work island and shares an angled eating bar with the adjacent breakfast room.

- Breakfast Room: This room's bay window is gorgeous, and the door to the garage is practical.

- Master Suite: You'll love the 9-ft. boxed ceiling in the bedroom and the vaulted ceiling in the bath, which also includes two walk0in closets, a corner whirlpool tub, split vanities, a shower, and a separate toilet room.

- Workshop: A huge workshop with half-bath is ideal for anyone who loves to build or repair.

Main Bathroom

Kitchen

Master Bedroom

69'-2"

Copyright by designer/architect.

WORK SHOP / GARAGE
23'-0" X 20'-0"

COVERED GRILLING PORCH
30'-6" X 12'-6"

GAS BIBB

STRG.

GARAGE
23'-0" X 22'-4"

BRKFAST RM.
12'-4" X 9'-6"

WHP TUB

M.BATH
15'-2" X 18'-0"

LIN

GREAT RM.
17'-0" X 22'-8"
9' BOXED CEILING

REF

DW

CT

OPT. ISLAND

OVEN

PAN

LAU.

W

D

BEDROOM 3
11'-8" X 14'-8"

KITCHEN
12'-4" X 12'-0"

GALLERY

BOOK SHELVES

BOOK SHELVES

FOYER
9' CEILING

MASTER SUITE
15'-2" X 16'-0"
9' BOXED CEILING

COVERED PORCH
17'-0" X 5'-0"
9' CEILING

DINING RM.
12'-4" X 12'-0"
9' BOXED CEILING

BEDROOM 2
13'-4" X 10'-8"

74'-10"

54'-6"

Your Private Sanctuary

E-mails. Voice mails. Blackberries. Text messages. Today, you have the capability to reach people at any moment. Unfortunately, this miracle of modern communication means that everyone can reach you just as easily. The stress that this adds to daily life seems like a steep price to pay for today's technological advancements.

Is it any surprise, then, that some days all you want to do is escape from the constant jangling of your cell phone to a place where no one can bother you?

Enter the master bathroom, the one room in the house where seclusion still reigns supreme. Even in today's high-style homes—increasingly designed for public display and admiration—the master bath is for your eyes only.

In the not-too-distant past, bathrooms were strictly utilitarian. Today, many homeowners are building master baths with all the accoutrements of a luxurious hotel or spa. This upscale trend is far more than an extravagant indulgence; it's a wise investment in one's health, happiness, and well-being. A beautiful master bathroom is a sanctuary where you can fortify your mind and body in order to meet the rigorous demands of contemporary life.

Defining Your Escape Plan

The first step in creating the grand master bath of your dreams is to compile a wish list. What does your fantasy bathroom look like? Do you imagine a romantic setting,

Nothing soothes the soul like Mother Nature, top right. For maximum comfort, think light and bright, and let simple elements like water and space define your bath's ambience.

Positioning a tub to take advantage of natural light, right, makes a daily bath a delightful treat.

complete with soaking tub, scented candles, and soft mood lighting? Or would you prefer a peaceful place to practice your yoga poses before jumping into a bracing steam shower? Perhaps your idea of sybaritic perfection is to sip your first cup of coffee, watch the the morning news, and check the day's stock prices, all from the comfort of a bubbling spa tub.

Think about a bathroom you enjoyed while vacationing at a resort or spa. What impressed you most? Was it the heated floors? The towel warmers? The two-person shower with personalized water-temperature controls? The generous vanity and storage space? Or was it the elegant little extras, such as a built-in magnifying mirror, his and her sinks, silent exhaust fan, or crystal-encrusted faucets?

Don't rule out anything that might seem unattainable; there's technology out there that will astound you, and much of it is less expensive than you might think. Even if an option you like is out of your price range, don't abandon your dream: a good designer who understands what you'd like to accomplish may help you come up with an affordable alternative that can capture the essence of your vision.

Next, do some research. Page through interior design books and magazines; visit model homes and show houses in your area; check out design Web sites; and peruse a few bath and decorative plumbing and hardware showrooms. Attending open houses in upscale neighborhoods will also help you build your idea file. Once you have a better sense of what you like, make a list of the amenities you want most in

SMARTtip

Space Savers

While it's wonderful to have a palatial bathroom, never let a lack of space prevent you from having the grand master bath of your dreams. Clever design features come in all shapes and sizes, and many of the best luxury amenities take up no space at all!

order of their priority. Next, ask yourself what you dislike about your bathroom in your current residence. Is the space cramped or poorly configured? Does it suffer from a lack of storage, light, or counter space? If multiple users share your bath, can two people get ready simultaneously, or do you get in each other's way?

This is also a good time to address future safety problems. For example, choose a bathroom floor that is not slippery when wet. Select medicine cabinets that can't be opened by small children. Verify your new faucet won't go from cold to scalding hot for no apparent reason. And remember to include a grab bar for the shower. Don't worry—you won't ruin your beautiful new bathroom. The newest grab bars are a testament to high style, and they will protect you and your family from dangerous falls. In fact, many top designers insist on including them in every new bath project.

Finally, decide on the overall feeling you want your new bath to conjure. Because your ideal retreat should provide both emotional and physical comfort, consider whether you want your bath to be soft and soothing, subtly elegant, or lively and invigorating. As later chapters discuss how to combine elements such as color, lighting, and materials, you will learn how to construct a space that evokes the responses you desire.

Elegant light fixtures, opposite top, highlight this bath's striking mirror, making it a visual focal point, while draped window treatments "frame" the spectacular tub.

Blending materials such as glass and metal lends dimension to your bath design, opposite bottom. Here, the wall-mounted faucet adds a sophisticated touch.

This bath, right, provides a streamlined look while maintaining separate his and hers spaces to simplify the morning routine.

Design for Life

When planning your dream bath, it's very easy to be seduced by the endless array of choices. How can you not be enticed by a jetted tub that incorporates mood lighting, surround-sound, and Internet access?

It's important to remember that your design plan should reflect your lifestyle. Sure, that deep soaking tub is gorgeous, but if you haven't found time for a long soak since 1993, maybe you'd be happier if you chose a spacious shower with all the upgrades.

Similarly, if your morning routine involves six different hair products and enough makeup to stock a department store, stark minimalism is probably not the style for you. Instead, think about incorporating an expansive grooming station with plenty of organized storage areas.

Do you head to your bathroom to relax, rejuvenate, and escape from the rest of the world? If so, why not maximize your precious "me" time with piped-in audio, a sitting area, a deep soaking tub, or even a fireplace? Conversely, if your morning routine is all about speed, choose a shower with temperature presets, so you needn't waste time fiddling to get the water just right.

Consider maintenance issues, too, especially if your bath will have multiple users. High-gloss surfaces, leather tiles, or intricately styled faucets with lots of tiny crevices all make gorgeous design statements, but they require extra upkeep to keep them looking great.

Remember, your master bath should be a place that helps you unwind; not one that adds more stress to your life; so be sure that your design incorporates all the elements you require for comfort and relaxation.

Size Matters

Once you've completed your wish list, it's time to ponder the question of square footage. Does your new bath meet your space requirements? Is it too small or, even, too large? House plans can be modified prior to construction.

Like the old adage that you can never be too thin or too rich, many people assume that you can never have a bathroom that is "too big." In truth, an overly large space may actually be quite uncomfortable. Just as a tiny room can be confining, a giant area can make you feel exposed and uneasy. What's more, bathrooms that are too large can echo unpleasantly, creating a feeling of coldness rather than warmth.

Obviously, a super-size bathroom can also be a wonderful luxury. Given ample room, you can pick and choose from a host of delightful amenities. Abundant counter and storage space is chief among them, but how about a two-person tub or shower (or both), dual grooming stations, a private bidet, or even a mini-kitchen, exercise area, or spa? Just keep in mind that with a large floor plan, you'll need to separate your master bath into functional areas, or zones, either through fixture placement or the artful use of color and materials. By doing so, you'll maintain a sense of warmth, create a better flow, and muffle excess sound.

Of course, square footage is not the sole feature that makes a bath luxurious, nor does a shortage of space mean you can't have a stunning and stylish retreat. If space is at a premium, you still have several options.

SMARTtip

Conceptualize

The essence of good design begins with the concept. The ambiance, the mood, the palette—all contribute to the success of the space. Think relaxation, luxury, and function when you plan your master bath.

Steal from existing space. Talk with a designer, prior to construction, about the many clever ways you can borrow space from an extra bedroom, closet, or hallway, or even create shared closet space between rooms.

Use space-saving products and solutions. If you modify the plans, but are limited to the current footprint, consider such options as a corner tub, pocket doors, wall-mounted faucets, and pedestal sinks, all designed to take up minimal square footage. Replacing an regular tub with a luxurious shower is another increasingly popular solution. If your home plan has a second bathroom with a tub you won't use, this may be an excellent space-saving idea that doesn't sacrifice anything you really want.

Get creative with storage. Lack of floor space doesn't mean you can't have plenty of functional storage. There are many ways to build storage space into your bath that don't waste precious square footage. These solutions are light years beyond a few shelves above the toilet or a wicker basket on the floor for storing extra towels. For example, there are new cabinet styles that come in an L-shape configuration that sits on two walls, doubling the storage capacity of a standard cabinet. Some new tubs offer built-in storage, and many showers feature recessed niches for soaps and shampoos. There are even full-length, door-hung mirrors on the market that open to reveal storage space for jewelry and medicine.

Let your bath transport you to the place you love best, whether it's a simple beach-side cottage or a romantic villa in Tuscany, opposite top.

Mixing classic white with eye-catching patterned tile in soft shades of brown makes this space feel serene without sacrificing visual interest, opposite bottom. Open storage and soft curves add to the bath's appeal.

If simplicity is your goal, consider built-in storage in the tub surround, an ingenious way to preserve the clean lines of the space, above.

Designer Insights

How do you create the master bath of your dreams? Designer Carol J. Weissman Kurth, AIA, Allied Member ASID, offers these suggestions that pertain to any bathroom:

- **Luxury doesn't need to be large.** Instead, it's the quality of the space that counts. Interesting ceilings, textures, and details all add to the depth and quality of the design.
- **Build upon the theme.** Layer and integrate design elements to enhance the architecture of the room and capture your unique personality.
- **Display special collectibles.** Niches for candles and towels and other creative ideas are all important facets of good bathroom design.
- **Eliminate clutter.** Cabinetry and places for toiletries ensure that everything is in its rightful place.
- **Use a variety of lighting.** From task lights for shaving to decorative lights that create magical moods, the importance of the right lighting cannot be overstated.

Style Sensations

Not so long ago, bathroom designs fell into very specific categories. There were two major style choices—traditional and contemporary—with a specific delineation between the two that left no room for a middle ground. The prevailing rules of interior decor also dictated that your bathroom had to match the style of the rest of your home, regardless of how well this met your needs.

Thankfully, there has been a growing movement in the last few years toward "transitional" design, which incorporates the best elements of contemporary and traditional styles. Combine this with the equally hot trend of mixing and matching materials, and today's design choices have become more fluid, not only in a specific room, but also from room to room.

The ABCs of Bath Design
Translating Professional Certifications

If you decide to modify your home plans bath design, get advice from a professional in the field. When checking out designers, don't be surprised if the letters after their names read a bit like alphabet soup. Many designers are members of professional associations that help them to further their education and skills. Others pursue special certifications as proof of their knowledge and experience.

How does all this translate into finding the right designer for you? It pays to know what their designations mean. For instance, some associations require little more than annual dues, while others monitor their members to ensure that they maintain high-quality standards. Likewise, certification requirements can range from a specified number of classroom hours to proof of specialized knowledge in a variety of areas. These requirements will vary based on the governing body.

Here are some of the common abbreviations you'll see and what they mean. For more information about each organization, visit the following Web sites.

· AIA: Member of the American Institute of Architects; www.aia.org
· ASID: Member of the American Society of Interior Designers; www.asid.org
· CBD: Certified Bath Designer; www.nkba.org
· CMKBD: Certified Master Kitchen and Bath Designer; www.nkba.org
· CKBR: Certified Kitchen and Bath Remodeler; www.nari.org
· CPBD: Certified Professional Building Designer; www.ncbdc.com
· CR: Certified Remodeler; www.nari.org
· DPHA: Member of the Decorative Plumbing & Hardware Association; www.dpha.net
· GCP: Green Certified Professional; www.nari.org
· NARI: Member of the National Association of the Remodeling Industry; www.nari.org
· NKBA: Member of the National Kitchen & Bath Association; www.nkba.org

But why go for "matchy-matchy" when you can layer different textures and materials that add depth, dimension, and your own personal flair? Today, it's perfectly okay to mix natural stone, bronze, glass, and mahogany or to combine Italian tile with a clean-lined, wall-mounted faucet.

That's not to suggest that anything goes. Combining a hodgepodge of styles and materials without a basic understanding of design principles can result in a big mess. That's why it's a good idea to consult with a qualified design professional for guidance if you decide to modify the bath design on your home plan.

Picking a Pro

You wouldn't entrust your health to a guy who sells miracle cures on late-night television. Neither would you assign your master bath redesign to someone who is not a licensed, experienced professional. Hiring a designer with a good track record and strong professional partnerships helps to minimize problems and ensure that your project gets done quickly and efficiently. Interview several designers; study their portfolios; visit jobs they've completed; and discuss in detail what you have in mind.

Transitional style is both timeless and versatile, making it a perfect choice to complement almost any decor, opposite top.

Contrasting the rich warmth of wood with the natural variations of stone adds, opposite bottom, depth and dimension to this impressive master bath.

Why not add a bit of "retro" glamour to your private sanctuary, right? Here, a private grooming nook features an ornately designed mirror and glittery, metallic tiles.

Plan #161016

Dimensions: 59'4" W x 58'8" D

Levels: 1.5

Heated Square Footage: 2,101

Main Level Sq. Ft.: 1,626

Upper Level Sq. Ft.: 475

Bedrooms: 3

Bathrooms: 2½

Foundation: Basement; crawl space option available for fee

Materials List Available: No

Price Category: D

Note: Home in photo reflects a modified garage entrance.

Images provided by designer/architect.

Features:

- **Great Room:** Made for relaxing and entertaining, the great room is sunken to set it off from the rest of the house. A balcony from the second floor looks down into this spacious area, making it easy to keep track of the kids while they are playing.

- **Kitchen:** Convenience marks this well laid-out kitchen where you'll love to cook for guests and for family.

- **Master Suite:** A vaulted ceiling complements the unusual octagonal shape of the master bedroom. Located on the first floor, this room allows some privacy from the second floor bedrooms. It is also ideal for anyone who no longer wishes to climb stairs to reach a bedroom.

You'll love the exciting roofline that sets this elegant home apart from its neighbors as well as the embellished, solid look that declares how well-designed it is—from the inside to the exterior.

CAD FILE AVAILABLE

Left Side Elevation

Rear Elevation

Right Side Elevation

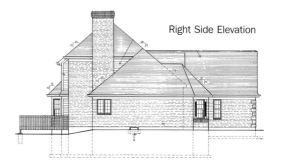

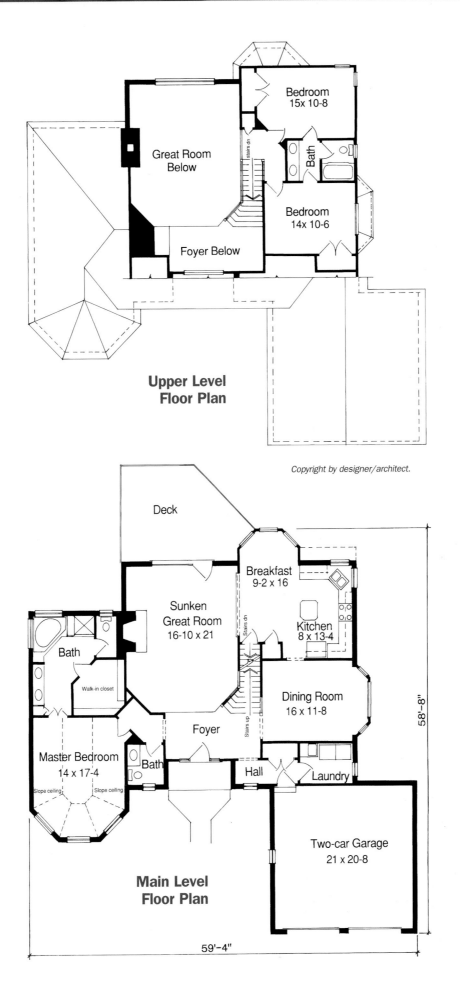

Bedroom
15x 10-8

Great Room
Below

Stairs dn

Bath

Bedroom
14x 10-6

Foyer Below

**Upper Level
Floor Plan**

Copyright by designer/architect.

Deck

Breakfast
9-2 x 16

Sunken
Great Room
16-10 x 21

Stairs dn

Kitchen
8 x 13-4

Bath

Walk-in closet

Foyer

Stairs up

Dining Room
16 x 11-8

Master Bedroom
14 x 17-4

Bath

Hall

Laundry

Slope ceiling   Slope ceiling

Two-car Garage
21 x 20-8

**Main Level
Floor Plan**

58'-8"

59'-4"

Plan #151731

Dimensions: 55' W x 58'6" D
Levels: 1.5
Heated Square Footage: 2,099
Main Level Sq. Ft.: 2,099
Upper Level Future Sq. Ft.: 480
Bedrooms: 3
Bathrooms: 2
Foundation: Crawl space or slab; basement or walkout for fee
CompleteCost List Available: Yes
Price Category: D

Images provided by designer/architect.

CAD FILE AVAILABLE

Main Level Floor Plan

Upper Level Floor Plan

Copyright by designer/architect.

Plan #371081

Dimensions: 54'6" W x 41'10" D
Levels: 2
Heated Square Footage: 2,143
Main Level Sq. Ft.: 1,535
Upper Level Sq. Ft.: 608
Bedrooms: 4
Bathrooms: 3
Foundation: Slab or basement
Materials List Available: No
Price Category: D

Images provided by designer/architect.

CAD FILE AVAILABLE

Main Level Floor Plan

Upper Level Floor Plan

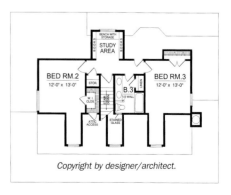

Copyright by designer/architect.

Rear Elevation

Main Level Floor Plan

Copyright by designer/architect.

Dining 13' x 15'

Breakfast 15'2" x 9'

Kitchen 16'6" x 9'

Laun.

Hall

Great Room 16' x 23'10"

Dressing

walk-in closet

Raised Foyer

Two-car Garage 22' x 22'

Porch

Master Bedroom 13'2" x 16'

Upper Level Floor Plan

Bedroom 12'10" x 11'6"

Bedroom 11' x 11'6"

Bath

Great Room Below

Balcony

walk-in closet

Bonus Room 11' x 11'11"

Plan #161034

Dimensions: 56' W x 53' D
Levels: 2
Heated Square Footage: 2,156
Main Level Sq. Ft.: 1,605
Upper Level Sq. Ft.: 551
Bedrooms: 3
Bathrooms: 2½
Foundation: Basement
Materials List Available: No
Price Category: D

Images provided by designer/architect.

Rear View

Plan #121117

Dimensions: 76' W x 46' D
Levels: 1
Heated Square Footage: 2,172
Bedrooms: 4
Bathrooms: 3
Foundation: Basement; crawl space for fee
Material List Available: Yes
Price Category: D

Images provided by designer/architect.

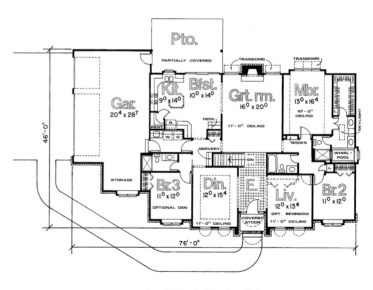

Pto.
PARTIALLY COVERED

TRANSOMS

TRANSOMS

Gar. 20'4 x 28'7

Kit. 9'0 x 14'0

Bfst. 10'0 x 14'0

Grt. rm. 16'0 x 20'0
11'-0" CEILING

Mbr. 13'0 x 16'4
10'-0" CEILING

DESK

SKYLIGHT

BOOKS

PANT.

W.D.

SERVERY

STORAGE

Br. 3 11'0 x 12'0
OPTIONAL DEN

Din. 12'0 x 15'4

Liv. 12'0 x 13'4
OPT. BEDROOM

Br. 2 11'0 x 12'0

WHIRL-POOL

DN

COVERED STOOP

11'-0" CEILING

11'-0" CEILING

11'-0" CEILING

46'-0"

76'-0"

Copyright by designer/architect.

Images provided by designer/architect.

Plan #191001

Dimensions: 62' W x 72' D

Levels: 1

Heated Square Footage: 2,156

Bedrooms: 4

Bathrooms: 3

Foundation: Crawl space, slab, or basement

Materials List Available: No

Price Category: D

This lovely home has the best of old and new — a traditional appearance combined with fabulous comforts and conveniences.

Features:

- **Great Room:** A tray ceiling gives stature to this expansive room, and its many windows let natural light stream into it.

- **Kitchen:** When you're standing at the sink in this gorgeous kitchen, you'll have a good view of the patio. But if you turn around, you'll see the island cooktop, wall oven, walk-in pantry, and snack bar, all of which make this kitchen such a pleasure.

- **Master Suite:** Somewhat isolated for privacy, this area is ideal for an evening or weekend retreat. Relax in the gracious bedroom or luxuriate in the spa-style bath, with its corner whirlpool tub, large shower, two sinks, and access to the walk-in closet, which measures a full 8 ft. x 10 ft.

- **Mudroom:** No matter whether you live where mud season is as reliable as spring thaws or where rain is a seasonal event, you'll love having a spot to confine the muddy mess.

Front View

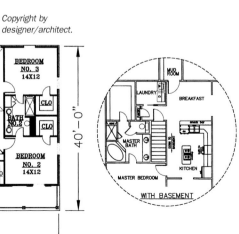

Plan #181085

Dimensions: 56'4" W x 44' D

Levels: 2

Heated Square Footage: 2,183

Main Level Sq. Ft.: 1,232

Second Level Sq. Ft.: 951

Bedrooms: 3

Bathrooms: 2½

Foundation: Basement

Materials List Available: Yes

Price Category: E

This country home features an inviting front porch and a layout designed for modern living.

CAD FILE AVAILABLE

Images provided by designer/architect.

Features:

- Ceiling Height: 8 ft.
- Solarium: Sunlight streams through the windows of this solarium at the front of the house.
- Living Room: Walk through French doors, and you will enter this inviting living room. Family and friends will be drawn to the corner fireplace.
- Formal Dining Room: Usher your guests directly from the living room into this formal dining room. The kitchen is located on the

other side of the dining room for convenient service.

- Kitchen: This generously sized kitchen is a delight, it offers a center island, separate eat-in area, and access to the back deck.
- Bonus Room: This room just off the entry hall can become a family room, a bedroom, or an office.
- Master Suite: Curl up by the corner fireplace in this master retreat, with its walk-in closet and lavish bath with separate shower and tub.

Main Level Floor Plan

44'-0"
13,2 m

56'-4"
16,9 m

Upper Level Floor Plan

Copyright by designer/ architect.

Plan #101011

Dimensions: 71'2" W x 58'1" D

Levels: 1

Heated Square Footage: 2,184

Bedrooms: 3

Bathrooms: 3

Foundation: Crawl space, slab, basement, or walkout

Materials List Available: Yes

Price Category: E

A classic design and spacious interior add up to a flexible design suitable to any modern lifestyle.

Features:

- Ceiling Height: 9 ft. unless otherwise noted.

- Dining Room: A decorative square column and a tray ceiling adorn this elegant dining room.

- Screened Porch: Enjoy summer breezes in style by stepping out of the French doors into this vaulted screened porch.

- Kitchen: Does everyone want to hang out in the kitchen while you are cooking? No problem. True to the home's country style, this huge 14-ft.-3-in. x 22-ft.-6-in. kitchen has plenty of room for helpers. This area is open to the vaulted family room.

Images provided by designer/architect.

- Patio or Deck: This pleasant outdoor area is accessible from both the screened porch and the master bedroom.

- Master Suite: This luxurious suite includes a double tray ceiling, a sitting area, two walk-in closets, and an exquisite bath.

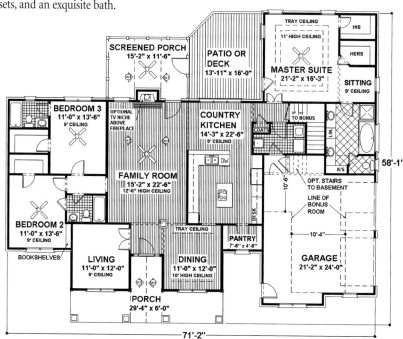

Copyright by designer/architect.

Kitchen

Dining Room

Family Room

Living Room

Master Bath

Master Bedroom

1,501–2,500 sq. ft.

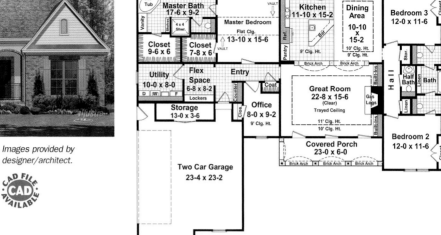

Copyright by designer/architect.

Screened Porch
15-4 x 9-8

Master Bath
17-6 x 9-2

Jet Tub
Vanity

Master Bedroom
Flat Clg.
13-10 x 15-6

Kitchen
11-10 x 15-2

Dining
Area
10-10
x
15-2
10' Clg. Ht.

Bedroom 3
12-0 x 11-6

Closet
9-6 x 6

Closet
7-8 x 6

Pantry
Ref.

9' Clg. Ht.

Brick Arch   Brick Arch

Hall

Stor.

Half
Bath   Bath

Linen

Utility
10-0 x 8-0

Flex
Space
6-8 x 8-2

Entry

Lockers

Coat

Great Room
22-8 x 15-6
(Clear)
Trayed Ceiling

11' Clg. Ht.
10' Clg. Ht.

Gas
Logs

Built-Ins

Built-Ins

Storage
13-0 x 3-6

Office
8-0 x 9-2
9' Clg. Ht.

Bedroom 2
12-0 x 11-6

Closet

Two Car Garage
23-4 x 23-2

Covered Porch
23-0 x 6-0

Brick Arch   Brick Arch   Brick Arch

Plan #351085

*Images provided by
designer/architect.*

Dimensions: 70'6" W x 65' D

Levels: 1

Heated Square Footage: 2,200

Bedrooms: 3

Bathrooms: 2½

Foundation: Crawl space or slab

Material List Available: Yes

Price Category: F

 CAD FILE AVAILABLE

Rear
Elevation

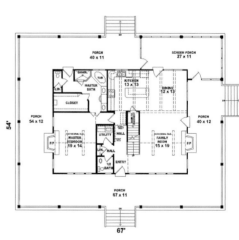

Main Level Floor Plan

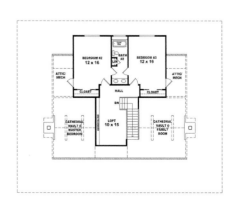

Upper Level
Floor Plan

Copyright by designer/architect.

Plan #651079

*Images provided by
designer/architect.*

Dimensions: 67' W x 54' D

Levels: 1.5

Heated Square Footage: 2,207

Main Level Sq. Ft.: 1,466

Upper Level Sq. Ft.: 741

Bedrooms: 3

Bathrooms: 2½

Foundation: Crawl space or basement

Material List Available: No

Price Category: E

CAD FILE AVAILABLE

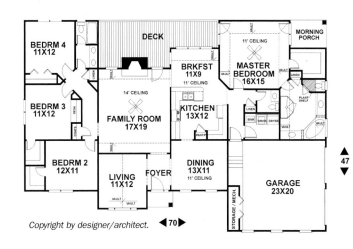

BEDRM 4
11X12

DECK

MORNING PORCH

11' CEILING

MASTER BEDROOM
16X15

BEDRM 3
11X12

BRKFST
11X9

11' CEILING

14' CEILING

FAMILY ROOM
17X19

KITCHEN
13X12

LINEN

SINK DSHWSHR DRYER

PANTRY

PLANT SHELF

BEDRM 2
12X11

LIVING
11X12

FOYER

DINING
13X11

11' CEILING

GARAGE
23X20

STORAGE / MECH

47

Copyright by designer/architect.

◄ 70 ►

Plan #101010

Dimensions: 70' W x 47' D
Levels: 1
Heated Square Footage: 2,187
Bedrooms: 4
Bathrooms: 2½
Foundation: Crawl space, slab, or basement
Materials List Available: Yes
Price Category: E

Images provided by designer/architect.

CAD FILE AVAILABLE — CAD

SMARTtip
Using Slipcovers in Your Dining Area

Change the look of your dining room by slipcovering chairs. Short-skirted slipcovers give a more informal appearance; fabrics in graphic patterns, such as checks or floral prints, complement this style of slipcover best. Long-skirted covers are elegant additions to a formal dining room, particularly in solid color or tone-on-tone fabrics. Ties, buttons, or trim can add personality.

Plan #111015

Dimensions: 64' W x 58' D
Levels: 1
Heated Square Footage: 2,208
Bedrooms: 4
Bathrooms: 2
Foundation: Slab
Materials List Available: No
Price Category: F

Images provided by designer/architect.

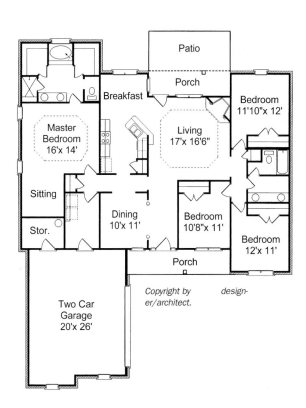

Patio

Porch

Breakfast

Bedroom
11'10" x 12'

Master Bedroom
16' x 14'

Living
17' x 16'6"

Sitting

Dining
10' x 11'

Bedroom
10'8" x 11'

Bedroom
12' x 11'

Stor.

Porch

Two Car Garage
20' x 26'

Copyright by designer/architect.

Plan #151113

Dimensions: 62'10" W x 91'4" D

Levels: 1

Heated Square Footage: 2,186

Bedrooms: 4

Bathrooms: 3

Foundation: Crawl space, slab, or basement

CompleteCost List Available: Yes

Price Category: D

The porch on this four-bedroom ranch welcomes you home.

Features:

- **Great Room:** You'll find this large room just off the foyer.

- **Dining Room:** This room, with a view of the side yard, is located adjacent to the kitchen and the great room.

- **Kitchen:** This island kitchen, with a built-in pantry, is open to the breakfast area.

- **Master Suite:** This suite features his and her walk-in closets and a private bathroom with double vanities and whirlpool tub.

- **Bedrooms:** Three secondary bedrooms have large closets and share a hall bathroom.

Images provided by designer/architect.

CAD FILE AVAILABLE

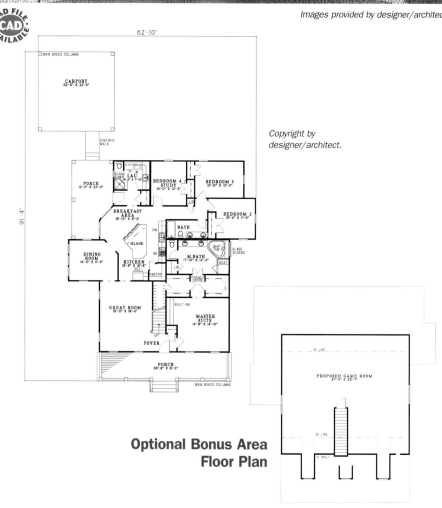

Copyright by designer/architect.

Optional Bonus Area Floor Plan

Images provided by designer/architect.

Plan #311015

Dimensions: 72'10" W x 56'6" D
Levels: 1
Heated Square Footage: 2,197
Bedrooms: 3
Bathrooms: 2½
Foundation: Crawl space, slab or basement
Material List Available: No
Price Category: D

The elegant exterior of this home will enhance any neighborhood.

Features:

- **Porches:** Two porches, one at the front and one at the back of the home, are wonderful for enjoying fresh air and relaxing.

- **Great Room:** This beautiful great room has a cathedral ceiling, a fireplace flanked by built-in cabinets, and access to the porch at the rear of the home.

- **Kitchen:** Surrounded by counter space, you'll always have room to prepare meals in this kitchen. The adjoining breakfast room shares a door to the porch with the great room, which is perfect for meals outside.

- **Master Suite:** Located away from the busier areas of the home, this master suite features a large bedroom area, two spacious closets, and two vanities.

Copyright by designer/architect.

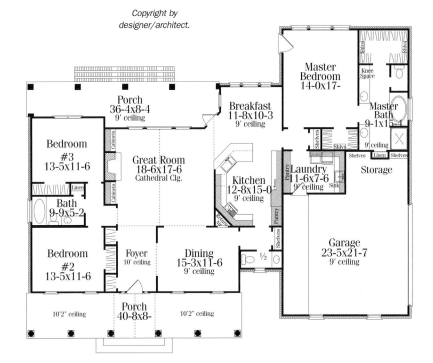

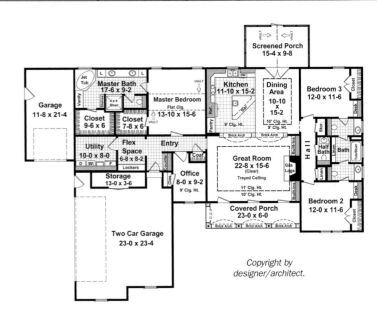

Copyright by designer/architect.

Plan #351086

Dimensions: 82'6" W x 65' D

Levels: 1

Heated Square Footage: 2,201

Bedrooms: 3

Bathrooms: 2½

Foundation: Crawl space or slab

Material List Available: Yes

Price Category: F

Images provided by designer/architect.

CAD FILE AVAILABLE

Rear Elevation

Main Level Floor Plan

Plan #161038

Dimensions: 58'6" W x 49' D

Levels: 2

Heated Square Footage: 2,209

Main Level Sq. Ft.: 1,542

Upper Level Sq. Ft.: 667

Bedrooms: 3

Bathrooms: 2½

Foundation: Basement

Materials List Available: Yes

Price Category: E

Images provided by designer/architect.

Upper Level Floor Plan

Copyright by designer/architect.

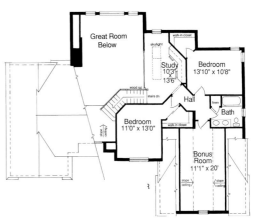

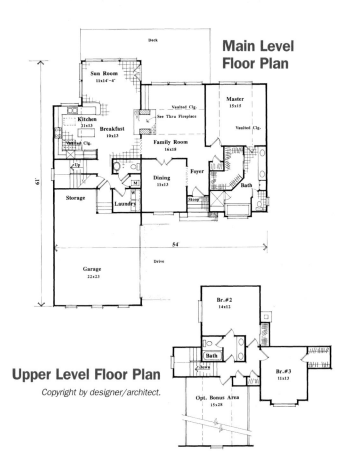

Main Level Floor Plan

Deck

Sun Room
11x14'-4"

Kitchen
11x13

Breakfast
10x13

Vaulted Clg.

See Thru Fireplace

Master
15x15

Vaulted Clg.

Vaulted Clg.

Family Room
16x18

Dining
11x13

Foyer

Bath

Storage

Laundry

Stoop

Garage
22x23

Drive

54'

61'

Images provided by designer/architect.

Br.#2
14x12

Bath

Br.#3
11x13

Opt. Bonus Area
15x28

Upper Level Floor Plan

Copyright by designer/architect.

Plan #251014

Dimensions: 54' W x 61' D

Levels: 2

Heated Square Footage: 2,210

Main Level Sq. Ft.: 1,670

Upper Level Sq. Ft.: 540

Bedrooms: 3

Bathrooms: 2½

Foundation: Crawl space, basement

Materials List Available: Yes

Price Category: E

Plan #371059

Dimensions: 77'8" W x 56'6" D

Levels: 1

Heated Square Footage: 2,240

Bedrooms: 4

Bathrooms: 2½

Foundation: Slab

Materials List Available: No

Price Category: E

Images provided by designer/architect.

CAD FILE AVAILABLE

BATH 1

3 CAR GARAGE
21'-0" x 31'-0"

WORK BENCH

SEE THRU FIREPLACE

STEP-UP CLG.
MASTER SUITE
14'-0" x 17'-0"

PORCH

BED RM.2
12'-0" x 11'-0"

B.3

UTIL.

11'-0" HIGH CLG.
LIVING RM.
20'-0" x 16'-0"

B.2

BED RM.3
12'-0" x 11'-0"

NOOK
8'-0" X 8'-0"

KITCH.
12'-0" x 11'-0"

11'-0" HIGH CLG.
DINING RM.
11'-0" x 15'-0"

ENT.

BED RM.4
11'-8" x 10'-0"

CLG. SLOPES

CLG. SLOPES

CLG. SLOPES

BONUS RM.
21'-4" x 14'-0"

STAIR DOWN

WOOD RAIL

CLG. SLOPES

Bonus Area

Copyright by designer/architect.

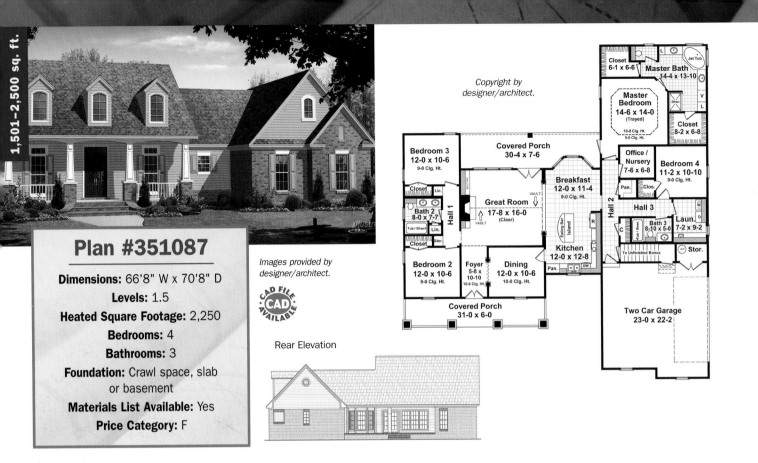

Plan #351087

Dimensions: 66'8" W x 70'8" D

Levels: 1.5

Heated Square Footage: 2,250

Bedrooms: 4

Bathrooms: 3

Foundation: Crawl space, slab or basement

Materials List Available: Yes

Price Category: F

Images provided by designer/architect.

Rear Elevation

Plan #351007

Dimensions: 73'8" W x 53'2" D

Levels: 1

Heated Square Footage: 2,251

Bedrooms: 3

Bathrooms: 2½

Foundation: Crawl space, slab, or basement

Materials List Available: Yes

Price Category: F

Images provided by designer/architect.

Bonus Room

Copyright by designer/architect.

Plan #161115

Dimensions: 79'8" W x 44'2" D

Levels: 1

Heated Square Footage: 2,253

Bedrooms: 4

Bathrooms: 3

Foundation: Walkout basement

Material List Available: Yes

Price Category: E

Images provided by designer/architect.

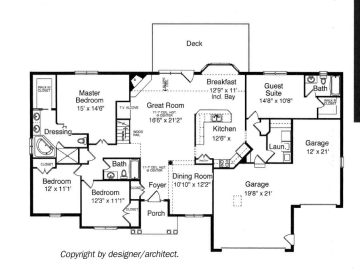

Copyright by designer/architect.

Rear Elevation

Plan #101012

Dimensions: 69'4" W x 62'9" D

Levels: 1

Heated Square Footage: 2,288

Bedrooms: 3

Bathrooms: 2½

Foundation: Crawl space, slab, basement, or walkout

Materials List Available: No

Price Category: E

Images provided by designer/architect.

Copyright by designer/architect.

Living Room

Plan #351055

Dimensions: 73'8" W x 58'4" D
Levels: 1
Heated Square Footage: 2,251
Bedrooms: 3
Bathrooms: 2½
Foundation: Crawl space, slab, or basement
Materials List Available: No
Price Category: F

This beautiful and versatile plan features three bedrooms, two baths, and a three-car garage.

Features:

• Great Room: Featuring a 12-ft.-high raised ceiling and a gas fireplace, this large gathering area is open to the kitchen.

• Kitchen: This peninsula kitchen has a walk-in pantry and a raised bar, which is open into the great room.

• Master Suite: An office/lounge, jetted tub, large walk-in shower, large walk-in closet, and privacy porch set this suite apart.

• Bedrooms: The two secondary bedrooms have large closets and share a common bathroom.

Images provided by designer/architect.

Main Level Floor Plan

Bonus Area Floor Plan

Copyright by designer/architect.

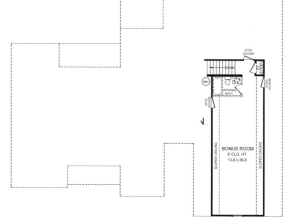

Plan #171004

Dimensions: 72' W x 52' D
Levels: 1
Heated Square Footage: 2,256
Bedrooms: 3
Bathrooms: 2
Foundation: Crawl space, slab
Materials List Available: Yes
Price Category: E

Images provided by designer/architect.

This home greets you with a front porch featuring a high roofline and stucco columns.

Features:

• Ceiling Height: 9 ft. unless otherwise noted.

• Foyer: Step through the front porch into this impressive foyer, which opens to the formal dining room and the study.

• Dining Room: This dining room's 12-ft. ceiling enhances its sense of spaciousness, with plenty of room for large dinner parties.

• Family Room: With plenty of room for all kinds of family activities, this room also has a 12-ft. ceiling, a fireplace, and two paddle fans.

• Kitchen: This kitchen has all the counter space you'll need to prepare your favorite recipes. There's a pantry, desk, and angled snack bar.

• Master Bedroom: This master retreat is separate from the other bedrooms for added privacy. It has an elegant, high step-up ceiling and a paddle fan.

• Master Bath: This master bath features a large walk-in closet, deluxe corner bath, walk-in shower, and his and her vanities.

Copyright by designer/architect.

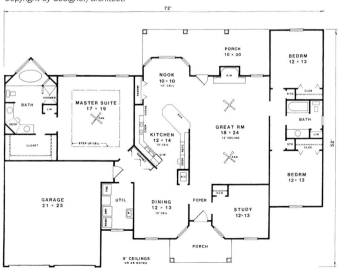

SMARTtip

Windows – Privacy

You can easily stencil a work of art onto a windowpane, perhaps only as a border around the edge. Choose or create a design that gives you as little or as much privacy and light control as you need. Use a ready-made stencil or a piece of openwork fabric such as lace, or mask a design onto the glass using tape and a razor knife. Then apply glass paint or frosted glass spray, referring to the instructions and guidelines that come with the product.

Plan #311007

Dimensions: 71'2" W x 62' D

Levels: 1

Heated Square Footage: 2,267

Bedrooms: 4

Bathrooms: 2½

Foundation: Crawl space, slab or basement

Material List Available: Yes

Price Category: E

Images provided by designer/architect.

This house has large areas that can be used for entertaining guests or as relaxing oasis.

Features:

- **Great Room:** A soaring cathedral ceiling and a fireplace enhance this spacious great room. It is connected to the dining room, which completes a wonderful layout for entertaining.

- **Kitchen:** The kitchen has two entrances-one leading to the breakfast room and another connecting to the dining room-ensuring that whatever your destination you will not have to walk far with dishes.

- **Laundry Room:** Conveniently located between the kitchen and the master suite, this large laundry room includes counter space, a sink, and a second pantry for the kitchen.

- **Master Suite:** You will not have to share in this master suite! Two closets and separate vanities ensure stress-free mornings.

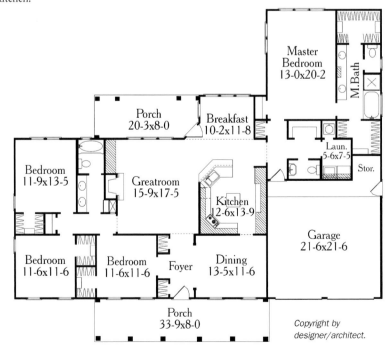

Copyright by designer/architect.

Images provided by designer/architect.

Plan #451231

Dimensions: 53' W x 42' D
Levels: 2
Heated Square Footage: 2,281
Main Level Sq. Ft.: 1,436
Upper Level Sq. Ft.: 845
Bedrooms: 3
Bathrooms: 2½
Foundation: Walkout basement
Materials List Available: No
Price Category: E

Boasting a craftsman-accent look, this home will be the talk of the neighborhood.

CAD FILE AVAILABLE

Features:

- **Great Room:** As you enter this large gathering area from the foyer, the warmth of the fireplace welcomes you home. The two-story-high ceiling gives the area an open feeling.

- **Kitchen:** An efficient space, this kitchen features a snack bar and walk-in pantry, and it is located near the laundry room, the great room, and the dining room. The glass doors in the dining room function to extend and open the kitchen area.

- **Master Suite:** This main-level suite contains a large sleeping area and access to the rear deck. The master bath has a marvelous whirlpool tub, dual vanities, and a stall shower.

- **Upper Level:** Two bedrooms, with large closets, share a common bathroom. The loft has a view down into the great room.

Images provided by designer/architect.

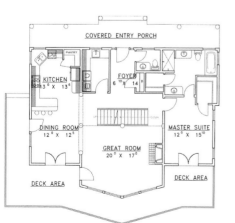

Main Level Floor Plan

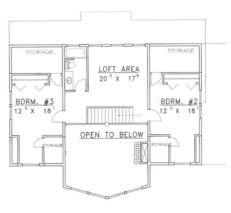

Upper Level Floor Plan

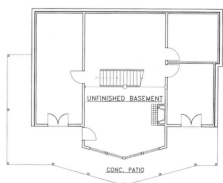

Lower Level Floor Plan

Plan #311030

Dimensions: 76'10" W x 55'6" D

Levels: 1

Heated Square Footage: 2,286

Main Level Sq. Ft.: 2,286

Opt. Bonus Sq. Ft.: 443

Bedrooms: 3

Bathrooms: 2½

Foundation: Basement, crawl space, or slab

Materials List Available: No

Price Category: E

Images provided by designer/architect.

If you're looking for a home you can expand in coming years, this gorgeous plan might be the answer to your dreams.

Features:

- **Foyer:** A 10-ft. ceiling sets the tone for the fabulous spaces in this home.

- **Great Room:** You'll love the cathedral ceiling, great windows, and fireplace flanked by built-ins.

- **Dining Room:** Ample dimensions make it easy to create a somewhat formal dining area here.

- **Kitchen:** The family cook will love the angled work area and ample storage space.

- **Breakfast Room:** Expansive windows add a note of cheer to this room, which opens to the porch.

- **Master Suite:** A wall of windows and door to the backyard brighten the sizable bedroom, and the bath features two walk-in closets, two vanities, a garden tub, and a separate shower.

Rear Elevation

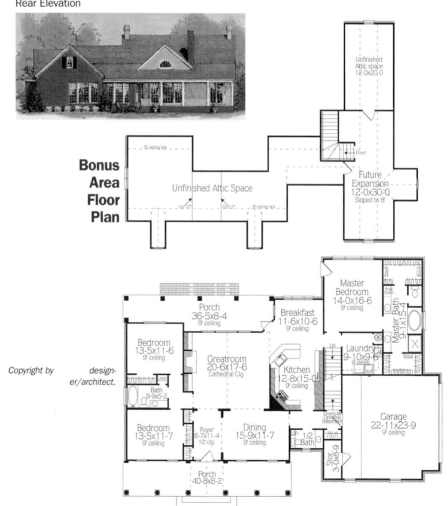

Copyright by designer/architect.

Plan #451249

Dimensions: 52' W x 54'8" D
Levels: 2
Heated Square Footage: 2,281
Main Level Sq. Ft.: 1,436
Upper Level Sq. Ft.: 845
Bedrooms: 3
Bathrooms: 3
Foundation: Walkout basement
Materials List Available: No
Price Category: E

CAD FILE AVAILABLE

This is the perfect house for a sloping lot, perhaps with a mountain view.

Features:

- **Entry:** The covered front porch welcomes you to the lovely home; in the foyer, you'll find a coat closet and a half bathroom.

- **Kitchen:** As you leave the foyer and arrive in this open kitchen, you'll be impressed by all of the cabinets and counter space. The raised bar is open to the dining room. The built-in pantry is a much-welcome bonus.

- **Master Suite:** This main-level oasis is separated from the other bedrooms, which are located upstairs. The French doors open from the sleeping area onto the rear deck. The two walk-in closets are the perfect size. The master bath boasts a stall shower, oversized tub, and his and her vanities.

- **Upper Level:** Two secondary bedrooms with nicely sized closets share a full bathroom.

The loft area, with a view down into the great room, will be the perfect area to relax.

- **Lower Level:** This future space may have a wet bar, recreation room, full bathroom, and office space. The French door to the lower patio will be a welcome breath of fresh air.

Images provided by designer/architect.

Front/Side View

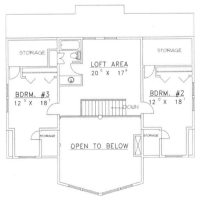

Main Level Floor Plan

Basement Level Floor Plan

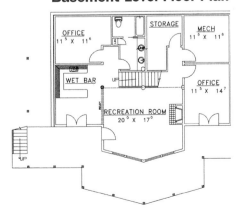

Upper Level Floor Plan

Copyright by designer/architect.

Images provided by designer/architect.

Plan #181151

Dimensions: 50' W x 46' D

Levels: 2

Heated Square Footage: 2,283

Main Level Sq. Ft.: 1,274

Second Level Sq. Ft.: 1,009

Bedrooms: 3

Bathrooms: 2½

Foundation: Basement

Materials List Available: Yes

Price Category: F

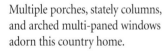

Multiple porches, stately columns, and arched multi-paned windows adorn this country home.

Features:

- Ceiling Height: 8 ft. unless otherwise noted.

- Great Room: The second-floor mezzanine overlooks this great room. With its soaring ceiling, this dramatic room is the centerpiece of a spacious and flowing design that is just as suited to entertaining as it is to family life.

- Dining Area: Guests will naturally flow into this dining area when it is time to eat. After dinner they can step directly out onto the porch to enjoy coffee and dessert when the weather is fair.

- Kitchen: This efficient and well-designed kitchen has double sinks and offers a separate eating area for those impromptu family meals.

- Master Suite: This master retreat has a walk-in closet and its own sumptuous bath.

- Home Office: Whether you work at home or just need a place for the family computer and keeping track of family finances, this home office fills the bill.

Front View

Main Level Floor Plan

21'-0" X 20'-8"
6,30 X 6,20

46'-0"
13,8 m

17'-0" X 11'-8"
5,10 X 3,50

9'-8" X 8'-8"
2,90 X 2,60

9'-0" X 10'-0"
2,70 X 3,00

10'-0" X 12'-0"
3,00 X 3,60

9'-8" X 9'-4"
2,90 X 2,80

12'-0" X 20'-8"
3,60 X 6,20

50'-0"
15,0 m

Upper Level Floor Plan

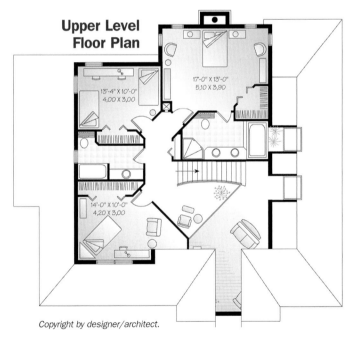

13'-4" X 10'-0"
4,00 X 3,00

17'-0" X 13'-0"
5,10 X 3,90

14'-0" X 10'-0"
4,20 X 3,00

Copyright by designer/architect.

SMARTtip

Coping Chair Rails

If the teeth of your rasp tend to break out thin edges of the cope, try wrapping the rasp with sandpaper to make fine adjustments.

Dining Room

Living Room

Master Bath

Plan #351011

Dimensions: 73'8" W x 53'2" D
Levels: 1
Heated Square Footage: 2,251
Bedrooms: 3
Bathrooms: 2½
Foundation: Crawl space, slab, or basement
Materials List Available: Yes
Price Category: F

Images provided by designer/architect.

CAD FILE AVAILABLE · CAD

Bonus Room Floor Plan

Copyright by designer/architect.

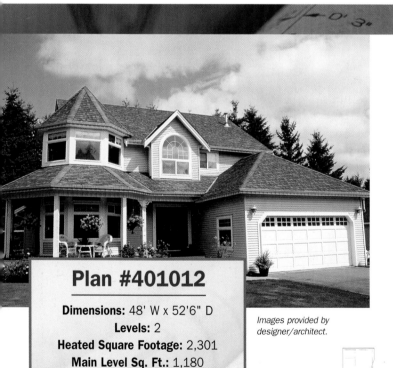

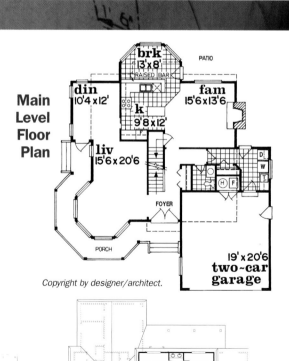

Plan #401012

Dimensions: 48' W x 52'6" D
Levels: 2
Heated Square Footage: 2,301
Main Level Sq. Ft.: 1,180
Upper Level Sq. Ft.: 1,121
Bedrooms: 3-4
Bathrooms: 2½
Foundation: Basement
Materials List Available: Yes
Price Category: E

Images provided by designer/architect.

Main Level Floor Plan

Copyright by designer/architect.

Optional Upper Level

Upper Level Floor Plan

Main Level Floor Plan

Plan #161039

Dimensions: 61' W x 41'8" D

Levels: 2

Heated Square Footage: 2,320

Main Level Sq. Ft.: 1,595

Upper Level Sq. Ft.: 725

Bedrooms: 4

Bathrooms: 2½

Foundation: Basement

Materials List Available: Yes

Price Category: E

Images provided by designer/architect.

Upper Level Floor Plan

Copyright by designer/architect.

Plan #121164

Dimensions: 74'11" W x 68'9½" D

Levels: 1

Heated Square Footage: 2,331

Bedrooms: 3

Bathrooms: 2½

Foundation: Slab; basement for fee

Material List Available: Yes

Price Category: E

Images provided by designer/architect.

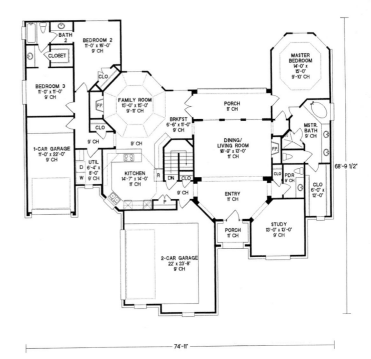

Copyright by designer/architect.

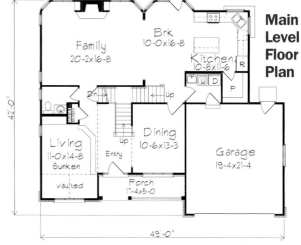

Main Level Floor Plan

Family 20-2x16-8

Brk 10-0x16-8

Kitchen 10-8x11-6

Dining 10-6x13-3

Living 11-0x14-8 Sunken

Entry

Garage 19-4x21-4

Porch 17-4x5-0

vaulted

42'-0"

49'-0"

Up

Dn

up

W D

P

Images provided by designer/architect.

CAD FILE AVAILABLE

Upper Level Floor Plan

Copyright by designer/architect.

Br 2 11-0x10-0

MBr 13-0x17-8 vaulted

Br 3 11-0x11-0

Br 4 10-6x11-0

open to below

vaulted

Dn Dn

Plan #321050

Dimensions: 49' W x 42' D

Levels: 2

Heated Square Footage: 2,336

Main Level Sq. Ft.: 1,291

Upper Level Sq. Ft.: 1,045

Bedrooms: 4

Bathrooms: 2½

Foundation: Basement

Materials List Available: Yes

Price Category: E

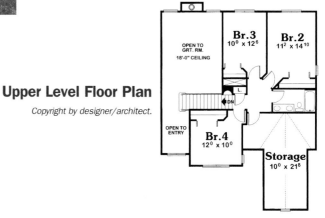

Main Level Floor Plan

Mbr. 13⁸ x 15⁰

Grt. Rm. 14⁰ x 18⁴ 18'-0" CEILING

Bfst. 10¹⁰ x 14⁸

RECYCLE SNACK BAR

Kit. 10⁸ x 15¹¹

Din. Rm. 11⁰ x 12⁴

Gar. 22⁰ x 22⁴

Study 13⁸ x 11⁰

WHIRLPOOL

E.

COVERED PORCH

UP

DN

P.

W.

D.

R.

45'-4"

54'-8"

Upper Level Floor Plan

Copyright by designer/architect.

OPEN TO GRT. RM. 18'-0" CEILING

Br.3 10⁰ x 12⁶

Br.2 11² x 14¹⁰

OPEN TO ENTRY

Br.4 12⁰ x 10⁰

Storage 10⁰ x 21⁸

DN

L

Plan #121032

Dimensions: 54' W x 45'4" D

Levels: 2

Heated Square Footage: 2,339

Main Level Sq. Ft.: 1,665

Upper Level Sq. Ft.: 674

Bedrooms: 4

Bathrooms: 2½

Foundation: Basement

Materials List Available: Yes

Price Category: E

Images provided by designer/architect.

CAD FILE AVAILABLE

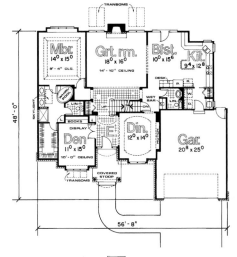

Main Level Floor Plan

Mbr. 14⁰ x 15⁰ — 8' - 4" CLG.
Grt. rm. 18⁰ x 16⁰ — 14' - 10" CEILING
Bfst. 10⁰ x 15⁶
Kit. 9⁴ x 12⁸
48' - 0"
WORK POOL
DESK
LIN.
BOOKS
DISPLAY
WET BAR
LIN.
P.
W.
D.
Den 11⁰ x 15⁰ — 10' - 0" CEILING
Din. 12⁰ x 14⁰
Gar. 20⁸ x 25⁰
COVERED STOOP
TRANSOMS
SKYLIGHT
56' - 8"

Plan #121088

Dimensions: 56'8" W x 48' D
Levels: 2
Heated Square Footage: 2,340
Main Level Sq. Ft.: 1,701
Upper Level Sq. Ft.: 639
Bedrooms: 4
Bathrooms: 2½
Foundation: Basement; slab for fee
Materials List Available: Yes
Price Category: E

Images provided by designer/architect.

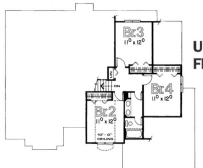

Upper Level Floor Plan

Br. 3 11⁰ x 12⁰
Br. 4 11⁰ x 12⁰
Br. 2 11⁰ x 12⁰ — 10' - 0" CEILING

Copyright by designer/architect.

Main Level Floor Plan

22'-0" X 14'-0" / 6,60 X 4,20
13'-0" X 17'-0" / 3,90 X 5,10
27'-0" X 20'-0" / 6,00 X 6,00
33'-0" / 9,9 m
20'-0" X 20'-0" / 6,00 X 6,00
10'-0" X 12'-0" / 3,00 X 3,60
10'-0" X 6'-0" / 3,00 X 1,80
58'-0" / 17,4 m

Plan #181081

Dimensions: 58' W x 33' D
Levels: 2
Heated Square Footage: 2,350
Main Level Sq. Ft.: 1,107
Second Level Sq. Ft.: 1,243
Bedrooms: 3
Bathrooms: 2½
Foundation: Basement
Materials List Available: Yes
Price Category: F

Images provided by designer/architect.

CAD FILE AVAILABLE

18'-0" X 14'-4" / 5,40 X 4,30
15'-0" X 15'-0" / 4,50 X 4,50
12'-8" X 16'-0" / 3,80 X 4,80
10'-0" X 12'-0" / 3,00 X 3,60
10'-0" X 12'-0" / 3,00 X 3,60

Upper Level Floor Plan

Copyright by designer/architect.

Plan #181053

Dimensions: 56' W x 53'2" D

Levels: 2

Heated Square Footage: 2,353

Main Level Sq. Ft.: 1,606

Upper Level Sq. Ft.: 747

Bedrooms: 4

Bathrooms: 2½

Foundation: Crawl space or basement, slab for fee

Material List Available: Yes

Price Category: E

Images provided by designer/architect.

This home has plenty of windows to let in the sunlight.

CAD FILE AVAILABLE

Features:

- **Great Room:** You will love to relax in this beautiful two-story great room, lounging in front of the fireplace or looking out at the yard.

- **Kitchen:** Plentiful amounts of space and work area define this kitchen, where there is lots of room for multiple helpers. The laundry area is conveniently located nearby, great for multi-tasking.

- **Master Suite:** After a long day, retire to this master suite, which includes a large sleeping area, a walk-in closet, a dual-sink vanity, a shower, and a tub.

- **Additional bedrooms:** Upstairs, two bedrooms share a common television area and a bath, perfect for siblings.

Rear View

Copyright by designer/architect.

Main Level Floor Plan

Upper Level Floor Plan

Plan #151172

Dimensions: 76'10" W x 53'4" D
Levels: 1.5
Heated Square Footage: 2,373
Main Level Sq. Ft.: 1,597
Upper Level Sq. Ft.: 776
Bedrooms: 4
Bathrooms: 3
Foundation: Crawl space, slab; basement or daylight basement for fee
Complete Cost List Available: Yes
Price Category: F

Images provided by designer/architect.

This lovely home easily accommodates a busy family, but it also allows expansion should you want a larger home in the future.

Features:

• **Great Room:** A wall of windows, fireplace, and media center are highlights in this spacious area.

• **Dining Room:** This lovely room is separated from the foyer by columns, and it opens to the kitchen.

• **Bedroom/Study:** Use the walk-in closet here for a computer niche if you can turn this room into a study.

• **Kitchen:** You'll love the angled snack bar in this well-designed step-saving kitchen.

• **Breakfast Room:** Large windows let natural light pour in, and a door leads to the rear grilling porch.

• **Master Suite:** The bedroom has a door to the rear porch and large corner windows, and the bath includes a corner whirlpool tub, shower with seat, two vanities, and walk-in closet.

Main Level Floor Plan

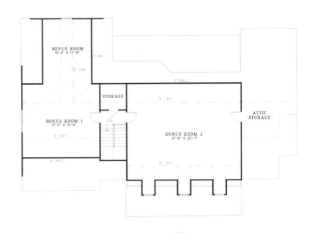

Upper Level Floor Plan

Copyright by designer/architect.

Plan #121017

Dimensions: 54' W x 50' D

Levels: 2

Heated Square Footage: 2,353

Main Level Sq. Ft.: 1,653

Upper Level Sq. Ft.: 700

Bedrooms: 4

Bathrooms: 2½

Foundation: Basement

Materials List Available: Yes

Price Category: E

Images provided by designer/architect.

CAD FILE **CAD** AVAILABLE

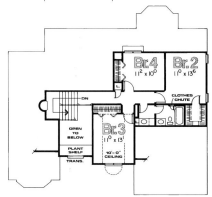

Main Level Floor Plan

Upper Level Floor Plan

Copyright by designer/architect.

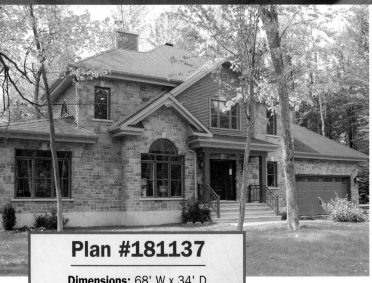

Plan #181137

Dimensions: 68' W x 34' D

Levels: 2

Heated Square Footage: 2,353

Main Level Sq. Ft.: 1,281

Upper Level Sq. Ft.: 1,072

Bedrooms: 3

Bathrooms: 2½

Foundation: Full basement

Materials List Available: Yes

Price Category: E

Images provided by designer/architect.

 CAD FILE **CAD** AVAILABLE

Main Level Floor Plan

Upper Level Floor Plan

Copyright by designer/architect.

Plan #191027

Dimensions: 62' W x 42' D

Levels: 1

Heated Square Footage: 2,354

Bedrooms: 4

Bathrooms: 2½

Foundation: Crawl Space or slab

Materials List Available: No

Price Category: E

Images provided by designer/architect.

Copyright by designer/architect.

Plan #271069

Dimensions: 63'5" W x 51'8" D

Levels: 2

Heated Square Footage: 2,376

Main Level Sq. Ft.: 1,248

Upper Level Sq. Ft.: 1,128

Bedrooms: 4

Bathrooms: 2½

Foundation: Crawl space, basement

Materials List Available: No

Price Category: E

Images provided by designer/architect.

Main Level Floor Plan

Upper Level Floor Plan

Copyright by designer/architect.

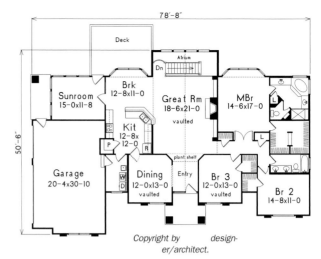

Copyright by designer/architect.

Plan #321037

Dimensions: 78'8" W x 50'6" D

Levels: 1

Heated Square Footage: 2,397

Bedrooms: 3

Bathrooms: 2

Foundation: Basement or walkout

Materials List Available: Yes

Price Category: F

Images provided by designer/architect.

CAD FILE AVAILABLE

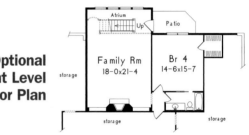

Optional Basement Level Floor Plan

Plan #151870

Dimensions: 66'4" W x 67'2" D

Levels: 1

Heated Square Footage: 2,405

Bedrooms: 4

Bathrooms: 3

Foundation: Crawl space or slab; basement or walkout for fee

CompleteCost List Available: Yes

Price Category: E

Images provided by designer/architect.

CAD FILE AVAILABLE

Bonus Area

Copyright by designer/architect.

**Main Level
Floor Plan**

*Images provided by
designer/architect.*

**CAD FILE
AVAILABLE**

Plan #181136

Dimensions: 52' W x 46'8" D

Levels: 2

Heated Square Footage: 2,426

Main Level Sq. Ft.: 1,319

Upper Level Sq. Ft.: 1,107

Bedrooms: 3

Bathrooms: 2½

Foundation: Basement

Materials List Available: Yes

Price Category: E

**Upper Level
Floor Plan**

*Copyright by design-
er/architect.*

*Images provided by
designer/architect.*

**CAD FILE
AVAILABLE**

Upper Level Floor Plan

Plan #371127

Dimensions: 85'2" W x 42'4 1/2" D

Levels: 2

Heated Square Footage: 2,427

Main Level Sq. Ft.: 1,788

Upper Level Sq. Ft.: 639

Bedrooms: 4

Bathrooms: 3

Foundation: Crawl space, slab,
or basement

Material List Available: No

Price Category: E

Main Level Floor Plan

*Copyright by
designer/architect.*

Main Level Floor Plan

TERRACE

optional reflecting pool

2-CAR GAR. 20 x 20

heat-circ. f.p.

FAM. RM 19-6 x 13

wet bar

DINETTE 9-8 x 11

KIT. 12-6 x 15-8

dw

D W

LAUN

ref.

cl.

pant.

dn.

L. R. 12-6 x 16-8

up

2 STOR. FOYER

cl.

D. R. 12-6 x 14

This home, as shown in the photograph, may differ from the actual blueprints. For more detailed information, please check the floor plans carefully.

Plan #131051

Dimensions: 64'4" W x 53'4" D

Levels: 2

Heated Square Footage: 2,431

Main Level Sq. Ft.: 1,293

Upper Level Sq. Ft.: 1,138

Bedrooms: 4

Bathrooms: 2½

Foundation: Crawl space, slab, or basement

Materials List Available: Yes

Price Category: F

Images provided by designer/architect.

Optional 3rd Level Floor Plan

dn.

open railing

storage

24'

storage

ALL PURPOSE RM 22

roof window

roof

optional fireplace

whirlpool tub

M. B. R. 18-7 x 13 AV. high ceiling

B. R. 12-6 x 10-9

w.i.c.

well rail

dn.

up

BALC.

w.i.c.

lin.

w.i.c.

cl.

B. R. 12-6 x 10-8

open to below

B. R. 12-6 x 11

roof

Upper Level Floor Plan

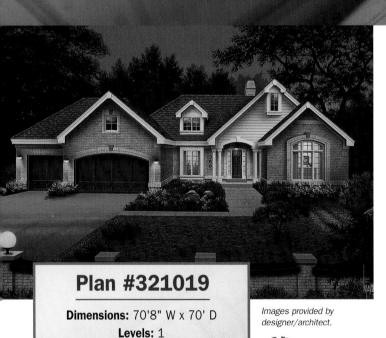

Plan #321019

Dimensions: 70'8" W x 70' D

Levels: 1

Heated Square Footage: 2,452

Bedrooms: 4

Bathrooms: 2½

Foundation: Basement

Materials List Available: Yes

Price Category: E

Images provided by designer/architect.

CAD FILE AVAILABLE CAD

70'-8"

70'-0"

Deck

Brk 13-6x12-0

Great Rm 19-4x18-0 vaulted

MBr 13-6x19-8 vaulted

Kitchen 13-6x14-7

Dining 13-0x12-0

Br 2 13-6x11-0

Foyer

Br 3 11-8x11-0

Garage 29-4x21-4

Porch

Home Office 17-4x12-0 vaulted

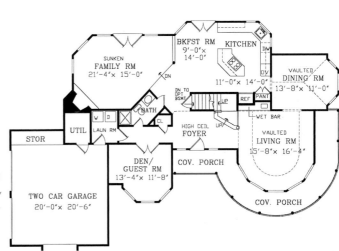

Upper Level Floor Plan

Plan #131032

Dimensions: 69'2" W x 46' D

Levels: 2

Heated Square Footage: 2,455

Main Level Sq. Ft.: 1,499

Upper Level Sq. Ft.: 956

Bedrooms: 4

Bathrooms: 3

Foundation: Crawl space, slab, or basement

Materials List Available: Yes

Price Category: F

Images provided by designer/architect.

Main Level Floor Plan

Copyright by designer/architect.

Upper Level Floor Plan

Plan #161051

Dimensions: 57'8" W x 58' D

Levels: 2

Square Footage: 2,484

Main Level Sq. Ft.: 1,710

Upper Level Sq. Ft.: 774

Bedrooms: 4

Bathrooms: 3½

Foundation: Basement; crawl space for fee

Materials List Available: Yes

Price Category: E

Images provided by designer/architect.

Main Level Floor Plan

Copyright by designer/architect.

Plan #151179

Dimensions: 66'4" W x 67'2" D
Levels: 1.5
Heated Square Footage: 2,405
Opt. Bonus Level Sq. Ft.: 358
Bedrooms: 4
Bathrooms: 3
Foundation: Crawl space, slab;
basement or walkout for fee
CompleteCost List Available: Yes
Price Category: E

Images provided by designer/architect.

As beautiful inside as it is outside, this home will delight the most discerning family.

Features:

- Great Room: This room has a 10-ft. ceiling, door to the porch, fireplace, and built-ins.

- Dining Room: You'll love the way the columns set off this room from the great room and foyer.

- Kitchen: An L-shaped work area, central dining, and working island add to your efficiency.

- Hearth Room: A fireplace and computer center make this room a natural gathering spot.

- Breakfast Room: This lovely room is lit by large windows and a door that opens to the rear porch.

- Master Suite: You'll love the sitting room in the bayed area, walk-in closet, and luxury bath.

- Rear Porch: Use this porch for grilling, dining, and just relaxing—it's large enough to do it all.

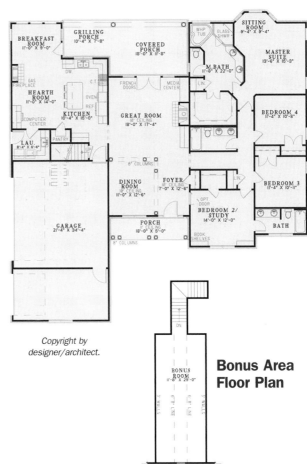

Copyright by designer/architect.

Bonus Area Floor Plan

Plan #151002

Dimensions: 67' W x 66' D
Levels: 1
Heated Square Footage: 2,444
Bedrooms: 3
Bathrooms: 2½
Foundation: Crawl space, slab, or basement
CompleteCost List Available: Yes
Price Category: F

Images provided by designer/architect.

• Kitchen: An eat-in bar is a great place to snack, and the handy computer nook allows the kids to do their homework while you cook.

• Breakfast Room: Opening from the kitchen, this area gives added space for the family to gather any time.

• Master Suite: Featuring a 10-ft. boxed ceiling, the master bedroom also has a door way that opens onto the covered rear porch. The master bathroom has a step-up whirlpool tub, separate shower, and twin vanities with a makeup area.

This gracious, traditional home is designed for practicality and convenience.

Features:

• Ceiling Height: 9-ft. except as noted below.

• Great Room: This room is ideal for entertaining, thanks to its lovely fireplace and French doors that open to the covered rear porch. Built-in cabinets give convenient storage space.

• Family Room: With access to the kitchen as well as the rear porch, this room will become your family's "headquarters."

• Study: Enjoy the quiet in this room with its 12-ft. ceiling and doorway to a private patio on the side of the house.

• Dining Room: Take advantage of the 8-in. wood columns and 12-ft. ceilings to create a formal dining area.

Copyright by designer/architect.

Images provided by designer/architect.

Plan #131030

Dimensions: 51' W x 41'10" D
Levels: 2
Heated Square Footage: 2,470
Main Level Sq. Ft.: 1,290
Upper Level Sq. Ft.: 1,180
Bedrooms: 4
Bathrooms: 2½
Foundation: Crawl space, slab, basement, or walkout
Materials List Available: Yes
Price Category: F

This home, as shown in the photograph, may differ from the actual blueprints. For more detailed information, please check the floor plans carefully.

Master Bedroom

Master Bathroom

Entry

If high ceilings and spacious rooms make you happy, you'll love this gorgeous home.

Features:

- **Family Room:** An 18-ft. vaulted ceiling that's open to the balcony above, a corner fireplace, and a wall of windows make this room feel special.

- **Dining Room:** This formal room, which flows into the living room, also opens to the front porch and optional backyard deck.

- **Kitchen:** A bright breakfast room joins with this kitchen and opens to the backyard deck.

- **Master Suite:** You'll smile when you see the 11-ft. vaulted ceiling, stunning arched window, and two walk-in closets in the bedroom. A skylight lets natural light into the private bath, with its spa tub, separate shower, and dual-sink vanity.

- **Bedrooms:** To reach these three charming bedrooms, you'll admire the view into the family room below as you walk along the balcony hall.

Main Level Floor Plan

OPT WOOD DECK

9' HIGH CLG
DINING RM
12'-0" x 13'-4"

9' HIGH CLG
KITCHEN
18'-8" x 16'-0"

9' HIGH CLG
BKFST RM

VAULTED CLG
FAMILY RM
18'-0" x 15'-0"

REF

PANT

LAV

LAUN RM
W D

9' HIGH CLG
LIVING RM
13'-0" x 16'-6"

DN

UP

2 STORY
HIGH
FOYER
CL

STOR

TWO CAR GARAGE
21'-8" x 20'-0"

COVERED PORCH

UP

Upper Level Floor Plan

SKYLITE

MSTR
BATH

WICL

LIN

WICL WICL

BEDRM #2
12'-0" x
11'-0"

UPPER
FAMILY RM

RAIL

LIN

BATH
#2

VAULTED CLG
MSTR BEDRM
13'-0" x 19'-0"

BALC

DN

CL

CL

UPPER
FOYER

BEDRM #4
10'-0" x
12'-0"

BEDRM #3
11'-4" x
12'-0"

Copyright by designer/architect.

Kitchen/Breakfast Area

Dining Room

Living Room

Kitchen/Breakfast Area

Plan #151237

Dimensions: 57'4" W x 55'10" D
Levels: 2
Heated Square Footage: 2,481
Main Level Sq. Ft.: 2,084
Upper Level Sq. Ft.: 397
Bedrooms: 4
Bathrooms: 3
Foundation: Crawl space, slab; basement or walkout for fee
CompleteCost List Available: Yes
Price Category: E

This beautiful home includes all of the features you may need.

Images provided by designer/architect.

Features:

- Porches: Two porches, one at the front and one at the back of the house, provide space for relaxing or having a barbecue with friends.
- Great Room: This two-story great room, overlooked by a balcony above, features a fireplace and French doors that open out to the grilling porch.
- Kitchen: Connected to a breakfast room, this kitchen includes a pantry, an eating bar, and an island.
- Master Suite: End your day relaxing in this master suite, which is home to a whirlpool tub, a walk-in closet, a glass shower, and a dual-sink vanity.

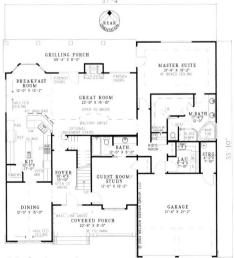

**Main Level
Floor Plan**

**Upper Level
Floor Plan**

Copyright by designer/architect.

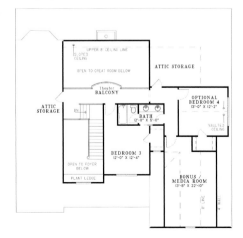

Plan #321005

Dimensions: 69' W x 53'8" D
Levels: 1
Heated Square Footage: 2,483
Bedrooms: 3
Bathrooms: 2
Foundation: Basement
Materials List Available: Yes
Price Category: F

Images provided by designer/architect.

You'll love the grand feeling of this home, which combines with the very practical features that make living in it a pleasure.

Features:

- **Porch:** The open brick arches and Palladian door set the tone for this magnificent home.

- **Great Room:** An alcove for the entertainment center and vaulted ceiling show the care that went into designing this room.

- **Dining Room:** A tray ceiling sets off the formality of this large room.

- **Kitchen:** The layout in this room is designed to make your work patterns more efficient and to save you steps and time.

- **Study:** This quiet room can be a wonderful refuge, or you can use it for a fourth bedroom if you wish.

- **Master Suite:** Made for relaxing at the end of the day, this suite will pamper you with luxuries.

Copyright by designer/architect.

Patio

Brkfst 14-9x13-0 vaulted clg

MBr 16-7x16-0 vaulted clg

Great Rm 19-6x23-10 vaulted clg

Kitchen 14-4x12-11 vaulted clg

Br 2 12-0x11-0

Dn

Menu Desk

Laundry

Br 3 12-0x11-5

Entry

Dining 12-0x15-0 tray clg

Study 14-4x11-0 vaulted clg

Porch

Garage 22-4x20-4

53'-8"

69'-0"

SMARTtip

Art in Pools

The tiled walls and floor of a pool make great canvases for art, so incorporate a serious or whimsical design. Also, make the stairs wide and shallow to form a wading area for kids.

Plan #151633

Dimensions: 59'6" W x 64'2" D

Levels: 1

Heated Square Footage: 2,486

Bedrooms: 4

Bathrooms: 3

Foundation: Crawl space or slab

CompleteCost List Available: Yes

Price Category: E

A charming exterior gives this home excellent curb appeal.

Features:

- **Entry:** Round columns on the front porch welcome your guests into this beautiful foyer.

- **Great Room:** This spacious room, with its optional built-ins and a gas fireplace, is sure to be the envy of all who see it.

- **Kitchen:** With this step-saving kitchen, adjoining breakfast room, and nearby grilling porch, the lack of space will never be an issue when it comes to entertaining or family gatherings.

- **Master Suite:** This suite is privately tucked away on the opposite side of this home and features a 10-ft.-high boxed ceiling. The bath boasts a walk-in closet, split vanities, and a corner whirlpool tub.

- **Bedrooms:** Two additional bedrooms with a shared bathroom and a guest room lend to plenty of sleeping accommodations.

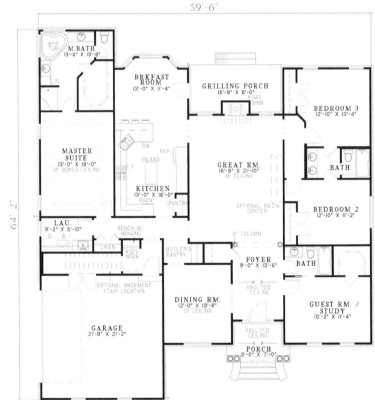

Copyright by designer/architect.

Plan #121003

Dimensions: 76' W x 55'4" D

Levels: 1

Heated Square Footage: 2,498

Bedrooms: 4

Bathrooms: 2½

Foundation: Basement; crawl space or slab for fee

Materials List Available: Yes

Price Category: E

Images provided by designer/architect.

Copyright by designer/architect.

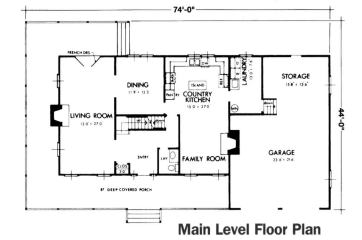

Main Level Floor Plan

Plan #271049

Dimensions: 74' W x 44' D

Levels: 2

Heated Square Footage: 2,464

Main Level Sq. Ft.: 1,288

Upper Level Sq. Ft.: 1,176

Bedrooms: 4

Bathrooms: 2½

Foundation: Basement, crawl space

Materials List Available: Yes

Price Category: E

Images provided by designer/architect.

Upper Level Floor Plan

Copyright by designer/architect.

Plan #241018

Dimensions: 83'7" W x 64'10" D

Levels: 1½

Heated Square Footage: 2,519

Main Level Sq. Ft.: 2,096

Upper Level Sq. Ft.: 423

Bedrooms: 4

Bathrooms: 4

Foundation: Slab

Materials List Available: No

Price Category: E

Images provided by designer/architect.

The wraparound veranda tells you how comfortable you'll be in this friendly home.

Features:

- Great Room: A fireplace, wet bar, and door to the rear porch make this room the heart of the home.

- Dining Room: A door to the veranda gives versatility to this lovely room.

- Kitchen: The cooks will love the U-shaped counter, center island, desk, and eating bar.

- Breakfast Room: The door to the porch makes it easy to enjoy dining outside in fine weather.

- Master Suite: The spacious bedroom is complemented by a walk-in closet and bath with vaulted ceiling and both tub and shower.

- Upper Floor: Both bedrooms have a dormer seat, large closet, and private bath. The balcony over the foyer is lovely, and the game room is a pleasure for the entire family.

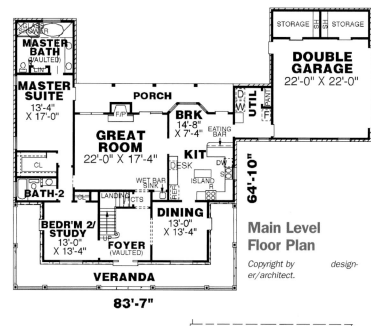

Main Level Floor Plan

Copyright by designer/architect.

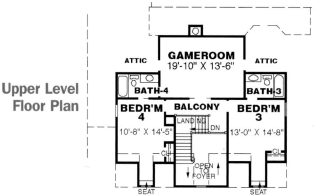

Upper Level Floor Plan

Plan #351089

Dimensions: 79'4" W x 53'6" D
Levels: 1
Heated Square Footage: 2,505
Bedrooms: 3
Bathrooms: 3
Foundation: Crawl space or slab
Material List Available: Yes
Price Category: G

Images provided by designer/architect.

CAD FILE AVAILABLE

Copyright by designer/architect.

Bonus Area Floor Plan

Rear View

Plan #441038

Dimensions: 59' W x 51'6" D
Levels: 2
Heated Square Footage: 2,518
Main Level Sq. Ft.: 1,464
Upper Level Sq. Ft.: 1,054
Bedrooms: 4
Bathrooms: 3
Foundation: Crawl space; slab or basement available for fee
Materials List Available: Yes
Price Category: E

Images provided by designer/architect.

CAD FILE AVAILABLE

Rear Elevation

Main Level Floor Plan

Copyright by designer/architect.

Upper Level Floor Plan

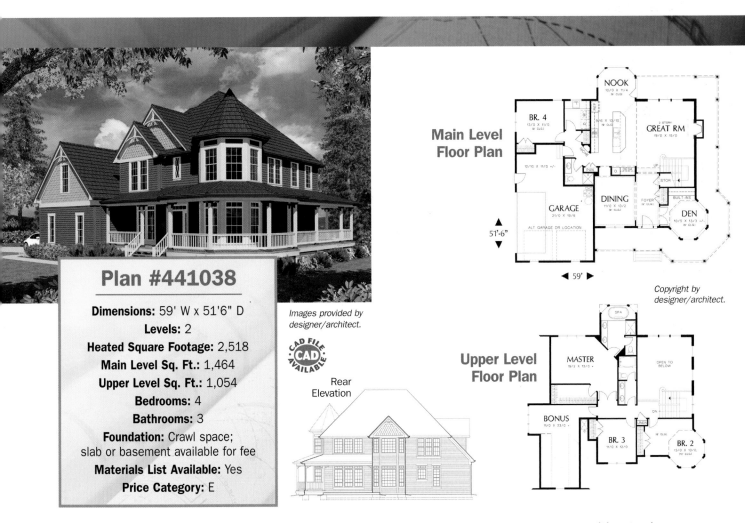

Plan #151188

Dimensions: 63'4" W x 59'10" D
Levels: 1
Heated Square Footage: 2,525
Bedrooms: 3
Bathrooms: 2½
Foundation: Crawl space, slab, basement or walkout
CompleteCost List Available: Yes
Price Category: E

This Southwestern-inspired home has a beautiful layout that you will love.

Features:

- **Great Room:** Opening out from the gallery, this great room is truly at the heart of this home. Built-in shelves and a media center flank a fireplace for a lovely setting.

- **Kitchen:** This kitchen features plenty of counter space for all of your needs. A center island provides additional space for prepping meals or holding dishes.

- **Master Suite:** Unwind in this wonderful master suite, complete with a whirlpool tub, a glass shower, separate vanities, and a spacious walk-in closet.

- **Secondary Bedrooms:** Located near the master suite, two secondary bedrooms are perfect for siblings. A shared bath features a private toilet and bath area.

Plan #241008

Dimensions: 65' W x 56'8" D
Levels: 1
Heated Square Footage: 2,526
Bedrooms: 4
Bathrooms: 3
Foundation: Crawl space, slab, or basement
Materials List Available: No
Price Category: E

A covered back porch—with access from the master suite and the breakfast area—makes this traditional home ideal for sitting near a golf course or with a backyard pool.

Features:

• Great Room: From the foyer, guests enter this spacious and comfortable great room, which features a handsome fireplace.

• Kitchen: This kitchen—the hub of this family-oriented home—is a joy in which to work, thanks to abundant counter space, a pantry, a convenient eating bar, and an adjoining breakfast area and sunroom.

• Master Suite: Enjoy the quiet comfort of this coffered-ceiling master suite, which features dual vanities and separate walk-in closets.

• Additional Bedrooms: Two secondary bedrooms, which share a full bath, are located at the opposite end of the house from the master suite. Bedroom 4—in front of the house—can be converted into a study.

Images provided by designer/architect.

Copyright by designer/architect.

Optional Bonus Area Floor Plan

SMARTtip

Traditional-Style Kitchen Cabinetry

You can modify stock kitchen cabinetry to enjoy fine furniture-quality details. Prefabricated trims may be purchased at local lumber mills and home centers. For example, crown molding, applied to the top of stock cabinetry and stained or painted to match the door style, may be all you need. Likewise, you can replace hardware with reproduction polished-brass door and drawer knobs or pulls for a finishing touch.

This article was reprinted from *Eat-In Kitchens* (Creative Homeowner 2009).

The Healthy Eat-In Kitchen

Perhaps you can't buy good health, but you can certainly create an eat-in kitchen that supports a wholesome lifestyle. Today's cutting-edge kitchen designs offer an innovative range of safe, eco-friendly products, such as bacteria-fighting surfaces, air-cleansing ventilation systems, and nontoxic paints, flooring, and cabinetry—all geared to your family's well being.

In addition to improving quality of life, today's health-conscious cabinets, counter-tops, backsplashes, floors, faucets, and ventilation systems look terrific. Once you become acquainted with the ever-expanding range of green products available for your eat-in kitchen, it's likely that you'll choose to incorporate as many as possible. Approach your new kitchen design the same way you would prepare a nourishing meal for your family: select the healthiest ingredients you can find, and combine them in a way that is enticing and visually appealing. And because a sun-filled kitchen is the warmest welcome, be sure to plan for an abundance of natural light streaming through windows and skylights. As you'll see on the following pages, healthy design works on all sorts of levels. Salud!

Ventilation

Only the cat enjoys waking up to the smell of last night's flounder. Fortunately, good kitchen ventilation banishes odors and grease and replaces stale air with fresh.

Mounted over the cooktop, a range hood of sufficient size and power pulls in moisture, smells, and smoke and exhausts them through a duct to the outside. Even when the weather outside is frightful and opening a window isn't an option, the ventilation system still does its job of providing fresh outdoor air. In the process, the system also controls mold-producing steam and moisture generated by cooking and dishwashing, dilutes chemical emissions and gases from building materials in the home,

and reduces pet dander and dust. Some of the more expensive ventilation systems also act as safety-conscious watchdogs, activating automatically when heat is sensed. Another helpful feature offered by a number of systems alerts the owner when the filter needs a good cleaning.

Range Hoods

Thanks to striking designs and state-of-the-art technology, range hoods can easily steal the eat-in kitchen spotlight. In stainless steel, copper, ceramic tile, and even wood with carved embellishments, the perfect range hood can be purchased ready-made or customized to suit your particular

kitchen's style, from country cottage to country estate, French Provincial to Arts and Crafts, Old World to industrial modern. The range hood is just as likely to appear over a center-island cooktop as it is wall mounted over the stove.

When needed, certain downdraft systems pop up behind the cooktop to do their work, and then lower themselves out of view. Prices can vary from less than $100 for a simple wall-mounted hood to several hundred dollars for a model equipped with lights, timers, and other bells and whistles. When the hood is custom made, the ventilation system is often purchased separately.

Opening the windows, above, is the most direct way to add fresh air to the eat-in kitchen.

In a hood suspended over a cooktop, a recirculating updraft system pulls air through a grease filter and then recycles the air in the kitchen, left.

Ventilation Systems

The air in well-ventilated kitchens is not only free from stale cooking odors but cleaner, which means less greasy residue on kitchen surfaces—and less cleanup. Refreshing the air in your eat-in kitchen has a design benefit as well, since many of today's range hoods are attractive works of art.

Wall- or ceiling-mounted **updraft** systems inside range hoods are the most popular form of kitchen ventilation for a good reason: the updraft system pulls smoke, grease, and moisture into the hood, ridding the house of stale air. This is achieved by exhausting the polluted air outside, or—with a **ductless** or **recirculating updraft system**—pulling the air through a grease filter (some with an optional odor-killing charcoal filter) and then recycling the cleaned air back into the kitchen. Because a ductless system does not exhaust the air to the outside, it can be an unsatisfactory choice for eliminating steam and moisture.

A third choice, the **hoodless downdraft system,** which may be installed in base cabinets close to the cooktop, uses a fan to draw air downward and vent it outside through ductwork. Downdraft systems work best over an island or peninsula cooktop where an overhead hood might not fit. Though the downdraft system is not as effective as a hooded system, it does a better job than a ductless system.

Sizing the Fan

While the hood may be gorgeous, it's the fan in the ventilation system that does the heavy work. Fans are sized according to the amount of air they can move in cubic feet per minute (CFM). The higher the CFM rating, the more air the system will move.

In general, the hood should extend beyond the edge of the cooktop and have a fan with power to properly match the hood's size. For example, a 36-inch commercial stove should have at least an 800-CFM system. When a high-powered system pulls too much air out of the house, a make-up air system, which guards against negative pressure, may be necessary. The competition for indoor air may cause appliances, such as hot water heaters and furnaces, to "backdraft," a dangerous condition that can bring harmful fumes and combustion byproducts, such as carbon monoxide into the home. As a safety precaution, consult a kitchen ventilation specialist to determine the right size for you.

Noise Control

Surprisingly, the noise from a ventilation system is not caused by the fan. The racket—which can sometimes sound like an airplane readying for takeoff—is caused by air being pulled through the filters. When shopping for a kitchen ventilation system, check the sone (sound level) rating. Ideally, you want a sone rating of 5.5 or less.

For the sake of efficiency, the stainless-steel hood, left, extends beyond the cooktop's edge.

The hood, like this one clad in trimwork, often becomes the focal point of the kitchen, below.

Mounted in back of the cooktop, right, a hoodless downdraft system draws air down and out of the house through ductwork.

Windows and Skylights

Sunlight streaming through the windows of an eat-in kitchen can be the most irresistible of invitations to come in, sit down, and enjoy the moment. We crave sunlight because it warms the body and feeds the psyche. And because realtors declare without hesitation that "the kitchen sells the house," it's no surprise that a home with a bright, light-filled kitchen ranks near the top of nearly every home buyer's wish list.

The kitchen is also the room that receives the prime location in most building and design plans. No other room makes better use of natural light, capturing the sun's rays for early morning coffee, reading a recipe, finding a kitchen tool, and feeding one's body and soul until sunset.

While studies report that exposure to natural light positively affects emotional and physical health, most of us spend a majority of time working or going to school in environments with artificial lighting. No doubt that's why adding more windows ranks so high on the list of modifications to home plans.

Replacing or adding kitchen windows is the starting point in most kitchen redesigns. Fortunately, it's possible to bring in all the sunlight you want and do it beautifully. Although many window styles may look custom made, most are available in affordable standard sizes.

Sometimes relocating windows is all that's needed to alter the ambiance of the kitchen. You can change a kitchen from twentieth-century traditional to twenty-first-century contemporary simply by installing sleek casement-style windows.

If you want to add a sense of history to the new kitchen, install double-hung windows with snap-in muntins. Stir up drama by grouping transom windows along the top of a wall. Incorporate a bay window or glass doors near the table area in your redesign. Make a bright design statement using a large bank of windows to create a wall of glass.

SMARTtip

Limit the size and number of east- and west-facing windows to keep down heating and cooling costs. Shades on south-facing windows can be added in summer, then removed to welcome the sun's heat in winter.

A trio of fixed windows provides an abundance of natural light and dramatic architectural elements to this eat-in kitchen.

There's a window style for every sensibility, too. The gardener in the family may want a greenhouse window to keep plants—and thumb—green year-round; the architecturally inspired homeowner might choose to feature a Frank Lloyd Wright-style leaded-glass window.

When selecting windows for the kitchen, keep your home's design in mind. Choose windows that match or are compatible with one another. Because windows are grouped in a pattern, be sure the exterior look of the house is not adversely affected by adding new ones.

Imagine the view from the window. The neighbor's driveway isn't high on anyone's list of favorite sights. However, a view of nature—no matter what season—is always pleasing. Improve a good view with a larger window. Add light and make a style statement with the addition of an arched design. Window treatments can help define a room's style as much as they control natural light.

Select energy-efficient windows that require minimal maintenance. A wood-frame window with a vinyl-coated exterior supplies good energy efficiency, low maintenance, and the appeal of a natural-wood interior finish.

"Open the window, please" is a simple request, and one of the most cost-efficient methods for keeping the air fresh in your eat-in kitchen.

GREENtip

Natural Cooling

Reduce air-conditioning costs in summer by shading sunny windows with overhangs, awnings, shade screens, and trees.

Energy-efficient windows bring light into the kitchen without wasting energy, above left.

The feeling of dining alfresco can be achieved by opening the double-hung windows that border this kitchen table, left.

SMARTtip

Lighten the heft of your energy bills by as much as $400 annually by replacing single-pane windows with Energy Star-qualified windows. These windows use low-e (low-emissivity) glass, which helps reduce year-round heating and cooling costs.

Skylights and Roof Windows

Operable skylights and roof windows can be excellent alternatives to more traditional windows. Not only do they look wonderful, but they also preserve your kitchen's wall space. Experts also claim that skylights can supply up to 30 percent more light than vertical windows, and if that's not enough of a selling point, they make the kitchen appear larger.

Windows installed along a roof slope or on a flat roof are generally unreachable. However, venting (operable) skylights that are hinged at the top can be operated with an electric wall switch, motorized or manual handcrank, or remote-control device to control fresh air and ventilation. Roof windows (the term is sometimes used for operable skylight as well) are generally set lower in the roofline than skylights and, as a result, are easier to reach. Their sashes are designed to pivot so that the outside glass can be cleaned from inside the house. Overall, the views from windows and skylights bring nature closer and improve moods. A ceiling fan can quietly circulate the air they provide throughout the kitchen.

Room-brightening roof windows, left, add light without using up valuable wall space.

Skylights work as part of an overall lighting scheme that incorporates chandeliers, windows, and recessed downlights, below.

Sanitary Surfaces

Nonporosity is crucial for keeping food preparation and cooking surfaces sanitary. Porous materials absorb water and increase the chance of cross-contamination from growing bacteria. Healthy, nonporous, and eco-friendly choices for countertops and backsplashes are abundant, including stained concrete, glass, fired clay, stainless steel, copper, vitreous china, and certain imported and indigenous stone, such as granite, provided it is sealed. All are water-resistant, durable, and rely on nontoxic natural pigments. Nonporous soapstone, an indigenous stone, is also resistant to acids and alkalis; its natural patina can be maintained organically by applying mineral oil.

Countertops made from recycled paper or glass are not only sanitary green materials but are often uniquely attractive. Whatever your choice, make sure the material is well sealed to prevent staining and that countertop seams are a minimum of 2 feet away from the sink.

Antimicrobial Countertops and Backsplashes

Composite stone—usually quartz bonded with powders and resins—is a popular engineered option to indigenous stone. It is completely nonporous and never requires sealing. In addition, manufacturers of composite-stone countertops now offer antimicrobial protection that prevents the growth of harmful bacteria and molds. Keep in mind that while this feature guards against the most common bacteria, yeasts, molds, and fungi that cause stains and odors, it is not designed to protect users from disease-causing microorganisms such as salmonella.

Bacteria-Fighting Tiles and Grout

Some natural stone tiles now have antimicrobial protection and a permanent waterproofing treatment mixed in during the manufacturing process. This technique makes the tiles resistant to stain-causing mold and mildew.

Copper, a Natural Antimicrobial

Copper, a soft metal, is long-wearing yet can dent and scratch fairly easily. It's determined by the eye of the beholder whether such tendencies give it character or lessen its appeal as a countertop material. A major plus is that copper is resistant to minor staining. However, copper's greatest advantage is that it's a naturally antimicrobial material. Experts tell us that untreated copper has powerful natural antimicrobial properties, as does stainless steel (another hygienic countertop material). Using salvaged copper is a good way to save money and also help the environment. Many older homes have copper kitchen countertops, so look for demolition work in older neighborhoods.

Hands Off

Who hasn't tried to turn on the faucet without cross contaminating it with messy hands? Thankfully, there's no longer a need to wrestle with the faucet handle. Hands-free faucets, ubiquitous in public places, are now appearing in home kitchens. Not only are they more sanitary, but hands-free faucets are also an eco-friendly windfall, automatically shutting off the water when the sensor detects it's not needed. Other hands-free developments include trashcans, soap dispensers, and light switches. Could hands-free cooktops and refrigerators be next?

Composite-stone countertops, which are totally nonporous and never need sealing, contain antimicrobial protection against bacteria and molds.

Safe Haven

Here's an easy-to-follow recipe for creating a safe kitchen for the cook, family, and friends:

- General and task lighting should be free of glare and shadows.
- Electrical switches, plugs, and lighting fixtures should not be close to water. Avoid touching with wet hands.
- A fire extinguisher should be easily accessible.
- Flooring and rugs should be slip resistant.
- Be sure to regulate water temperature. If you can, purchase a faucet that comes with internal antiscald dials.
- Select a safe cooktop featuring controls in front or along the side, and burners that are staggered or in a single row.
- Divert traffic away from the cooking zone. Avoid placing the range near kitchen doorways.
- Create storage that keeps cleaning supplies, sharp implements, and appliance cords away from children.
- It's fine to locate prep and cleanup surfaces near windows or skylights, but the cooktop should never be directly under a window.

Breathing Easy

Volatile organic compounds (VOCs) produce potentially harmful gasses that not only reduce air quality but may be detrimental to health. The best defense is to abstain from buying building materials, finishes, and cabinetry that emit formaldehyde and other noxious chemicals. Opt instead for zero- or low-VOC products. Though cabinets made with particleboard or fiberboard may contain urea formaldehyde; they can be sealed with low-VOC paints, stains, or finishes. If your plan calls for new cabinets, check out solid-wood cabinet lines that have low-VOC emissions. As another option, choose cabinetry made with wheatboard or strawboard, combinations of agricultural fibers and sustainable binders that work best in areas that don't get wet. A majority of major cabinet manufacturers now offer eco-friendly cabinetry lines with zero VOC off-gassing.

Keep in mind that wall paints and finishes may contain high levels of VOCs. Opt for the many low- and no-VOC paints available wherever most paints are sold. Most are nearly odor free.

On the Floor

Because vinyl flooring can emit chemical fumes, safer choices are stone, tile, natural linoleum, or reclaimed wood. While cork and bamboo are the reigning alternatives to endangered wood species, such as mahogany and teak, reclaimed wood has an innate beauty of its own. Aged timbers are supplied from old mills and barns, river bottoms, swamps, even pickle vats. Visit the Internet to find reclaimed wood, such as quartersawn antique heart pine, sinker cypress, antique white oak, pickle-vat redwood, barn red oak, barn white oak, American chestnut, and tobacco-barn beech.

Reuse and Recycle

If you want to add vintage accessories to your new kitchen, consider recycled material. There are salvage yards in nearly every locale. Their main mission is to recycle used building materials. Simply do an Internet search for those recycling organizations closest to you and find out how to incorporate recycled cabinetry, countertops, and other reusable materials into a redesign of your new home plan. Habitat for Humanity, for instance, operates retail centers throughout the United States and Canada called ReStores, which sell used and surplus building materials donated by building supply stores, contractors, and other supporters to the public at a fraction of normal prices. Proceeds from those sales help build decent, affordable housing for families in need.

Plan #131027

Dimensions: 62'4" W x 53'6" D
Levels: 1.5
Heated Square Footage: 2,567
Main Level Sq. Ft.: 2,017
Upper Level Sq. Ft.: 550
Bedrooms: 4
Bathrooms: 3
Foundation: Crawl space, slab, or basement
Materials List Available: Yes
Price Category: F

This home, as shown in the photograph, may differ from the actual blueprints. For more detailed information, please check the floor plans carefully.

Images provided by designer/architect.

The features of this home are so good that you may have trouble imagining all of them at once.

Features:

- Great Room: Imagine a stepped ceiling, corner fireplace, built-media center, and wall of windows with a glass door to the backyard—in one room.

- Dining Room: A stepped ceiling and server with a sink add to the elegance of this formal room.

- Breakfast Room: Eat at the bar this room shares with the island kitchen, and admire the 12-ft. cathedral ceiling and bayed group of 8- and 9-ft. windows. Or go through the sliding glass door to the covered side porch.

- Master Suite: The bedroom has a tray ceiling and cozy sitting area, and a whirlpool tub, shower, and walk-in closet are in the skylighted bath.

- Optional Study: The private bath in bedroom 2 makes it ideal for a study or home office.

Breakfast Nook

Rear View

Great Room

Main Level Floor Plan

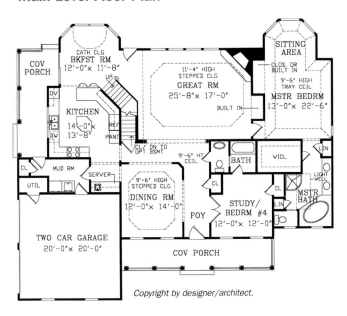

Copyright by designer/architect.

Upper Level Floor Plan

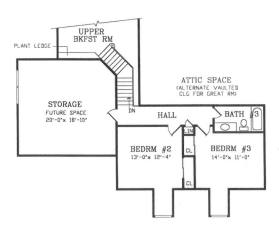

Painting Tips

As with any skill, there is a right and a wrong way to paint. There is a right way to hold a brush, a right way to maneuver a roller, a right way to spray a wall, etc. Follow these basic professional tips:

Brushing vs. Rolling. Some painters insist that only a brush-painted job looks right. However, most painters will "cut in" the edges with a brush, and then finish the main body of a wall or ceiling using a roller. Brushing alone can be time-consuming, and it is typically reserved for architectural woodwork.

Using the Right Brush. Use the largest brush with which you are comfortable. Professional painters seldom pick up anything smaller than a 4-inch brush. Most homeowners will achieve good results using a 4-inch brush for "cutting in" and for large surfaces, and an angled 2½- to 3-inch sash brush for trim around windows and doors. Be sure, also, to use brushes that are appropriate for the type of paint being applied. Oil-based paints require a natural bristle (also called "China bristles"), while water-based paints are applied with a synthetic bristle brush.

Handling a Brush. Many people grip a paintbrush as if they were shaking someone's hand. It is better to grip a brush more like a pencil, with the fingers and thumb wrapped around the metal ferrule. This grip provides the hand and wrist with a wider range of motion and therefore greater speed and precision. If your hand cramps, switch hands or switch temporarily to the handshake grip.

Wiping Rags. Before you begin painting, put a dust rag in your pocket. This is helpful for clearing away cobwebs and dust before painting. It is also handy for wiping off paint drips before they have a chance to dry.

Paint Hooks. When working on a ladder, use a good-quality paint hook to secure the paint bucket to your ladder. Avoid makeshift hooks made with wire or coat hangers. Paint hooks are inexpensive and available at virtually all paint and hardware stores.

Images provided by designer/architect.

Plan #151383

Dimensions: 70'4" W x 57'2" D
Levels: 1
Heated Square Footage: 2,534
Bedrooms: 3
Bathrooms: 2
Foundation: Crawl space or slab
CompleteCost List Available: Yes
Price Category: G

The arched entry of the covered porch welcomes you to this magnificent home.

Features:

- Foyer: Welcome your guests in this warm foyer before leading them into the impressive dining room with magnificent columns framing the entry.

- Great Room: After dinner, your guests will enjoy conversation in this spacious room, complete with fireplace and built-ins.

- Study: Beautiful French doors open into this quiet space, where you'll be able to concentrate on that work away from the office.

- Rear Porch: This relaxing spot may be reached from the breakfast room or your secluded master suite.

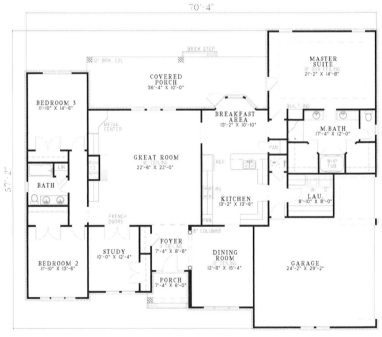

Copyright by designer/architect.

Front View

Plan #271081

Dimensions: 86' W x 54' D
Levels: 1
Heated Square Footage: 2,539
Bedrooms: 3
Bathrooms: 2
Foundation: Slab
Materials List Available: No
Price Category: E

This traditional home is sure to impress your guests and even your neighbors.

CAD FILE AVAILABLE

Features:

- **Living Room:** This quiet space off the foyer is perfect for pleasant conversation.

- **Family Room:** A perfect gathering spot, this room is nicely enhanced by a fireplace.

- **Kitchen:** This room easily serves the bayed morning room and the formal dining room.

- **Master Suite:** The master bedroom overlooks a side patio, and boasts a private bath with a skylight and a whirlpool tub.

- **Library:** This cozy room is perfect for curling up with a good novel. It would also make a great extra bedroom.

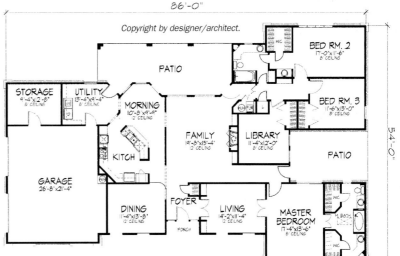

86'-0"

Copyright by designer/architect.

54'-0"

SMARTtip

Determining Curtain Length

Follow length guidelines for foolproof results, but remember that they're not rules. Go ahead and play with curtain and drapery lengths. Instead of shortening long panels at the hem, for instance, take up excess material by blousing them over tiebacks for a pleasing effect.

Plan #151063

Dimensions: 64' W x 60'2" D
Levels: 1
Heated Square Footage: 2,554
Bedrooms: 4
Bathrooms: 2½
Foundation: Crawl space or slab; basement or walkout for fee
CompleteCost List Available: Yes
Price Category: E

This home boasts a beautiful arched entry on the covered porch.

Features:

- Dining Room: Set off by columns, this room will impress your dinner guests. The triple window gives a front-yard view while allowing natural light into the space.

- Entertaining: Your family and friends will love to gather in the hearth room and the great room, which share a see-through fire place. The hearth room has access to the grilling porch for outdoor entertaining.

- Kitchen: Centrally located, this island kitchen is open to the dining room in the front and the hearth room in the rear. It features a raised bar into the hearth room.

- Master Suite: This secluded retreat resides on the opposite side of the home from the secondary bedrooms. The large master bath features a whirlpool tub, two walk-in closets, and dual vanities.

This home, as shown in the photograph, may differ from the actual blueprints. *Images provided by designer/architect.*
For more detailed information, please check the floor plans carefully.

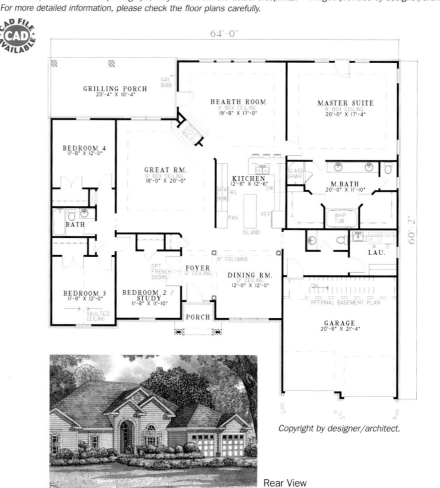

Rear View

Copyright by designer/architect.

Plan #151486

Dimensions: 74'7" W x 70'6" D
Levels: 1
Heated Square Footage: 2,556
Bedrooms: 4
Bathrooms: 3
Foundation: Crawl space or slab
CompleteCost List Available: Yes
Price Category: E

Images provided by designer/architect.

From the moment you step on the covered front porch, you will revel in the comfort of this home.

Features:

- **Great Room:** This great room boasts a cozy fireplace to keep you warm on cold nights.

- **Kitchen:** The kitchen welcomes you to dine at the raised snack bar open to the breakfast room. The grilling porch at the rear of the house is a wonderful space to enjoy a barbecue on a warm summer evening.

- **Master Suite:** You'll love the several amenities this master suite boasts, including the large walk-in closet, whirlpool tub, and a fireplace.

- **Secondary Bedrooms:** Two additional bedrooms, each with their own walk-in closet, share their own bath.

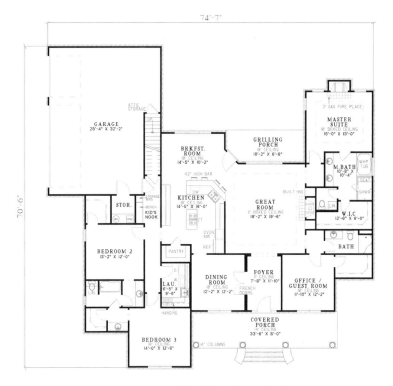

Copyright by designer/architect.

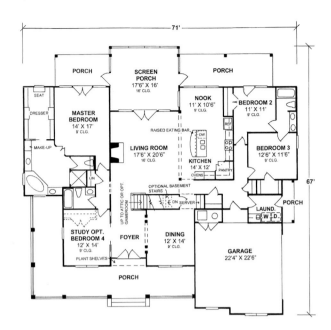

Plan #121196

Dimensions: 71' W x 67' D

Levels: 1

Heated Square Footage: 2,512

Bedrooms: 3

Bathrooms: 3

Foundation: Slab; basement for fee

Material Take-off Included: Yes

Price Category: E

Images provided by designer/architect.

PORCH · **SCREEN PORCH** 17'6" X 16' 16' CLG. · **PORCH**

SEAT · DRESSER

MASTER BEDROOM 14' X 17' 9' CLG.

MAKE-UP

NOOK 11' X 10'6" 9' CLG.

BEDROOM 2 11' X 11' 9' CLG.

RAISED EATING BAR

LIVING ROOM 17'6" X 20'6" 16' CLG.

DW · REF

BEDROOM 3 12'6" X 11'6" 9' CLG.

KITCHEN 14' X 12' · OVENS · PANTRY

UP TO ATTIC OR OPT. GAMEROOM

OPTIONAL BASEMENT STAIRS

DN · SERVER

LAUND. · W. D.

PORCH

STUDY OPT. BEDROOM 4 12' X 14' 9' CLG.

PLANT SHELVES

FOYER

DINING 12' X 14' 9' CLG.

GARAGE 22'4" X 22'6"

PORCH

Optional Floor Plan

Copyright by designer/architect.

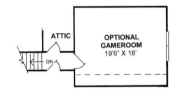

ATTIC · DN · **OPTIONAL GAMEROOM** 19'6" X 16'

Plan #121029

Dimensions: 58'8" W x 54' D

Levels: 1.5

Heated Square Footage: 2,576

Main Level Sq. Ft.: 1,735

Upper Level Sq. Ft.: 841

Bedrooms: 4

Bathrooms: 2½

Foundation: Basement

Materials List Available: Yes

Price Category: E

Images provided by designer/architect.

Upper Level Floor Plan

OPEN TO BELOW · 19'-0" CEILING

Br.3 13³ x 12⁰

DESK

DN

Br.2 14⁰ x 13⁰

Br.4 13³ x 11⁰

OPEN TO BELOW

OPTIONAL STUDY · BOOKS · BOOKS

Main Level Floor Plan

Copyright by designer/architect.

WHIRLPOOL TUB

Grt. Rm. 16⁰ x 17¹⁰ 19'-0" CEILING

Bfst. 10⁸ x 16⁰

Kit. 11⁰ x 12⁰

CATHEDRAL CEILING

ENTERT. CENTER

SNACK BAR

DN · UP

P · R

Mbr. 14⁰ x 15² 10'-4" CEILING

BOOKS · BOOKS

E.

CURIO · CURIO

Din. 14⁰ x 13⁰

STOOP

W. D.

Gar. 22⁰ x 23⁰

54'-0"

58'-8"

Main Level Floor Plan

Images provided by designer/architect.

COVERED PORCH

GREAT ROOM
25'-5"x15'-0"
(9' CLG)

KITCHEN
16'-6"x14'-1"
(9' CLG)

LNDRY

SHOP/STORAGE
11'-10"x19'-3"

OFFICE/BDRM #5/
HOME SCHOOL
13'-0"x11'-1"
(9' CLG)

FOYER
(9' CLG)

FORMAL DINING
13'-0"x13'-0"
(9' CLG)

GARAGE
24'-0"x24'-0"

COVERED PORCH

FOYER
(9' CLG)

REVERSED
STAIR OPTION

Upper Level Floor Plan

Copyright by designer/architect.

MASTER
BATH

W.I.C.

BEDROOM #2
13'-0"x12'-7"

BEDROOM #3
13'-0"x12'-7"

BONUS ROOM
20'-3"x18'-9"

MASTER BEDROOM
13'-0"x18'-0"
(VAULTED)

HALL
BATH

SITTING ROOM
14'-11"x14'-11"
(VAULTED)

STORAGE

Plan #421023

Dimensions: 72' W x 52'4" D

Levels: 2

Heated Square Footage: 2,579

Main Level Sq. Ft.: 1,399

Upper Level Sq. Ft.: 1,180

Bedrooms: 4

Bathrooms: 2½

Foundation: Crawl space, slab or basement

Material List Available: Yes

Price Category: E

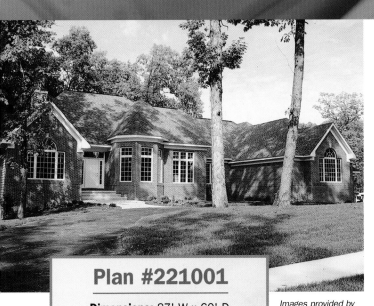

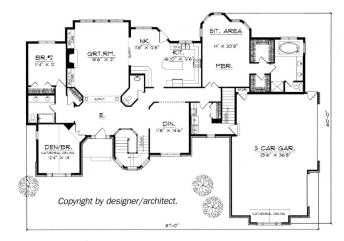

BR. #2
11'4" x 12'

GRT. RM.
18'6" x 21'

NK.
11'8" x 12'8"

KIT.
16'10" x 12'6"

SIT. AREA
14' x 20'8"

MBR.

DEN/BR.
CATHEDRAL CEILING
12'4" x 14'

DIN.
11'8" x 14'6"

3 CAR GAR.
25'6" x 36'8"

CATHEDRAL CEILING

87'-0"

Copyright by designer/architect.

Plan #221001

Dimensions: 87' W x 60' D

Levels: 1

Heated Square Footage: 2,600

Bedrooms: 3

Bathrooms: 2½

Foundation: Basement

Materials List Available: No

Price Category: F

Images provided by designer/architect.

CAD FILE AVAILABLE

Rear Elevation

Kitchen

Plan #101013

Dimensions: 72' W x 66' D
Levels: 1
Heated Square Footage: 2,564
Bedrooms: 3
Bathrooms: 2½
Foundation: Basement; slab
Materials List Available: Yes
Price Category: F

Images provided by designer/architect.

This exciting design combines a striking classic exterior with a highly functional floor plan.

CAD FILE AVAILABLE

Features:

- Ceiling Height: 9 ft. unless otherwise noted.

- Family Room: This warm and inviting room measures 18 ft. x 22 ft. It features a 14-ft. ceiling and a rear wall of windows. French doors lead to an enormous deck.

- Kitchen: This unique angled kitchen is open to the hearth room and eating areas, all of which enjoy vaulted ceilings and are surrounded by windows. The hearth room has a TV niche.

- Master Suite: This 19-ft. x 18-ft. master suite is truly sumptuous, with its 12-ft. ceiling, sitting area, two walk-in closets, and full-featured bath.

- Secondary Bedrooms: Each of the secondary bedrooms measures 11 ft. x 14 ft. and has direct access to a shared bath.

- Bonus Room: Just beyond the entry are stairs leading to this bonus room, which measures approximately 12 ft. x 21 ft.—plenty of room for storage or future expansion.

Master Bedroom

Copyright by designer/architect.

Plan #151537

Dimensions: 70'2" W x 53'4" D
Levels: 2
Heated Square Footage: 2,603
Main Level Sq. Ft.: 1,813
Upper Level Sq. Ft.: 790
Bedrooms: 4
Bathrooms: 2½
Foundation: Crawl space or slab
CompleteCost List Available: Yes
Price Category: F

Images provided by designer/architect.

Eye-catching covered porches and columns are used on both the front and rear of this traditional home.

Features:

• **Great Room:** A vaulted ceiling, balcony, and built-in media center enhance this great room, which is open to the kitchen and breakfast room.

• **Kitchen:** This large kitchen, with a raised bar, has an abundance of cabinets and a walk-in pantry.

• **Master Suite:** This suite and an additional bedroom or study are located on the main level for privacy and convenience.

• **Upper Level:** The upstairs has a balcony overlooking the great room. In addition, it has two bedrooms, a full bathroom, a built-in computer nook, and a large bonus room.

Main Level Floor Plan

Upper Level Floor Plan

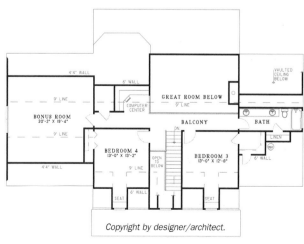

Copyright by designer/architect.

Plan #321051

Dimensions: 69'8" W x 46' D
Levels: 2
Heated Square Footage: 2,624
Main Level Sq. Ft.: 1,774
Upper Level Sq. Ft.: 850
Bedrooms: 4
Bathrooms: 2½
Foundation: Basement
Materials List Available: Yes
Price Category: F

The dramatic exterior design allows natural light to flow into the spacious living area of this home.

Features:

- **Entry:** This two-story area opens into the dining room through a classic colonnade.

- **Dining Room:** A large bay window, stately columns, and doorway to the kitchen make this room both beautiful and convenient.

- **Great Room:** Enjoy light from the fireplace or the three Palladian windows in the 18-ft. ceiling.

- **Kitchen:** The step-saving design features a walk-in pantry as well as good counter space.

- **Breakfast Room:** You'll love the light that flows through the windows flanking the back door.

- **Master Suite:** The vaulted ceiling and bayed areas in both the bed and bath add elegance. You'll love the two walk-in closets and bath with a sunken tub, two vanities, and separate shower.

This home, as shown in the photograph, may differ from the actual blueprints. For more detailed information, please check the floor plans carefully.   *Images provided by designer/architect.*

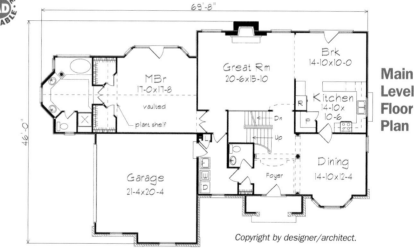

Main Level Floor Plan

Copyright by designer/architect.

Master Bath

Upper Level Floor Plan

Plan #121150

Dimensions: 68'7" W x 57'4" D
Levels: 2
Heated Square Footage: 2,639
Main Level Sq. Ft.: 2,087
Upper Level Sq. Ft.: 552
Bedrooms: 4
Bathrooms: 3½
Foundation: Slab; basement for fee
Material List Available: Yes
Price Category: F

Images provided by designer/architect.

Both the exterior and interior of this home are warm and inviting.

Features:

• **Entry:** Sunlight enters this area along with you and your guests, making your welcome home bright and cheerful. The adjoining staircase boasts an 18-ft.-high ceiling, giving it a grand and picturesque feel.

• **Family Room:** With its two-story cathedral ceiling, corner fireplace, and convenient connection to the kitchen, this family room is wonderful for both entertaining and relaxing.

• **Kitchen:** You will love to cook in this beautiful kitchen, which features a pantry and adjoining breakfast room.

• **Master Suite:** Secluded from the rest of the sleeping areas, this spacious master suite features two sinks, a walk-in closet, and access to the covered porch outside.

• **Guest Room:** Guests will love to stay over in your home! This guest room is a private refuge, offering visitors a large sleeping area, walk-in closet, and private bath with tub.

Main Level Floor Plan

Upper Level Floor Plan

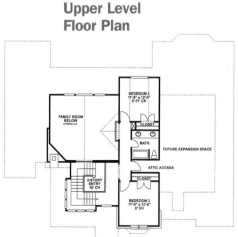

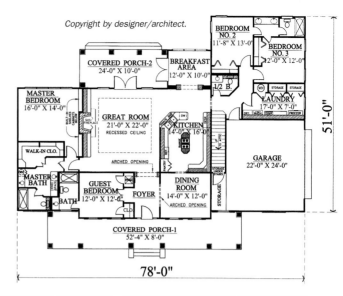

Copyright by designer/architect.

Images provided by designer/architect.

Plan #191017

Dimensions: 78' W x 51' D

Levels: 1

Heated Square Footage: 2,605

Bedrooms: 4

Bathrooms: 2½

Foundation: Crawl space, slab, or basement

Materials List Available: No

Price Category: F

Entry

Kitchen

Plan #121028

Dimensions: 54'8" W x 42' D

Levels: 2

Heated Square Footage: 2,644

Main Level Sq. Ft.: 1,366

Upper Level Sq. Ft.: 1,278

Bedrooms: 4

Bathrooms: 2½

Foundation: Basement

Materials List Available: Yes

Price Category: F

Images provided by designer/architect.

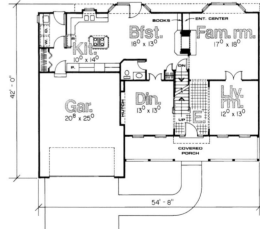

Main Level Floor Plan

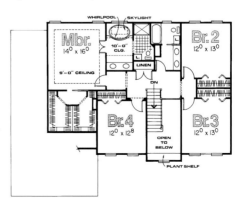

Upper Level Floor Plan

Copyright by designer/architect.

Plan #441009

Dimensions: 94' W x 53' D

Levels: 1

Heated Square Footage: 2,650

Bedrooms: 4

Bathrooms: 2½

Foundation: Crawl space; slab or basement available for fee

Materials List Available: Yes

Price Category: F

Images provided by designer/architect.

Copyright by designer/architect.

Rear Elevation

Plan #371008

Dimensions: 86'4" W x 45'4" D

Levels: 2

Heated Square Footage: 2,656

Main Level Sq. Ft: 1,969

Upper Level Sq. Ft.: 687

Bedrooms: 4

Bathrooms: 3

Foundation: Crawl space, slab, or basement

Materials List Available: No

Price Category: F

Images provided by designer/architect.

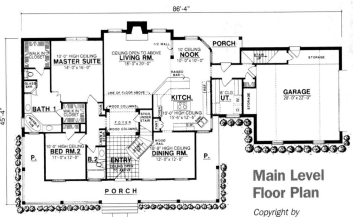

Main Level Floor Plan

Copyright by designer/architect.

Upper Level Floor Plan

Images provided by designer/architect.

CAD FILE AVAILABLE

Copyright by designer/architect.

Plan #661007

Dimensions: 66'4" W x 74'4" D

Levels: 1

Heated Square Footage: 2,660

Bedrooms: 4

Bathrooms: 3

Foundation: Slab

Material List Available: No

Price Category: F

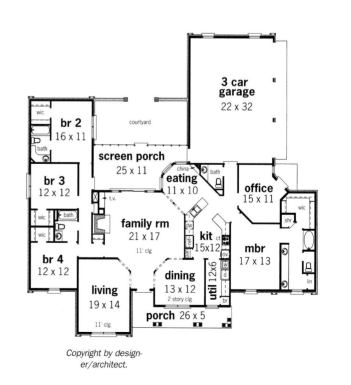

Images provided by designer/architect.

CAD FILE AVAILABLE

Copyright by designer/architect.

Plan #211062

Dimensions: 96'6" W x 43' D

Levels: 1

Heated Square Footage: 2,719

Bedrooms: 4

Bathrooms: 2½

Foundation: Slab

Materials List Available: Yes

Price Category: F

Plan #121079

Dimensions: 50' W x 60' D
Levels: 2
Heated Square Footage: 2,688
Main Level Sq. Ft.: 1,650
Upper Level Sq. Ft.: 1,038
Bedrooms: 4
Bathrooms: 3½
Foundation: Slab
Materials List Available: Yes
Price Category: F

Images provided by designer/architect.

This home, as shown in the photograph, may differ from the actual blueprints. For more detailed information, please check the floor plans carefully.

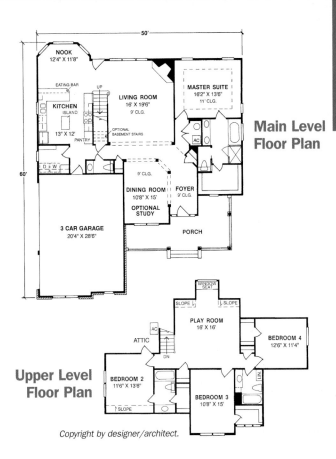

Main Level Floor Plan

Upper Level Floor Plan

Copyright by designer/architect.

Plan #121091

Dimensions: 56' W x 50' D
Levels: 2
Heated Square Footage: 2,689
Main Level Sq. Ft.: 1,415
Upper Level Sq. Ft.: 1,274
Bedrooms: 4
Bathrooms: 2½
Foundation: Basement
Materials List Available: Yes
Price Category: F

Images provided by designer/architect.

This home, as shown in the photograph, may differ from the actual blueprints. For more detailed information, please check the floor plans carefully.

Main Level Floor Plan

Upper Level Floor Plan

Copyright by designer/architect.

Images provided by designer/architect.

Plan #121163

Dimensions: 65'10" W x 75'6" D
Levels: 1
Heated Square Footage: 2,679
Bedrooms: 4
Bathrooms: 3
Foundation: Slab; basement for fee
Material List Available: Yes
Price Category: F

Large rooms give this home a spacious feel in a modest footprint.

Features:

- **Family Room:** This area is the central gathering place in the home. The windows to the rear fill the area with natural light. The fireplace take the chill off on cool winter nights.

- **Kitchen:** This peninsula kitchen with raised bar is open into the family room and the breakfast area. The built-in pantry is a welcomed storage area for today's family.

- **Master Suite:** This secluded area features large windows with a view of the backyard. The master bath boasts a large walk-in closet, his and her vanities and a compartmentalized lavatory area.

- **Secondary Bedrooms:** Bedroom 2 has its own access to the main bathroom, while bedrooms 3 and 4 share a Jack-and-Jill bathroom. All bedrooms feature walk-in closets.

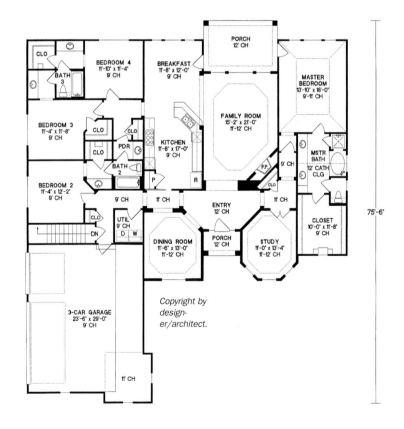

Copyright by designer/architect.

Plan #321007

Dimensions: 76' W x 55'2" D

Levels: 1

Heated Square Footage: 2,695

Bedrooms: 3

Bathrooms: 2½

Foundation: Base,emt

Material List Available: Yes

Price Category: G

Images provided by designer/architect.

You'll lve the way this spacious rand reminds you of a French country home.

Features:

- Foyer: come into this lovely home's foyer and be greeted with a view of the gracious staircase and the great room just beyond.

- Great Room: Settle down by the cozy fireplace in cool weather, and reach for a book on the built-in shelves that surround it.

- Kitchen: Designed for efficient work patterns, this large kitchen is open to the great room.

- Breakfast Room: Just off the kitchen, this sunny room will be a family favorite all through the day.

- Master Suite: A bay window, walk-in closet, and shower built for two are highlights of this area.

- Additional Bedrooms: These large bedrooms both have walk-in closets and share a Jack-and-Jill bath for total convenience.

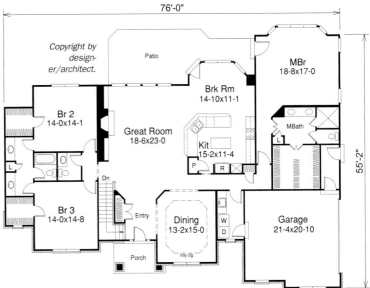

SMARTtip

Decorative Poles

Drapery poles are supported by the brackets fastened to the window frame or wall. The brackets that are provided with the poles generally coordinate and blend in with the pole finish. Brackets can be simple but also decorative. If you opt for a spectacular, attention-getting bracket, consider chosing less showy finials for the ends of th e pole.

Images provided by designer/architect.

Plan #131028

Dimensions: 69'2" W x 50'2" D

Levels: 1.5

Heated Square Footage: 2,696

Main Level Sq. Ft.: 1,960

Upper Level Sq. Ft.: 736

Bedrooms: 4

Bathrooms: 3

Foundation: Crawl space, slab, or basement

Materials List Available: Yes

Price Category: G

Imagine owning a home with Victorian styling and a dramatic, contemporary interior design.

Features:

• Foyer: Enter from the curved covered porch into this foyer with its 17-ft. ceiling.

• Great Room: A vaulted ceiling sets the tone for this large room, where friends and family are sure to congregate.

• Dining Room: A 14-ft. ceiling here accentuates the rounded shape of this room.

• Kitchen: From the angled corner sink to the angled island with a snack bar, this room has character. A pantry adds convenience.

• Master Suite: A 13-ft. tray ceiling exudes elegance, and the bath features a tub and designer shower.

• Upper Level: The balcony hall leads to a turreted recreation room, two bedrooms, and a full bath.

Main Level Floor Plan

Upper Level Floor Plan

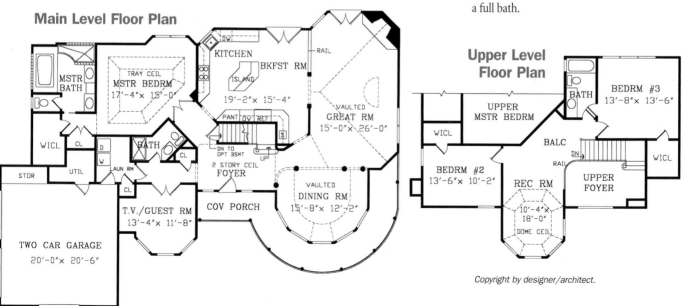

Copyright by designer/architect.

Plan #121067

imensions: 56' W x 59'4" D
Levels: 1.5
Heated Square Footage: 2,708
Main Level Sq. Ft.: 1,860
Upper Level Sq. Ft.: 848
Bedrooms: 4
Bathrooms: 3½
Foundation: Basement
Materials List Available: Yes
Price Category: F

Images provided by designer/architect.

You'll love this home because it is such a perfect setting for a family and still has room for guests.

Features:

- **Family Room:** Expect everyone to gather in this room, near the built-in entertainment centers that flank the lovely fireplace.

- **Living Room:** The other side of the see-through fireplace looks out into this living room, making it an equally welcoming spot in chilly weather.

- **Kitchen:** This room has a large center island, a corner pantry, and a built-in desk. It also features a breakfast area where friends and family will congregate all day long.

- **Master Suite:** Enjoy the oversized walk-in closet and bath with a bayed whirlpool tub, double vanity, and separate shower.

Main Level Floor Plan

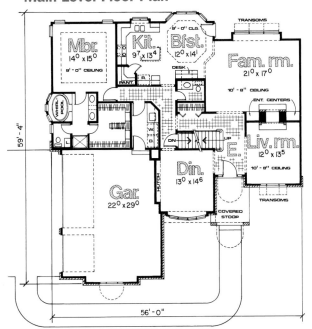

Upper Level Floor Plan

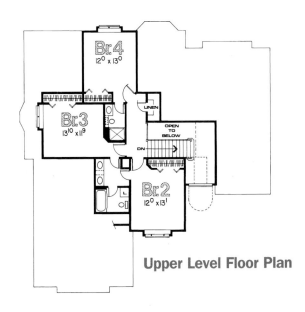

Copyright by designer/architect.

2,501-3,000 sq. ft.

Plan #131029

Dimensions: 56'4" W x 46'6" D
Levels: 2
Heated Square Footage: 2,936
Main Level Sq. Ft.: 1,680
Upper Level Sq. Ft.: 1,256
Bedrooms: 4
Bathrooms: 2½
Foundation: Crawl space, slab, or basement
Materials List Available: Yes
Price Category: G

Images provided by designer/architect.

Main Level Floor Plan

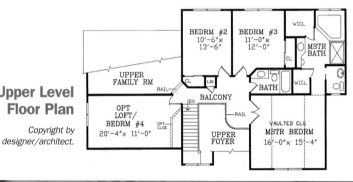

Upper Level Floor Plan

Copyright by designer/architect.

Plan #321028

Dimensions: 79' W x 64'2" D
Levels: 1
Heated Square Footage: 2,723
Bedrooms: 3
Bathrooms: 2½
Foundation: Basement
Materials List Available: Yes
Price Category: F

Images provided by designer/architect.

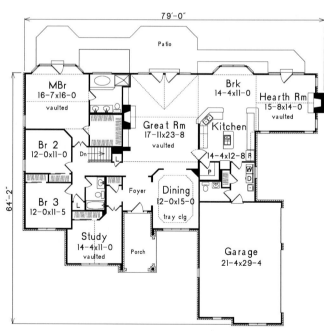

Copyright by designer/architect.

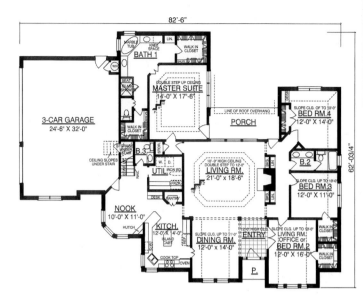

Plan #371095

Dimensions: 82'6" W x 62'0 3/4" D

Levels: 1

Heated Square Footage: 2,725

Bedrooms: 4

Bathrooms: 2½

Foundation: Crawl space, slab, or basement

Material List Available: No

Price Category: F

Images provided by designer/architect.

Bonus Area Floor Plan

Copyright by designer/architect.

Plan #151108

Dimensions: 84'6" W x 58'6" D

Levels: 1

Heated Square Footage: 2,742

Bedrooms: 4

Bathrooms: 2½

Foundation: Crawl space, slab, or basement

CompleteCost List Available: No

Price Category: G

Images provided by designer/architect.

Copyright by designer/architect.

Optional Bonus Space Floor Plan

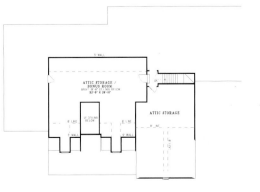

Plan #151118

Dimensions: 54'2" W x 73'6" D
Levels: 1.5
Heated Square Footage: 2,784
Main Level Sq. Ft.: 1,895
Upper Level Sq. Ft.: 889
Bedrooms: 4
Bathrooms: 2½
Foundation: Crawl space, slab, or basement
CompleteCost List Available: Yes
Price Category: F

Images provided by designer/architect.

The classic good looks of the exterior of this lovely home are matched inside by clean lines and contemporary comforts.

Features:

- Great Room: Opening from the foyer, this room contains a fireplace and media center, and it leads to the rear grilling porch.

- Living Room: A high ceiling sets an elegant tone in this spacious, formal room.

- Dining Room: Equally formal, this room is nicely adjacent to the kitchen for serving ease.

- Kitchen: Built for a gourmet cook, the kitchen has plenty of counter and cabinet space.

- Breakfast Area: Sharing a snack bar with the kitchen, this area also leads to the grilling porch.

- Master Suite: The bedroom features a bay window, and the bath has a walk-in closet, whirlpool tub, glass shower, and double vanity.

CAD FILE AVAILABLE

Main Level Floor Plan

Upper Level Floor Plan

Copyright by designer/architect.

Plan #151014

Dimensions: 70'2" W x 51'4" D

Levels: 1.5

Heated Square Footage: 2,698

Main Level Sq. Ft.: 1,813

Upper Level Sq. Ft.: 885

Bedrooms: 5

Bathrooms: 3

Foundation: Crawl space, slab; basement for fee

CompleteCost List Available: Yes

Price Category: F

Images provided by designer/architect.

A comfortable front porch welcomes you into this home that features a balcony over the great room, a study, and a kitchen designed for gourmet cooks.

CAD FILE AVAILABLE

Features:

- Ceiling Height: 9 ft.
- Front Porch: Stately 12-in.-wide pillars form the entryway.
- Foyer: Open to upper story.
- Great Room: A fireplace, vaulted 9-ft. ceiling, and balcony from the second floor add character to this lovely room.
- Dining Room: Open to the kitchen for convenience.
- Kitchen: A large walk-in pantry, well-designed work areas, and eat-in bar make this room a treasure.
- Breakfast Room: Enjoy this spot that opens to both the kitchen and a large covered porch at the rear of the house.
- Study: This quiet room has French doors leading to the yard.
- Master Suite: This spacious area has cozy window seats as well as his and her walk-in closets. The master bathroom is fitted with a whirlpool tub, a glass shower, and his and her sinks.

Upper Level Floor Plan

Main Level Floor Plan

Copyright by designer/architect.

2,501-3,000 sq. ft.

Bonus Area Floor Plan

Copyright by designer/architect.

Plan #151384

Dimensions: 76'8" W x 77'7" D
Levels: 1.5
Heated Square Footage: 2,742
Bedrooms: 3
Bathrooms: 2½
Foundation: Crawl space or slab
CompleteCost List Available: Yes
Price Category: F

Images provided by designer/architect.

CAD FILE AVAILABLE

Front View

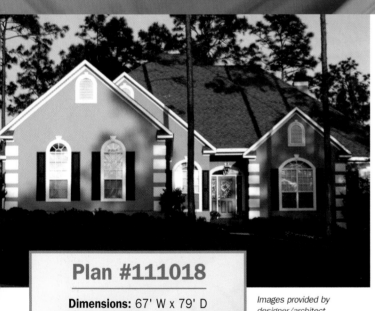

Rear Elevation

Copyright by designer/architect.

Plan #111018

Dimensions: 67' W x 79' D
Levels: 1
Heated Square Footage: 2,745
Bedrooms: 4
Bathrooms: 3½
Foundation: Basement
Materials List Available: No
Price Category: G

Images provided by designer/architect.

Copyright by designer/architect.

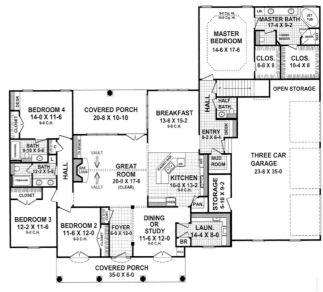

Bonus Area Floor Plan

Copyright by designer/architect.

UNFINISHED
BONUS ROOM
18'-8" X 18'-0"
(CLEAR)
8'-0" C.H.

Plan #351104

Dimensions: 84' W x 67'10" D
Levels: 1
Heated Square Footage: 2,755
Bedrooms: 4
Bathrooms: 3½
Foundation: Crawl space or slab
Material List Available: Yes
Price Category: G

Images provided by designer/architect.

CAD FILE AVAILABLE

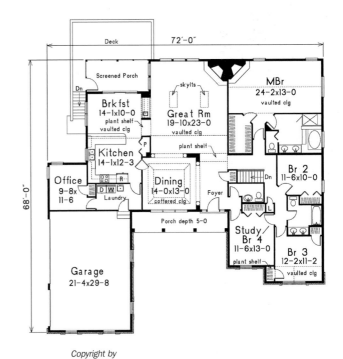

Copyright by designer/architect.

Plan #321027

Dimensions: 72' W x 68' D
Levels: 1
Heated Square Footage: 2,758
Bedrooms: 4
Bathrooms: 2½
Foundation: Basement
Materials List Available: Yes
Price Category: F

Images provided by designer/architect.

CAD FILE AVAILABLE

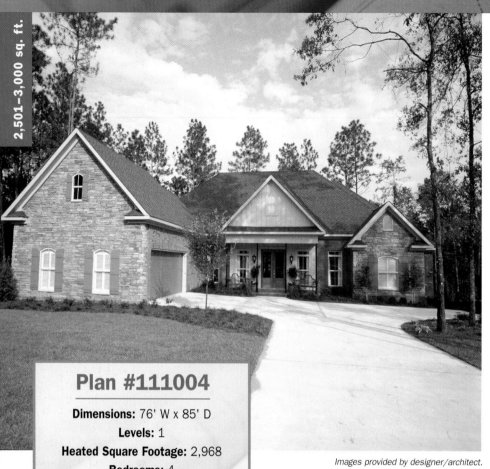

Images provided by designer/architect. Living Room

Plan #111004

Dimensions: 76' W x 85' D

Levels: 1

Heated Square Footage: 2,968

Bedrooms: 4

Full Bathrooms: 3½

Foundation: Crawl space or slab

Materials List Available: No

Price Category: G

If you've been looking for a home that includes a special master suite, this one could be the answer to your dreams.

Features:

• Living Room: Make a sitting area around the fireplace here so that the whole family can enjoy the warmth on chilly days and winter evenings. A door from this room leads to the rear covered porch, making this room the heart of your home.

• Kitchen: An island with a cooktop makes cooking a pleasure in this well-designed kitchen, and the breakfast bar invites visitors at all times of day.

• Utility Room: A sink and a built-in ironing board make this room totally practical.

• Master Suite: A private fireplace in the corner sets a romantic tone for this bedroom, and the door to the covered porch allows you to sit outside on warm summer nights. The bath has two vanities, a divided walk-in closet, a standing shower, and a deluxe corner bathtub.

CAD FILE AVAILABLE

Copyright by designer/architect.

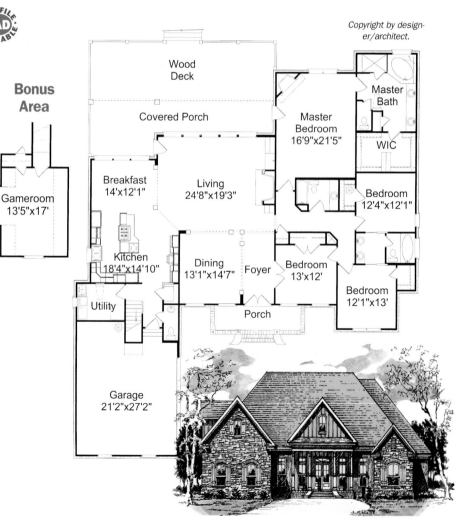

Bonus Area

Gameroom 13'5"x17'

Wood Deck

Covered Porch

Breakfast 14'x12'1"

Living 24'8"x19'3"

Master Bedroom 16'9"x21'5"

Master Bath

WIC

Bedroom 12'4"x12'1"

Kitchen 18'4"x14'10"

Dining 13'1"x14'7"

Foyer

Bedroom 13'x12'

Utility

Porch

Bedroom 12'1"x13'

Garage 21'2"x27'2"

Plan #101020

Dimensions: 55'8" W x 49'2" D
Levels: 2
Heated Square Footage: 2,972
Main Level Sq. Ft.: 1,986
Upper Level Sq. Ft.: 986
Bedrooms: 4
Bathrooms: 3½
Foundation: Basement, or walkout
Materials List Available: No
Price Category: F

Images provided by designer/architect.

This luxurious country home has an open-design main level that maximizes the use of space.

Features:

- **Ceiling Height:** 9 ft. unless otherwise noted.
- **Foyer:** Guests will be greeted by this grand two-story entry, with its graceful angled staircase.
- **Dining Room:** At nearly 12 ft. x 15 ft., this elegant dining room has plenty of room for large parties.
- **Family Room:** Everyone will be drawn to this 17-ft. x 19-ft. room, with its dramatic two-story ceiling and its handsome fireplace.
- **Kitchen:** This spacious kitchen is open to the family room and features a breakfast bar and built-in table in the cooktop island.
- **Master Suite:** This elegant retreat includes a bayed 18-ft.-5-in. x 14-ft.-9-in. bedroom and a beautiful corner his and her bath/closet arrangement.
- **Secondary Bedrooms:** Upstairs you'll find three spacious bathrooms, one with a private bath and two with access to a shared bath.

Main Level Floor Plan

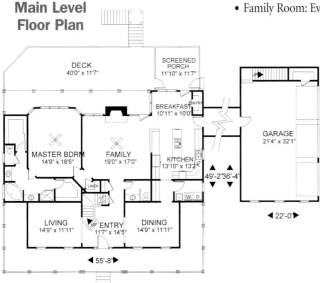

Upper Level Floor Plan

Copyright by designer/architect.

Plan #151015

Dimensions: 72'4" W x 48'4" D
Levels: 1.5
Heated Square Footage: 2,789
Main Level Sq. Ft.: 1,977
Upper Level Sq. Ft.: 812
Bedrooms: 4
Bathrooms: 3
Foundation: Crawl space, slab, or basement
CompleteCost List Available: Yes
Price Category: F

Images provided by designer/architect.

The spacious kitchen that opens to the breakfast room and the hearth room make this family home ideal for entertaining.

Features:

- **Great Room:** The fireplace will make a cozy winter focal point in this versatile space.
- **Hearth Room:** Enjoy the built-in entertainment center, built-in shelving, and fireplace here.
- **Dining Room:** A swing door leading to the kitchen is as attractive as it is practical.
- **Study:** A private bath and walk-in closet make this room an ideal spot for guests when needed.
- **Kitchen:** An island work area, a computer desk, and an eat-in bar add convenience and utility.
- **Master Suite:** Two vanities, two walk-in closets, a shower with a seat, and a whirlpool tub highlight this private space.

CAD FILE AVAILABLE

Main Level Floor Plan

Copyright by designer/architect.

Upper Level Floor Plan

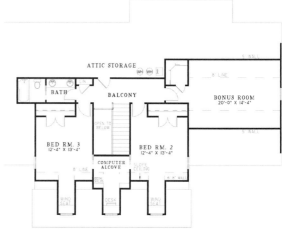

Plan #211011

Dimensions: 84' W x 54' D
Levels: 1
Heated Square Footage: 2,791
Bedrooms: 3 or 4
Bathrooms: 2
Foundation: Slab or crawl space
Materials List Available: Yes
Price Category: F

Images provided by designer/architect.

CAD FILE AVAILABLE · CAD ·

SMARTtip

Types of Decks

Ground-level decks resemble a low platform and are best for flat locations. They can be the most economical type to build because they don't require stairs.

Raised decks can rise just a few steps up or meet the second story of a house. Lifted high on post supports, they adapt well to uneven or sloped locations.

Multilevel decks feature two or more stories and are connected by stairways or ramps. They can follow the contours of a sloped lot, unifying the deck with the outdoors.

Plenty of room plus an open, flexible floor plan make this a home that will adapt to your needs.

Features:

• Ceiling Height: 8 ft. unless otherwise noted.

• Living Room: This distinctive room features a 12-ft. ceiling and is designed so that it can also serve as a master suite with a sitting room.

• Family Room: The whole family will want to gather in this large, inviting family room.

• Morning Room: The family room blends into this sunny spot, which is perfect for informal family meals.

• Kitchen: This spacious kitchen offers a smart layout. It is also contiguous to the family room.

• Master Suite: You'll look forward to the end of the day when you can enjoy this master suite. It includes a huge, luxurious master bath with two large walk-in closets and two vanity sinks.

• Optional Bedroom: This optional fourth bedroom is located so that it can easily serve as a library, den, office, or music room.

Copyright by designer/architect.

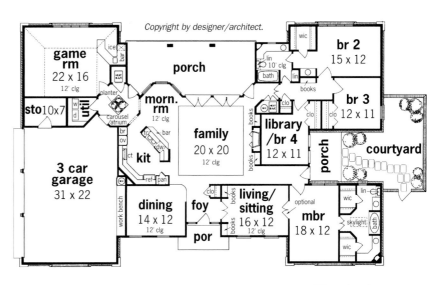

Plan #151101

Dimensions: 87'10" W x 54'6" D
Levels: 1
Heated Square Footage: 2,804
Bedrooms: 4
Bathrooms: 2½
Foundation: Slab
CompleteCost List Available: Yes
Price Category: F

Images provided by designer/architect.

This one-story home has everything you would find in a two-story house and more. This home plan is keeping up with the times.

Features:

- **Porches:** The long covered front porch is perfect for sitting out on warm evenings and greeting passersby. The back grilling porch, which opens through French doors from the great room, is great for entertaining guests with summer barbecues.

- **Utility:** Accessible from outside as well as the three-car garage, this small utility room is a multipurpose space. Through the breakfast area is the unique hobby/laundry area, a room made large enough for both the wash and the family artist.

- **Cooking and Eating Areas:** In one straight shot, this kitchen flows into both the sunlit breakfast room and the formal dining room,

for simple transitions no matter the meal. The kitchen features tons of work and storage space, as well as a stovetop island with a seated snack bar and a second eating bar between the kitchen and breakfast room.

- **Study:** For bringing work home with you or simply paying the bills, this quiet study sits off the foyer through French doors.

- **Master Suite:** A triplet of windows allows the

morning sun to shine in on this spacious, relaxing area. The full master bath features two separate vanities, a glass shower, a whirlpool tub, and a large walk-in closet.

- **Secondary Bedrooms:** Two of the three bedrooms include computer centers, keeping pace with the technological times, and all three-share access to the second full bathroom, with its dual sinks and whirlpool tub.

Copyright by designer/architect.

Plan #151032

Dimensions: 84'8" W x 48'4" D
Levels: 2
Heated Square Footage: 2,824
Main Level Sq. Ft.: 2,279
Upper Level Sq. Ft.: 545
Bedrooms: 4
Bathrooms: 3
Foundation: Crawl space, slab; basement option for fee
CompleteCost List Available: Yes
Price Category: F

CAD FILE AVAILABLE

Images provided by designer/architect.

This luxurious two-story home combines a stately exterior with a large, functional floor plan.

Features:

- **Great Room:** The spacious foyer leads directly into this room, which opens to the rear yard, providing natural light and views of the outdoors.

- **Kitchen:** This fully equipped kitchen is located to provide the utmost convenience in serving both the formal dining room and the informal breakfast area. The combination of breakfast room, hearth room, and kitchen creatively forms a comfortable family gathering place.

- **Master Suite:** Located on the main level for privacy, this private retreat has a boxed ceiling in the sleeping area. The master bath boasts a large tub, dual vanities, and a walk-in closet.

- **Upper Level:** This level is where you'll find the two secondary bedrooms. Each has ample space, and they share the full bathroom.

Upper Level Floor Plan

Main Level Floor Plan

Copyright by designer/architect.

Plan #611110

Dimensions: 61'8" W x 74'6" D

Levels: 1

Heated Square Footage: 2,762

Bedrooms: 5

Bathrooms: 3½

Foundation: Slab

Material List Available: No

Price Category: F

Images provided by designer/architect.

CAD FILE AVAILABLE

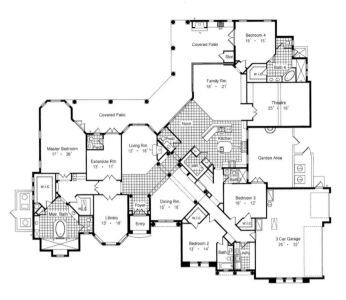

Copyright by designer/architect.

Plan #111001

Dimensions: 66'8" W x 76'11" D

Levels: 1

Heated Square Footage: 2,832

Bedrooms: 4

Bathrooms: 2½

Foundation: Crawl space or slab

Materials List Available: No

Price Category: G

Images provided by designer/architect.

Copyright by designer/architect.

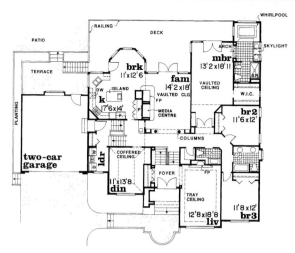

Plan #401023

Dimensions: 76' W x 63'4" D

Levels: 1

Heated Square Footage: 2,806

Bedrooms: 3

Bathrooms: 2½

Foundation: Basement, walkout

Materials List Available: Yes

Price Category: F

Images provided by designer/architect.

Optional Lower Level Floor Plan

Copyright by designer/architect.

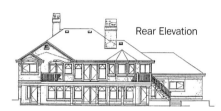

Rear Elevation

Plan #151225

Dimensions: 81'10" W x 67'2" D

Levels: 1

Heated Square Footage: 2,875

Bedrooms: 5

Bathrooms: 4

Foundation: Crawl space or slab

CompleteCost List Available: Yes

Price Category: F

Images provided by designer/architect.

CAD FILE **CAD** AVAILABLE

Bonus Area Floor Plan

Copyright by designer/architect.

Plan #161018

Dimensions: 74'4" W x 69'11" D

Levels: 1.5

Heated Square Footage: 2,816
+ 325 Sq. Ft. bonus room

Main Level Sq. Ft.: 2,231

Upper Level Sq. Ft.: 624

Bedrooms: 3

Bathrooms: 2 full, 2 half

Foundation: Basement or walkout

Materials List Available: No

Price Category: F

Images provided by designer/architect.

If you love classic European designs, look closely at this home with its multiple gables and countless conveniences and luxuries.

Features:

- Foyer: Open to the great room, the 2-story foyer offers a view all the way to the rear windows.

- Great Room: A fireplace makes this room cozy in any kind of weather.

- Kitchen: This large room features an island with a sink, and an angled wall with French doors to the back yard.

- Dining Room: The furniture alcove and raised ceiling make this room both formal and practical.

- Master Suite: You'll love the quiet in the bedroom and the luxuries — a tub, separate shower, and double vanities—in the bath.

- Basement: The door from the basement to the side yard adds convenience to outdoor work.

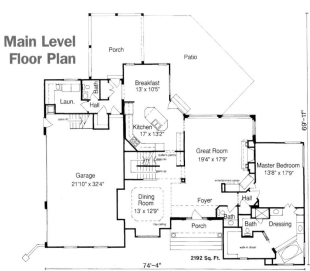

Main Level Floor Plan

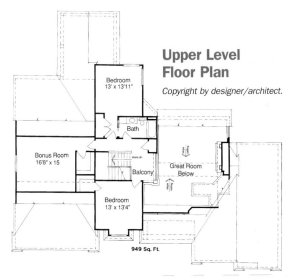

Upper Level Floor Plan

Copyright by designer/architect.

Rear View

Foyer/Dining Room

Rear Elevation

Living Room

Plan #151881

Dimensions: 42' W x 79'6" D

Levels: 2

Heated Square Footage: 2,889

Main Level Sq. Ft.: 1,819

Upper Level Sq. Ft.: 1,070

Bedrooms: 4

Bathrooms: 2½

Foundation: Crawl space or slab; basement or walkout for fee

CompleteCost List Available: Yes

Price Category: F

Main Level Floor Plan

Copyright by designer/architect.

Upper Level Floor Plan

Images provided by designer/architect.

Rear View

Plan #441011

Dimensions: 67' W x 46' D

Levels: 1

Heated Square Footage: 2,898

Main Level Sq. Ft.: 1,744

Basement Level Sq. Ft.: 1,154

Bedrooms: 3

Bathrooms: 2½

Foundation: Walkout basement

Materials List Available: Yes

Price Category: F

Main Level Floor Plan

Images provided by designer/architect.

Basement Level Floor Plan

Copyright by designer/architect.

Rear Elevation

Plan #121171

Dimensions: 66' W x 51' D
Levels: 1.5
Square Footage: 2,978
Main Level Sq. Ft.: 2,101
Upper Level Sq. Ft.: 877
Bedrooms: 4
Bathrooms: 3
Foundation: Slab; basement for fee
Material List Available: Yes
Price Category: F

Images provided by designer/architect.

Upper Level Floor Plan

Copyright by designer/architect.

Main Level Floor Plan

Plan #151057

Dimensions: 73'6" W x 80'6" D
Levels: 1
Heated Square Footage: 2,951
Bedrooms: 4
Bathrooms: 3
Foundation: Crawl space, slab, or basement
CompleteCost List Available: No
Price Category: F

Images provided by designer/architect.

CAD FILE AVAILABLE

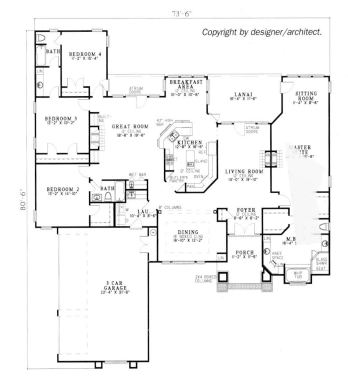

Copyright by designer/architect.

Images provided by designer/architect.

Plan #291015

Dimensions: 88'6" W x 58'3" D
Levels: 1.5
Heated Square Footage: 2,901
Main Level Sq. Ft.: 2,078
Upper Level Sq. Ft.: 823
Bedrooms: 3
Bathrooms: 2½
Foundation: Basement
Materials List Available: No
Price Category: F

Upon entering this home, a cathedral-like timber-framed interior fills the eye.

Features:

- **Great Room:** This large gathering area's ceiling rises up two stories and is open to the kitchen. The beautiful fireplace is the focal point of this room.

- **Kitchen:** This island kitchen is open to the great room and the breakfast nook. Warm woods of all species enhance the great room and this space.

- **Master Suite:** This suite has a sloped ceiling and adjoins a luxurious master bath with twin walk-in closets that open to a sunroom with a private balcony.

- **Upper Level:** This upper level has an open lounge that leads to two bedrooms with vaulted ceilings and a generous second bath.

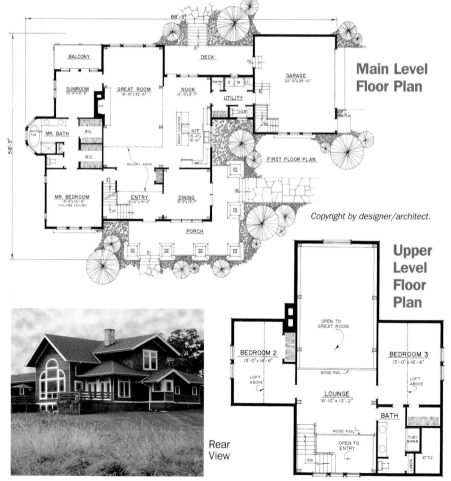

Main Level Floor Plan

Copyright by designer/architect.

Upper Level Floor Plan

Rear View

Plan #151183

Dimensions: 67'8" W x 60' D

Levels: 2

Heated Square Footage: 2,952

Main Level Sq. Ft.: 2,266

Upper Level Sq. Ft.: 686

Bedrooms: 4

Bathrooms: 3

Foundation: Crawl space, slab (basement or walk-out basement option for fee)

CompleteCost List Available: Yes

Price Category: F

Images provided by designer/architect.

This lovely home includes private spaces as well as large rooms that invite everyone to gather.

Features:

- Great Room: Look out to the grilling porch from the bank of windows in this two-story room with a fireplace and built-in media center.

- Dining Room: Columns set off this room, but it's an easy walk from the adjacent kitchen.

- Kitchen: Designed for a gourmet cook, the kitchen features an angled snack bar.

- Breakfast Room: Lit by expansive windows, this room opens to the rear grilling porch.

- Master Suite: A fireplace, expansive windows, and door to the porch accent this suite, which includes a private study, two walk-in closets, and bath with whirlpool tub, shower, and bidet.

- Upper Floor: Look down to the foyer and great room from the theater balconies here.

Main Level Floor Plan

Upper Level Floor Plan

Copyright by designer/architect.

Plan #101019

Dimensions: 58'4" W x 55'2" D
Levels: 2
Heated Square Footage: 2,954
Main Level Sq. Ft. 2,093
Upper Level Sq. Ft. 861
Bedrooms: 4
Bathrooms: 3½
Foundation: Basement
Materials List Available: No
Price Category: F

Images provided by designer/architect.

CAD FILE AVAILABLE

Main Level Floor Plan

DECK 22'11" x 9'6"

BRKFST 15'3" x 9'9"
VAULTED CEILING

TWO STORY CEILING

KITCHEN 15'3" x 17'0"

MASTER BDRM. 14'8" x 17'6"
TRAY CEILING
OPTIONAL POCKET DOORS

FAMILY 22'11" x 18'0"

55'2"

DINING 12'5" x 16'0"

TWO STORY CEILING

GARAGE 21'11" x 21'0"

STUDY 12'6" x 12'9"

ENTRY 9'10" x 12'6"

58'4"

Upper Level Floor Plan

OPEN BELOW

BEDRM 4 13'0" x 11'6"

OPEN BELOW

BEDRM 2 12'5" x 12'5"

PLANT SHELF

BEDRM 3 11'3" x 17'1"

Copyright by designer/architect.

Plan #661191

Dimensions: 58'8" W x 68' D
Levels: 2
Heated Square Footage: 2,998
Main Level Sq. Ft.: 2,227
Upper Level Sq. Ft.: 771
Bedrooms: 4
Bathrooms: 4
Foundation: Slab
Material List Available: No
Price Category: F

Images provided by designer/architect.

This home, as shown in the photograph, may differ from the actual blueprints. For more detailed information, please check the floor plans carefully.

CAD FILE AVAILABLE

Covered Patio

Master Suite 15'-10" x 16'-2"

Family Room 19'-8" x 16'-2"

Nook

Bath 2

Bedroom 2 11'-10" x 11'-0"

W.I.C.

Kitchen

Utility

Master Bath

Foyer

Dining Room 12'-8" x 13'-6"

pantry

Living Room 15'-8" x 12'-2"

Entry

2 Car Garage 21'-0" x 26'-6"

Main Level Floor Plan

Open Below

Bedroom 4 11'-10" x 9'-4"

Loft 24'-3" x 12'-10"

Bedroom 3 12'-8" x 11'-2"

Bath 3

Upper Level Floor Plan

Copyright by designer/architect.

Plan #441010

Dimensions: 108'6" W x 59' D
Levels: 1
Heated Square Footage: 2,973
Bedrooms: 4
Bathrooms: 4½
Foundation: Crawl space;
slab or basement available for fee
Materials List Available: Yes **Category:** F

Bordering on estate-sized, this plan borrows elements from Norman, Mediterranean, and English architecture.

Images provided by designer/architect.

Features:

- **Great Room:** This gathering area features a large bay window and a fireplace flanked with built-ins. The vaulted ceiling adds to the large feel of the area.

- **Kitchen:** This large island kitchen features a walk-in pantry and a built-in desk. The breakfast nook has access to the patio.

- **Master Suite:** This retreat features a vaulted ceiling in the sleeping area and access to the patio. The master bath boasts dual vanities, a stand-up shower, a spa tub, and a very large walk-in closet.

- **Bedrooms:** Two family bedrooms, each with its own private bathroom, have large closets.

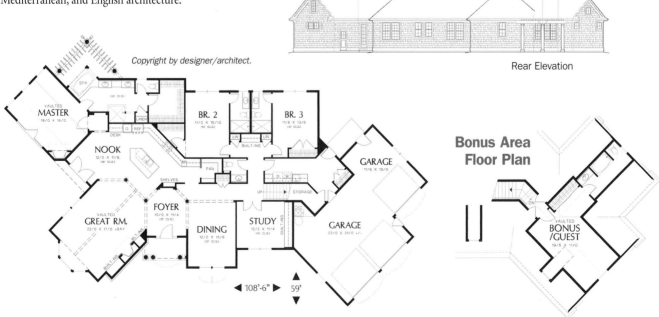

Rear Elevation

Copyright by designer/architect.

Bonus Area Floor Plan

Landscaping Ideas

L andscapes change over the years. As plants grow, the overall look evolves from sparse to lush. Trees cast cool shade where the sun used to shine. Shrubs and hedges grow tall and dense enough to provide privacy. Perennials and ground covers spread to form colorful patches of foliage and flowers. Meanwhile, paths, arbors, fences, and other structures gain the patina of age.

Constant change over the years—sometimes rapid and dramatic, sometimes slow and subtle—is one of the joys of landscaping. It is also one of the challenges. Anticipating how fast plants will grow and how big they will eventually get is difficult, even for professional designers.

To illustrate the kinds of changes to expect in a planting, these pages show a landscape design at three different "ages." Even though a new planting may look sparse at first, it will soon fill in. And because of careful spacing, the planting will look as good in 10 to 15 years as it does after 3 to 5. It will, of course, look different, but that's part of the fun.

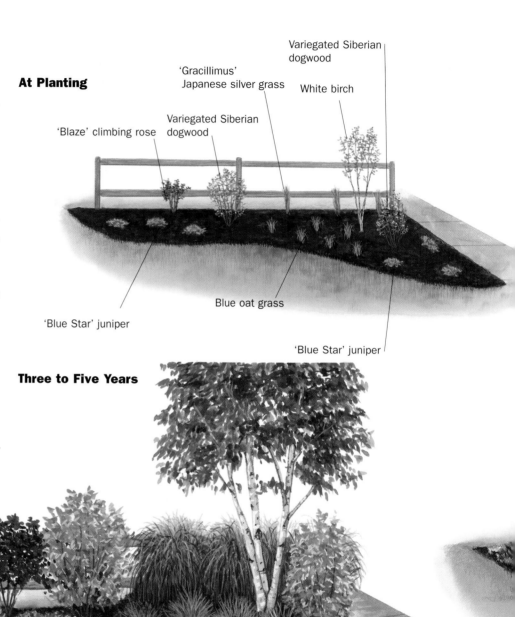

At Planting

'Blaze' climbing rose

Variegated Siberian dogwood

'Gracillimus' Japanese silver grass

Variegated Siberian dogwood

White birch

'Blue Star' juniper

Blue oat grass

'Blue Star' juniper

Three to Five Years

At Planting—Here's how the corner might appear in early summer immediately after planting. The white birch tree is only 5 to 6 ft. tall, with trunks no thicker than broomsticks. The variegated Siberian dogwoods each have a few main stems about 3 to 4 ft. tall. The 'Blaze' rose has just short stubs where the nursery cut back the old stems, but it will grow fast and may bloom the first year. The 'Blue Star' junipers are low mounds about 6 to 10 in. wide. The blue oat grass forms small, thin clumps of sparse foliage. The 'Gracillimus' Japanese silver grass may still be dormant, or it may have a short tuft of new foliage. Both grasses will grow vigorously the first year.

Three to Five Years—The birch tree has grown 1 to 2 ft. taller every year but is still quite slender. Near the base, it's starting to show the white bark typical of maturity. The variegated Siberian dogwoods are well established now. If you cut them to the ground every year or two in spring, they grow back 4 to 6 ft. tall by midsummer, with strong, straight stems. The 'Blaze' rose covers the fence, and you need to prune out a few of its older stems every spring. The slow-growing 'Blue Star' junipers make a series of low mounds; you still see them as individuals, not a continuous patch. The grasses have reached maturity and form lush, robust clumps. It would be a good idea to divide and replant them now, to keep them vigorous.

Ten to Fifteen Years—The birch tree is becoming a fine specimen, 20 to 30 ft. tall, with gleaming white bark on its trunks. Prune away the lower limbs up to 6 to 8 ft. above ground to expose its trunks and to keep it from crowding and shading the other plants. The variegated dogwoods and 'Blaze' rose continue to thrive and respond well to regular pruning. The 'Blue Star' junipers have finally merged into a continuous mass of glossy foliage. The blue oat grass and Japanese silver grass will still look good if they have been divided and replanted over the years. If you get tired of the grasses, you could replace them with cinnamon fern and astilbe, as shown here, or other perennials or shrubs.

Ten to Fifteen Years

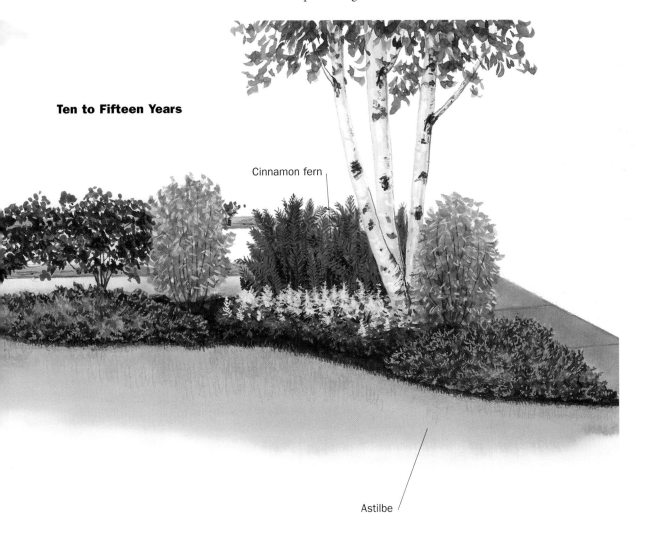

Cinnamon fern

Astilbe

A Warm Welcome
Make a Pleasant Passage to Your Front Door

Why wait until a visitor reaches the front door to extend a cordial greeting? Have your landscape offer a friendly welcome and a helpful "Please come this way." Well-chosen plants and a revamped walkway not only make a visitor's short journey a pleasant one, but they can also enhance your home's most public face.

This simple arrangement of plants and paving produces an elegant entrance that deftly mixes formal and informal elements.

A wide walk of neatly fitted flagstones and a rectangular bed of roses have the feel of a small formal courtyard, complete with a pair of "standard" roses in planters, each displaying a mound of flowers atop a single stem. Clumps of ornamental grass rise from the paving like leafy fountains.

Gently curving beds of low-growing evergreens and shrub roses edge the flagstones, softening the formality and providing a comfortable transition to the lawn.

Morning glories and clematis climb simple trellises to brighten the walls of the house.

Flowers in pink, white, purple, and violet are abundant from early summer until frost. They are set off by the rich green foliage of the junipers and roses and the gray leaves of the catmint edging.

Add a bench, as shown here, so you can linger and enjoy the scene; in later years, the lovely star magnolia behind it will provide comfortable dappled shade.

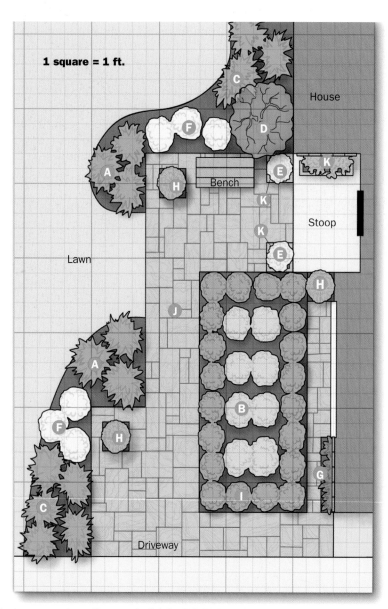

Plants and Projects

Once established, these shrubs and perennials require little care beyond deadheading and an annual pruning. Ask the nursery where you buy the standard roses for advice on how to protect the plants in winter.

Ⓐ 'Blue Star' juniper *Juniperus squamata* (use 6 plants)
The sparkly blue foliage of this low-growing evergreen shrub neatly edges the opening onto the lawn.

Ⓑ 'Bonica' rose *Rosa* (use 8)
This deciduous shrub blooms from June until frost, producing clusters of double, soft pink flowers.

Ⓒ Dwarf creeping juniper
Juniperis procumbens 'Nana' (use 8)
This low, spreading evergreen with prickly green foliage makes a tough, handsome ground cover.

Ⓓ Star magnolia *Magnolia stellata* (use 1)
This small, multitrunked deciduous tree graces the entry with lightly scented white flowers in early spring.

Ⓔ 'The Fairy' rose *Rosa* (use 2)
Clusters of small, double, pale pink roses appear in abundance from early summer to frost. Buy plants

trained as standards at a nursery. Underplant with impatiens.

Ⓕ 'White Meidiland' rose
Rosa (use 6)
A low, spreading shrub, it is covered with clusters of lovely single white flowers all summer.

Ⓖ Jackman clematis *Clematis x Jackmanii* (use 2)
Trained to a simple lattice, this deciduous vine produces large, showy, dark purple flowers for weeks in summer.

Ⓗ 'Gracillimus' Japanese silver grass *Miscanthus* (use 3)
The arching leaves of this perennial grass are topped by fluffy seed heads from late summer through winter.

Ⓘ 'Six Hills Giant' catmint
Nepeta x faassenii (use 20)
A perennial with violet-blue flowers and aromatic gray-green foliage edges the roses.

Ⓙ Flagstone paving
Rectangular flagstones in random sizes.

Ⓚ Planters
Simple wooden boxes contain blue-flowered annual morning glories (on the stoop, trained to a wooden lattice) and standard roses (in front of the stoop).

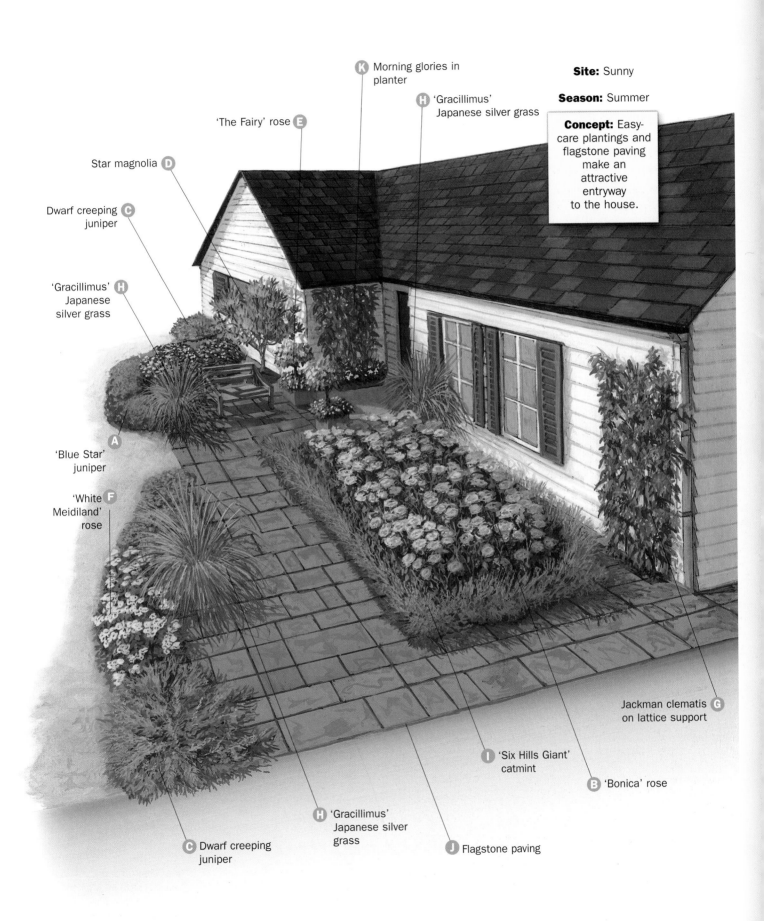

K Morning glories in planter

H 'Gracillimus' Japanese silver grass

Site: Sunny

Season: Summer

Concept: Easy-care plantings and flagstone paving make an attractive entryway to the house.

'The Fairy' rose **E**

Star magnolia **D**

Dwarf creeping juniper **C**

'Gracillimus' **H** Japanese silver grass

A 'Blue Star' juniper

F 'White Meidiland' rose

Jackman clematis **G** on lattice support

I 'Six Hills Giant' catmint

B 'Bonica' rose

C Dwarf creeping juniper

H 'Gracillimus' Japanese silver grass

J Flagstone paving

Up Front and Formal

Greet Visitors with Classic Symmetry

Formal gardens have a special appeal. Their simple geometry can be soothing in a hectic world, and the look is timeless, never going out of style. The front yard of a classical house, like the one shown here, invites a formal makeover. (A house with a symmetrical facade in any style has similar potential.)

In this design, a paved courtyard and a planting of handsome trees, shrubs, and ground covers have transformed a site typically given over to lawn and a cement walkway. The result is a more dramatic entry, but also one where you can happily linger with guests on a fine day.

Tall hedges on the borders of the design and the centrally placed redbud provide a modicum of privacy in this otherwise public space. Lower hedges along the sidewalk and front of the driveway allow a view of the street and make these approaches more welcoming.

A matched pair of viburnums make a lovely setting for the front door. To each side, layered groups of shrubs give depth and interest to the house's facade. From spring through fall, the planting's flowers and foliage make the courtyard a comfortable spot, and there is ample evergreen foliage to keep up appearances in winter. Completing the scene is an ornamental focal point and a bench for enjoying the results of your landscaping labors.

> **Site:** Sunny
>
> **Season:** Early summer
>
> **Concept:** Wide paving, hedges, trees, and shrubs create an appealing entry courtyard.

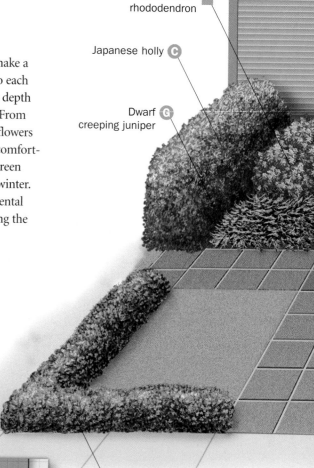

'Janet Blair' **F** rhododendron

Japanese holly **C**

Dwarf **G** creeping juniper

D 'Crimson Pygmy' Japanese barberry

Plants and Projects

Spring is the season for flowers in this planting, with redbud, rhododendron, and candytuft blossoms in shades of pink and white. The colorful leaves and berries of viburnum, redbud, and barberry brighten the fall. While the hedge plants are dependable and problem-free, you'll need to shear them at least once a year to maintain the formal shapes.

A **Redbud** *Cercis canadensis* (use 1 plant)
Small pink flowers line the branches of this deciduous tree in early spring before the foliage appears. The heart-shaped leaves emerge reddish, mature to a lustrous green, and turn gold in fall. Bare branches form an attractive silhouette in winter, especially as the tree ages.

House

Stoop

Lawn

Lawn

Driveway

Lawn

Lawn

Lawn

Sidewalk

1 square = 1 ft.

Note: All plants are appropriate for USDA Hardiness Zones 4, 5, and 6.

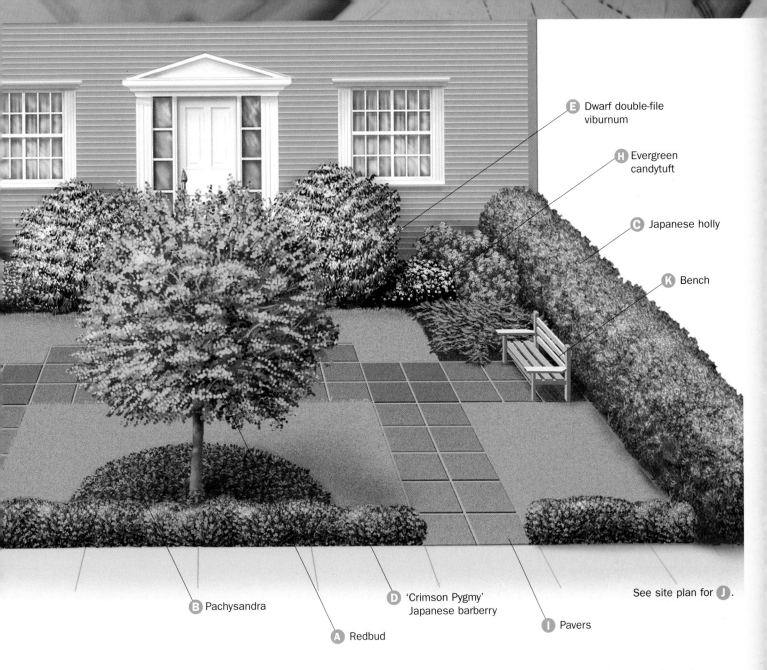

E Dwarf double-file viburnum

H Evergreen candytuft

C Japanese holly

K Bench

B Pachysandra

D 'Crimson Pygmy' Japanese barberry

A Redbud

I Pavers

See site plan for J.

B Pachysandra *Pachysandra terminalis* (use 250)
Hardy, adaptable evergreen ground cover that will spread in the shade of the redbud, forming an attractive, weed-smothering, glossy green carpet.

C Japanese holly *Euonymus alatus* 'Compactus' (use 19)
Choose an upright cultivar of this evergreen shrub to form a hedge of dark green leaves. In Zones 4 and 5 substitute the hardier compact burning bush, *Euonymus alatus* 'Compactus.'

D 'Crimson Pygmy' Japanese barberry *Berberis thunbergii* (use 34)
This rugged deciduous shrub puts on a colorful show, with small maroon leaves that turn red in fall when they're joined by bright red berries. A small rounded plant, it can be sheared, as shown here, or pruned lightly into an informal low hedge.

E Dwarf double-file viburnum *Viburnum plicatum* var. *tomentosum* (use 2)
A pair of these deciduous shrubs make an elegant frame for the door. Tiers of horizontal branches are smothered with small clusters of pure white flowers from May through fall. Large, crinkled leaves are medium green.

F 'Janet Blair' rhododendron *Rhododendron* (use 6)
The wonderful evergreen foliage and light pink flowers of this compact shrub anchor the planting at the corners of the house. Blooms in late spring. 'Mist Maiden' and 'Anna Hall' rhododendrons are good substitutes.

G Dwarf creeping juniper *Juniperus procumbens* 'Nana' (use 10)
Layered sprays of this evergreen shrub's prickly bright green foliage lay like thick rugs on the edge of the lawn. A lovely contrast to the dark green rhododendrons behind. For extra color in spring, plant handfuls of crocuses, snowdrops, or

grape hyacinths next to the junipers.

H Evergreen candytuft *Iberis sempervirens* (use 12)
An evergreen perennial ground cover, it forms a low, sprawling mound of glossy foliage next to the viburnums. Bears small white flowers for weeks in the spring.

I Pavers
The courtyard is surfaced with 2-ft.-square precast pavers. Use two complementary colors to create patterns, if you choose. Substitute flagstones or bricks if they would look better with your house.

J Ornament
An ornament centered in the courtyard paving provides a focal point. Choose a sculpture, sundial, reflecting ball, birdbath, or large potted plant to suit your taste.

K Bench
Enjoy the courtyard garden from a comfortable bench in a style that complements the garden and the house.

Landscaping a Low Wall

Two-Tier Garden Replaces a Short Slope

Some things may not love a wall, but plants and gardeners do. For plants, walls offer warmth for an early start in spring and good drainage for roots. Gardeners appreciate the rich visual potential of composing a garden on two levels, as well as the practical advantage of working on two relatively flat surfaces instead of a single sloping one. If you have a wall, or have a place to put one, grasp the opportunity for some handsome landscaping.

This design places two complementary perennial borders above and below a wall bounded at one end by a set of stairs. While each bed is narrow enough for easy maintenance, when viewed from the lower level they combine to form a border almost 8 ft. deep, with plants rising to eye level. The planting can be easily extended on both sides of the steps.

Building the wall that makes this impressive sight possible doesn't require the time or skill it once did. Nor is it necessary to scour the countryside for tons of fieldstone or to hire an expensive contractor. Thanks to precast retaining-wall systems, a knee-high do-it-yourself wall can be installed in as little as a weekend. More experienced or ambitious wall builders may want to tackle a natural stone wall, but anyone with a healthy back (or access to energetic teenagers) can succeed with a prefabricated system.

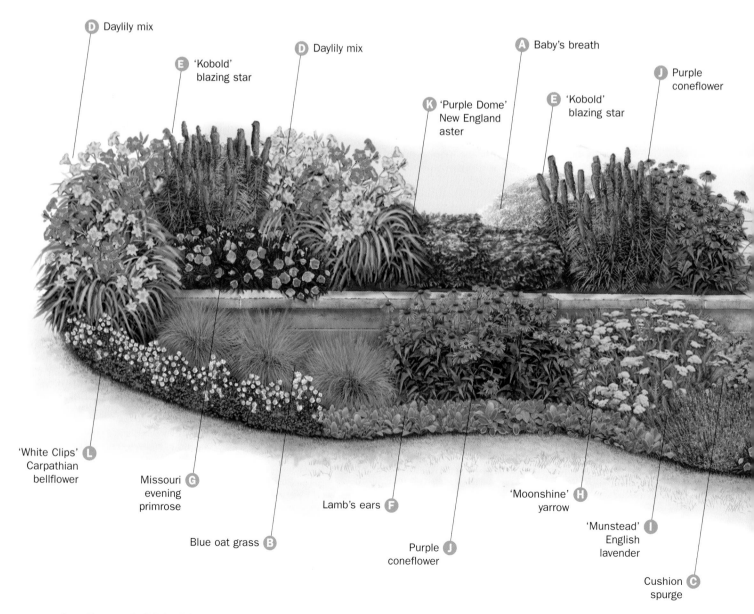

D Daylily mix

E 'Kobold' blazing star

D Daylily mix

A Baby's breath

J Purple coneflower

K 'Purple Dome' New England aster

E 'Kobold' blazing star

L 'White Clips' Carpathian bellflower

G Missouri evening primrose

F Lamb's ears

H 'Moonshine' yarrow

B Blue oat grass

J Purple coneflower

I 'Munstead' English lavender

C Cushion spurge

These plants provide color from spring until frost with little care from you. All are perennials or grasses that need minimal maintenance beyond clipping of spent blooms and a fall or spring cleanup. Several offer excellent flowers for cutting or drying.

A **Baby's breath** *Gypsophila paniculata* (use 3 plants)
This popular perennial produces a cloud of tiny white flowers in June and July that add an airy texture to the garden and are excellent for cutting. A good foil to the stronger colors and textures of the adjacent plants.

B **Blue oat grass** *Helictotrichon sempervirens* (use 3)
A carefree grass, it forms a neat, dense clump of thin blue leaves that maintain their color through winter.

C **Cushion spurge** *Euphorbia polychroma* (use 1)
The electric-yellow spring color of this showy perennial is produced by long-lasting flower bracts, not petals, so it serves as a garden focal point for weeks. Its mound of foliage neatly fills

the corner by the steps and turns red in fall.

D **Daylily mix** *Hemerocallis* (use 6)
For an extended show of lovely lilylike flowers, combine early- and late-blooming cultivars in a selection of your favorite colors. The grassy foliage of this perennial covers the end of the wall.

E **'Kobold' blazing star** *Liatris spicata* (use 6)
Magenta flower spikes of this durable perennial rise from a clump of dark green foliage from late July through August. A good mate for its prairie companion, purple coneflower. Flowers are great for cutting and drying, and butterflies love them.

F **Lamb's ears** *Stachys byzantina* (use 6)
The large soft leaves of this spreading perennial ground cover are a season-long presence; their silvery color is a nice foil to the blues and yellows nearby. Bears small purple flowers in early summer.

G **Missouri evening primrose** *Oenothera missouriensis* (use 6)
Large, glowing yellow flowers

cover the glossy foliage of this low spreading perennial, which will cascade over the wall. Blooms from late June through August.

H **'Moonshine' yarrow** *Achillea* (use 3)
This perennial's flat heads of lemon yellow flowers light up the center of the garden much of the summer. Grayish foliage is fragrant, surprisingly tough despite its lacy looks. Flowers are good for drying.

I **'Munstead' English lavender** *Lavandula angustifolia* (use 3)
The gray foliage of this classic bushy herb seems to deepen the greens nearby. Bears a profusion of fragrant pale lavender flower spikes in July, a pretty combination with the yellow yarrow and primroses.

J **Purple coneflower** *Echinacea purpurea* (use 6)
In July and August, stiff stalks carrying large daisylike pink flowers with dark brown cone-shaped centers rise above this native perennial's basal clump of rich green leaves. Leave some flower stalks standing for winter interest and to provide seeds for songbirds.

K **'Purple Dome' New England aster** *Aster novaeangliae* (use 2)
This native perennial makes a

mound of foliage and is covered with purple flowers in the fall, when the garden needs a shot of color.

L **'White Clips' Carpathian bellflower** *Campanula carpatica* (use 6)
A hardy little perennial with tufts of glossy green leaves and white cuplike flowers that stand out beside the blue oat grass from July until frost.

M **Wall and steps**
This wall and steps are built from a readily available prefabricated wall system. It is 15 ft. long and 24 in. high. Select a system to match the colors and style of your home.

N **Walkway**
This is built from flagstone dressed to random rectangular sizes. Precast concrete pavers or gravel would also go well with a prefabricated wall.

> **Site:** Sunny
>
> **Season:** Summer
>
> **Concept:** Low retaining wall creates easy-to-maintain beds for a distinctive two-level planting.

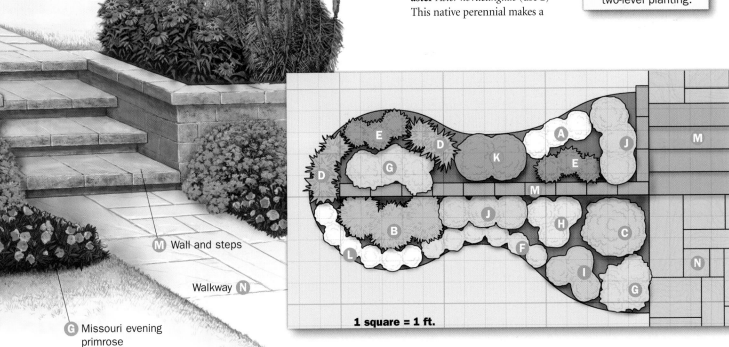

M Wall and steps

Walkway **N**

G Missouri evening primrose

1 square = 1 ft.

Note: All plants are appropriate for USDA Hardiness Zones 4, 5, and 6.

Plan #561002

Dimensions: 61' W x 75' D
Levels: 1.5
Square Footage: 3,416
Main Level Sq. Ft.: 2,479
Upper Level Sq. Ft.: 937
Bedrooms: 4
Bathrooms: 3½
Foundation: Basement
Material List Available: Yes
Price Category: G

Traditional Cape Cod styling provides this home with incredible street appeal.

Images provided by designer/architect.

Features:

- **Great Room:** There is plenty of room for your family and friends to gather in this large room. The fireplace will add a feeling of coziness to the expansive space

- **Kitchen:** Open to the great room and a dining area, this island kitchen adds to the open feeling of the home. Additional seating, located at the island, enables guests to mingle with the chef of the family without getting in the way.

- **Lower Level:** This level (finishing is optional) adds a fourth bedroom suite, enough space for a family room or media room, and a wet bar for entertaining.

- **Garage:** Split garages allow the daily drivers their spaces plus a separate garage for that special vehicle or even a golf cart.

Main Level Floor Plan

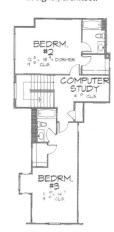

Upper Level Floor Plan

Copyright by designer/architect.

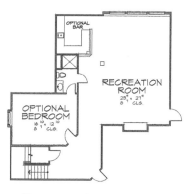

Basement Level Floor Plan

Great Room

Great Room

Kitchen

Office

Master Bedroom

Master Bath

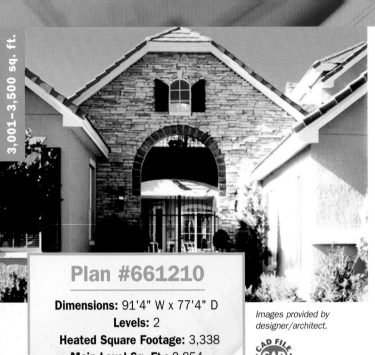

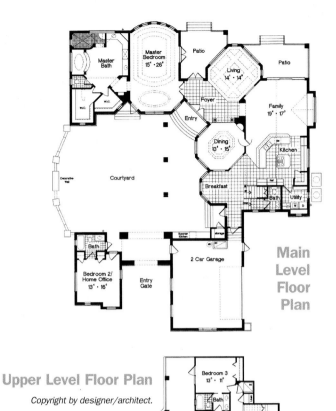

Plan #661210

Dimensions: 91'4" W x 77'4" D
Levels: 2
Heated Square Footage: 3,338
Main Level Sq. Ft.: 2,854
Upper Level Sq. Ft.: 484
Bedrooms: 4
Bathrooms: 3½
Foundation: Slab
Material List Available: No
Price Category: G

Images provided by designer/architect.

CAD FILE AVAILABLE

Main Level Floor Plan

Upper Level Floor Plan

Copyright by designer/architect.

Plan #221025

Dimensions: 69'8" W x 72' D
Levels: 2
Heated Square Footage: 3,009
Main Level Sq. Ft.: 2,039
Upper Level Sq. Ft.: 970
Bedrooms: 4
Bathrooms: 2½
Foundation: Basement
Materials List Available: No
Price Category: G

Images provided by designer/architect.

CAD FILE AVAILABLE

Upper Level Floor Plan

Main Level Floor Plan

Copyright by designer/architect.

Plan #121061

Dimensions: 56' W x 52' D
Levels: 2
Heated Square Footage: 3,025
Main Level Sq. Ft.: 1,583
Upper Level Sq. Ft.: 1,442
Bedrooms: 4
Bathrooms: 3½
Foundation: Basement
Materials List Available: Yes
Price Category: G

Images provided by designer/architect.

This large home with a contemporary feeling is ideal for the family looking for comfort and amenities.

Features:

• Entry: Stacked windows bring sunlight into this two-story entry, with its stylish curved staircase.

• Library: French doors off the entry lead to this room, with its built-in bookcases flanking a large, picturesque window.

• Family Room: Located in the rear of the home, this family room is sunken to set it apart. A spider-beamed ceiling gives it a contemporary feeling, and a bay window, wet bar, and pass-through fireplace add to this impression.

• Kitchen: The island in this kitchen makes working here a pleasure. The corner pantry joins a breakfast area and hearth room to this space.

Main Level Floor Plan

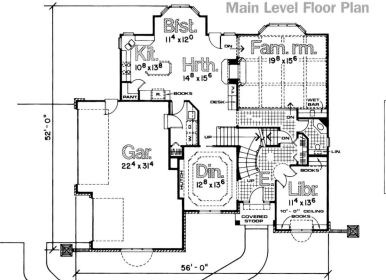

Copyright by designer/architect.

Upper Level Floor Plan

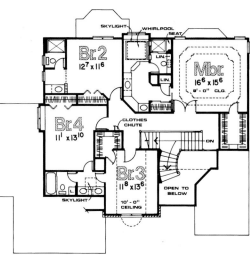

Plan #241013

Dimensions: 68' W x 46' D
Levels: 2
Heated Square Footage: 3,033
Main Level Sq. Ft.: 1,918
Upper Level Sq. Ft.: 1,115
Bedrooms: 4
Bathrooms: 3½
Foundation: Crawl space, slab, or walkout
Materials List Available: No
Price Category: G

The generous front porch and balcony of this home signal its beauty and comfortable design.

Features:

- **Great Room:** A large fireplace is the focal point of this spacious room, which opens from the foyer.

- **Kitchen:** Open to the dining room and breakfast room, the kitchen is designed for convenience.

- **Sunroom:** A fireplace and tray ceiling highlight this room that's just off the breakfast room.

- **Study:** Positioned for privacy, the study is ideal for quiet time alone.

- **Master Suite:** You'll love the decorative drop ceiling, huge walk-in closet, and bath with two vanities, a tub, and separate shower.

- **Playroom:** This enormous space gives ample room for play on rainy afternoons. Set up a media center here when the children have outgrown the need for a playroom.

Images provided by designer/architect.

Main Level Floor Plan

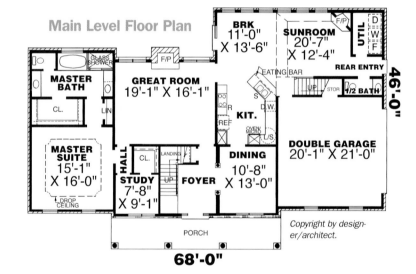

Copyright by designer/architect.

Upper Level Floor Plan

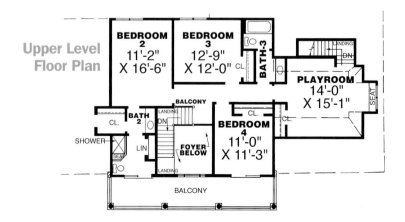

Plan #121024

Dimensions: 60' W x 58' D
Levels: 2
Heated Square Footage: 3,057
Main Level Sq. Ft.: 1,631
Second Level Sq. Ft.: 1,426
Bedrooms: 4
Bathrooms: 2½
Foundation: Basement;
crawl space for fee
Materials List Available: Yes
Price Category: G

Images provided by designer/architect.

This distinctive home offers plenty of space and is designed for gracious and convenient living.

Features:

- Ceiling Height: 8 ft. unless otherwise noted.

- Foyer: A curved staircase in this elegant entry will greet your guests.

- Living Room: This room invites you with a volume ceiling flanked by transom-topped windows that flood the room with sunlight.

- Screened Veranda: On warm summer nights, throw open the French doors in the living

room and enjoy a breeze on the huge screened veranda.

- Dining Room: This distinctive room is over-looked by the veranda.

- Family Room: At the back of the home is this comfortable family retreat with its soaring cathedral ceiling and handsome fireplace flanked by bookcases.

- Master Suite: This bayed bedroom features a 10-ft. vaulted ceiling.

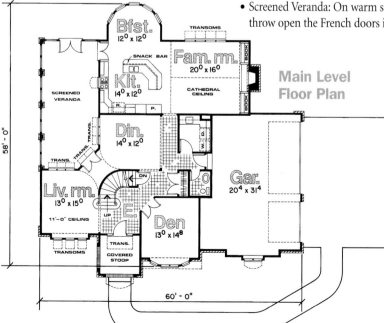

Main Level Floor Plan

Upper Level Floor Plan

Copyright by designer/architect.

Plan #181079

Dimensions: 60' W x 47'8" D
Levels: 2
Heated Square Footage: 3,016
Main Level Sq. Ft.: 1,716
Upper Level Sq. Ft.: 1,300
Bedrooms: 6
Bathrooms: 4½
Foundation: Crawl space
Materials List Available: Yes
Price Category: G

Images provided by designer/architect.

CAD FILE AVAILABLE

Main Level Floor Plan

Upper Level Floor Plan

Copyright by designer/architect.

Plan #121076

Dimensions: 64' W x 60'8" D
Levels: 2
Heated Square Footage: 3,067
Main Level Sq. Ft.: 2,169
Upper Level Sq. Ft.: 898
Bedrooms: 4
Bathrooms: 3½
Foundation: Basement
Materials List Available: Yes
Price Category: G

Images provided by designer/architect.

Main Level Floor Plan

Upper Level Floor Plan

Copyright by designer/architect.

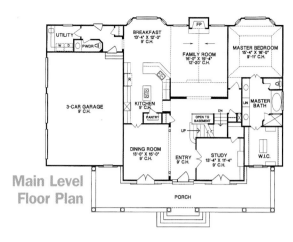

Main Level Floor Plan

Images provided by designer/architect.

CAD FILE AVAILABLE

Plan #121047

Dimensions: 67'8" W x 57' D
Levels: 1.5
Heated Square Footage: 3,072
Main Level Sq. Ft.: 2,116
Upper Level Sq. Ft.: 956
Bedrooms: 4
Bathrooms: 3½
Foundation: Slab; basement for fee
Materials List Available: Yes
Price Category: G

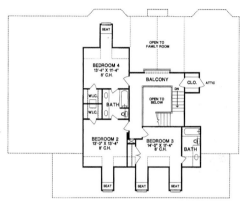

Upper Level Floor Plan

Copyright by designer/architect.

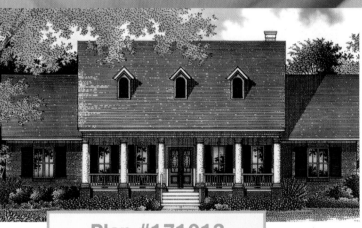

Plan #171013

Dimensions: 74' W x 72' D
Levels: 1
Heated Square Footage: 3,084
Bedrooms: 4
Bathrooms: 3½
Foundation: Crawl space or slab
Materials List Available: Yes
Price Category: G

Images provided by designer/architect.

Copyright by designer/architect.

Bonus Room

Copyright by designer/architect.

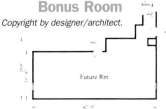

Future Rm

Plan #181122

Dimensions: 62' W x 36'4" D

Levels: 2

Heated Square Footage: 3,105

Main Level Sq. Ft.: 1,470

Upper Level Sq. Ft.: 1,635

Bedrooms: 4

Bathrooms: 3

Foundation: Walkout; crawl space or slab for fee

Material List Available: Yes

Price Category: G

You and your family and friends will love spending time in this vacation home.

CAD FILE AVAILABLE

Images provided by designer/architect.

Features:

- **Deck:** This large deck envelopes the front of this house, making it wonderful for relaxing. Stairs on the side of the house enable easy outdoor access between floors.

- **Great Rooms:** This house features two great rooms-one downstairs with a fireplace and the other upstairs close to the kitchen and dining area.

- **Kitchen:** This kitchen features a bar for some conversation while preparing meals in addition to an adjoining dining area.

- **Master Suite:** Located upstairs, this master suite has a private bath, two closets, and a dual-sink vanity.

Great Room

Main Level Floor Plan

Upper Level Floor Plan

Copyright by designer/architect.

Plan #151001

Dimensions: 70' W x 88' D
Levels: 1
Heated Square Footage: 3,124
Bedrooms: 4
Bathrooms: 3½
Foundation: Crawl space, slab
CompleteCost List Available: Yes
Price Category: G

CAD FILE AVAILABLE

From the double front doors to sleek arches, columns, and a gallery with arched openings to the bedrooms, you'll love this elegant home.

Features:

• Grand Room: With a 13-ft. pan ceiling and column entry, this room opens to the rear covered porch as well as through French doors to the bay-windowed morning room that, in turn, leads to the gathering room.

• Gathering Room: A majestic fireplace, built-in entertainment center, and book shelves give   comfort and ease.

• Kitchen: A double oven, built-in desk, and a work island add up to a design for efficiency.

• Master Suite: Enjoy the practicality of walk-in closets, the comfort of a private sitting area, and the convenience of an adjacent study or nursery. The bath features a step-up whirlpool tub and separate shower.

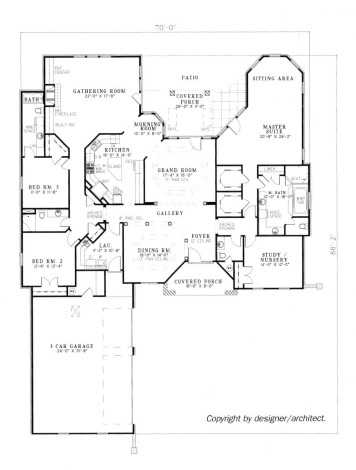

Copyright by designer/architect.

Plan #101024

Dimensions: 53' W x 57' D

Levels: 2

Heated Square Footage: 3,135

Main Level Sq. Ft.: 1,600

Upper Level Sq. Ft.: 1,535

Bedrooms: 5

Bathrooms: 4

Foundation: Basement

Materials List Available: No

Price Category: G

CAD FILE AVAILABLE

Images provided by designer/architect.

The amenities and conveniences inside this elegant home are perfect for an active family.

Features:

- Family Room: A fireplace, 18-ft ceiling, and door to the rear deck attract everyone to this room.
- Dining Room: Columns separate this room and the living room from the foyer, adding formality.
- Kitchen: A central island, walk-in pantry, and door to the deck will delight the whole family.
- Media Room: A large closet and door to the adjoining bath allow real versatility here.
- Master Suite: You'll love the corner fireplace and doors to the upper rear deck that open from the sitting room, the tray ceiling in the bedroom, and the luxury bath that leads to the spacious exercise room, walk-in closet, and storage room.
- Additional Bedrooms: Huge closets and doors to adjacent baths make each room a pleasure.

Main Level Floor Plan

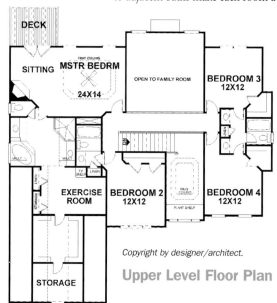

Copyright by designer/architect.

Upper Level Floor Plan

Plan #151180

Dimensions: 67'3" W x 68'6" D
Levels: 2
Heated Square Footage: 3,167
Main Level Sq. Ft.: 2,486
Upper Level Sq. Ft.: 681
Bedrooms: 4
Bathrooms: 3
Foundation: Crawl space, slab (basement or walkout basement option for fee)
CompleteCost List Available: Yes
Price Category: G

Images provided by designer/architect.

From one end to the other, this home is designed to give your friends and family total comfort.

Features:

• Great Room: This spacious room is visible from the second floor balconies, has a fabulous fireplace, and opens to the grilling porch.

• Dining Room: The columns here add a touch of formality around which you can decorate.

• Kitchen: The kitchen is designed for convenience and shares a snack bar with the breakfast room.

• Guest Room: The walk-in closet and bank of windows will welcome all of your friends.

• Breakfast Room: You'll love the natural lighting in this room, which leads to the grilling porch beyond.

• Master Suite: The high boxed ceiling and door to the grilling porch highlight the bedroom. The bath includes a walk-in closet, whirlpool tub, separate shower, and double vanity.

Main Level Floor Plan

Copyright by designer/architect.

Upper Level Floor Plan

Plan #151121

Dimensions: 66'8" W x 60'4" D
Levels: 2
Heated Square Footage: 3,108
Main Level Sq. Ft.: 2,107
Upper Level Sq. Ft.: 1,001
Bedrooms: 3
Bathrooms: 2½
Foundation: Crawl space, slab;
basement option for fee
CompleteCost List Available: Yes
Price Category: G

Images provided by designer/architect.

Upper Level Floor Plan

Main Level Floor Plan

Copyright by designer/architect.

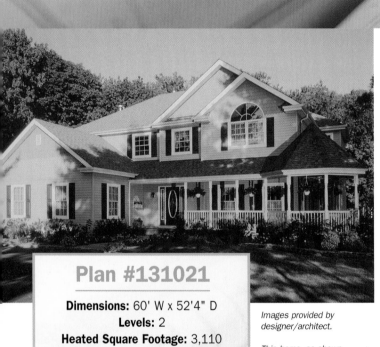

Plan #131021

Dimensions: 60' W x 52'4" D
Levels: 2
Heated Square Footage: 3,110
Main Level Sq. Ft.: 1,818
Upper Level Sq. Ft.: 1,292
Bedrooms: 5
Bathrooms: 2½
Foundation: Crawl space, slab,
or basement
Materials List Available: Yes
Price Category: H

Images provided by designer/architect.

This home, as shown in the photograph, may differ from the actual blueprints. For more detailed information, please check the floor plans carefully.

Main Level Floor Plan

Upper Level Floor Plan

Copyright by designer/architect.

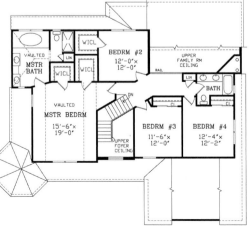

Main Level Floor Plan

sto 11 x 6 sto 11 x 6

3 car garage 22 x 30

deck 23 x 22

sunroom 23 x 10

util 12 x 12

mbr 16⁶ x 18⁶

family 25 x 15

kit 12 x 8⁶

eating 12 x 9

study 14 x 15

foy 6 x 15

dining 14 x 15

porch 34 x 8

Images provided by designer/architect.

CAD FILE AVAILABLE CAD

br 4 16 x 12

to attic   dn   to attic

br 3 14 x 12

br 2 14 x 12

Upper Level Floor Plan

Copyright by designer/architect.

Plan #211073

Dimensions: 66' W x 80' D
Levels: 1.5
Heated Square Footage: 3,119
Main Level Sq. Ft.: 2,092
Upper Level Sq. Ft.: 1,027
Bedrooms: 4
Bathrooms: 3½
Foundation: Crawl space, optional basement
Materials List Available: Yes
Price Category: G

Plan #331004

Dimensions: 81' W x 49'10" D
Levels: 2
Heated Square Footage: 3,125
Main Level Sq. Ft.: 2,147
Upper Level Sq. Ft.: 978
Bedrooms: 4
Bathrooms: 3½
Foundation: Crawl space, slab, or basement
Materials List Available: No
Price Category: G

Images provided by designer/architect.

This home, as shown in the photograph, may differ from the actual blueprints. For more detailed information, please check the floor plans carefully.

PATIO

3-CAR GARAGE 23' x 31⁵

BRKFST. 13⁴ x 11⁷

LIVING 21⁶ x 16⁸

MASTER SUITE 17⁸ x 16⁸

UTIL

KITCHEN 13⁴ x 14⁷

LOGGIA

PWDR

MASTER BATH

DINING 12⁸ x 14⁷

FOYER

LIBRARY 12⁸ x 17⁵

PORCH

Main Level Floor Plan

BEDRM 3 13⁴ x 12¹⁰

BONUS 15⁵ x 14⁸

BATH

BALCONY

BEDRM 2 14⁴ x 11¹⁰

BEDRM 4 12⁸ x 13⁵

BATH

Upper Level Floor Plan

Copyright by designer/architect.

Main Level Floor Plan

Upper Level Floor Plan

Copyright by designer/architect.

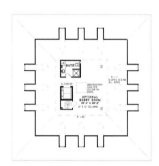

Lower Level Floor Plan

Optional Upper Level Floor Plan

Plan #151031

Dimensions: 60'2" W x 60'2" D
Levels: 2
Heated Square Footage: 3,130
Main Level Sq. Ft.: 1,600
Upper Level Sq. Ft.: 1,530
Bedrooms: 3
Bathrooms: 3½
Foundation: Crawl space, slab, or walkout
CompleteCost List Available: Yes
Price Category: F

Images provided by designer/architect.

CAD FILE AVAILABLE

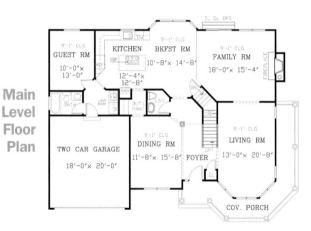

Main Level Floor Plan

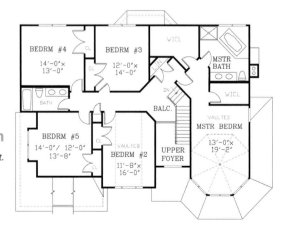

Plan #131069

Dimensions: 52' W x 38' D
Levels: 2
Heated Square Footage: 3,169
Main Level Sq. Ft.: 1,535
Upper Level Sq. Ft.: 1,634
Bedrooms: 5
Bathrooms: 3½
Foundation: Crawl space or basement
Material List Available: Yes
Price Category: H

Images provided by designer/architect.

Upper Level Floor Plan

Copyright by designer/architect.

Main Level Floor Plan

Plan #161056

Dimensions: 86'2" W x 63'8" D
Levels: 1
Heated Square Footage: 5,068
Main Level Sq. Ft.: 3,171
Basement Level Sq. Ft.: 1,897
Bedrooms: 4
Bathrooms: 3½
Foundation: Basement or walkout
Material List Available: Yes
Price Category: J

Images provided by designer/architect.

Basement Level Floor Plan

Copyright by designer/architect.

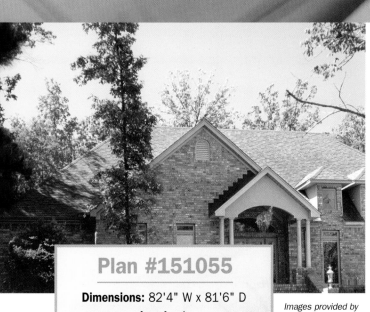

Plan #151055

Dimensions: 82'4" W x 81'6" D
Levels: 1
Heated Square Footage: 3,183
Bedrooms: 4
Bathrooms: 2½
Foundation: Crawl space or slab; basement or walkout available for fee
CompleteCost List Available: Yes
Price Category: E

Images provided by designer/architect.

CAD FILE AVAILABLE

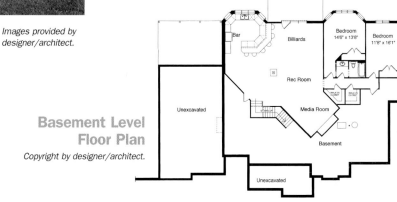

Copyright by designer/architect.

Front View

Plan #481035

Dimensions: 99' W x 64' D
Levels: 2
Heated Square Footage: 3,204
Main Level Sq. Ft.: 1,701
Upper Level Sq. Ft.: 1,503
Bedrooms: 3
Bathrooms: 2½
Foundation: Walkout
Material List Available: No
Price Category: G

Images provided by designer/architect.

Features:

- Foyer: This large foyer welcomes you home and provides a view through the home and into the family room. The adjoining study can double as a home office.

- Family Room: This two-story gathering space features a fireplace flanked by built-in cabinets. The full-height windows on the rear wall allow natural light to flood the space.

- Kitchen: This island kitchen flows into the nearby family room, allowing mingling between both spaces when friends or family are visiting. The adjacent dinette is available for daily meals.

- Master Suite: This private retreat waits for you to arrive home. The tray ceiling in the sleeping area adds elegant style to the area.

Distinctive design details set this home apart from others in the neighborhood.

Rear Elevation

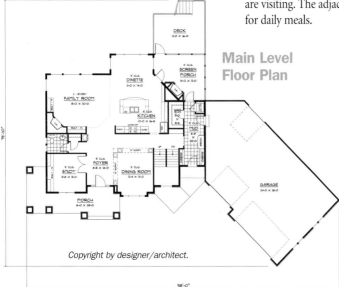

Main Level Floor Plan

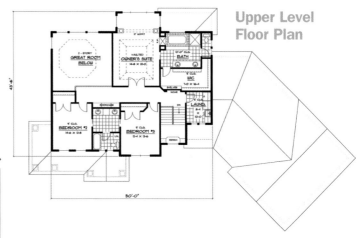

Upper Level Floor Plan

Copyright by designer/architect.

Plan #181260

Dimensions: 54' W x 43' D
Levels: 2
Heated Square Footage: 3,251
Main Level Sq. Ft.: 1,536
Upper Level Sq. Ft.: 1,715
Bedrooms: 4
Bathrooms: 3½
Foundation: Walkout; crawl space or slab for fee
Material List Available: Yes
Price Category: G

Features:

- **Decks:** This large deck area, spanning two levels of the home, is a wonderful place to entertain guests.

- **Kitchen:** This centrally located kitchen features a pantry, a center island, and an attached eating nook.

- **Master Suite:** Located upstairs, this master suite includes a large bedroom with a sitting area, an expansive walk-in closet, two vanities, and a tub.

- **Secondary Bedrooms:** Four additional bedrooms—three located upstairs and one downstairs—are wonderful for siblings or guests. Upstairs, one of the bedrooms has a private bath, and the other two bedrooms share a bath.

This contemporary home combines interesting architecture with useful features.

Main Level Floor Plan

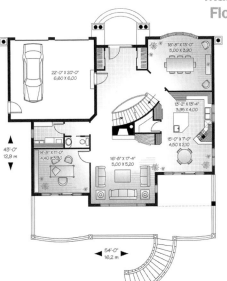

Upper Level Floor Plan

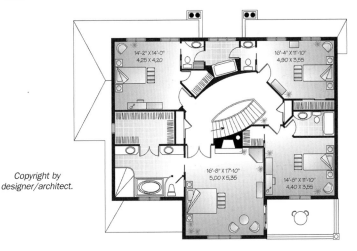

Plan #451321

Dimensions: 65' W x 56'6" D
Levels: 1
Heated Square Footage: 3,304
Main Level Sq. Ft.: 1,652
Lower Level Sq. Ft.: 1,652
Bedrooms: 2
Bathrooms: 3
Foundation: Slab or walkout
Material List Available: No
Price Category: G

If you're searching for an ideal vacation home that's inviting and spacious enough to accommodate loved ones, this is it.

CAD FILE AVAILABLE

Features:

- **Outdoor Living Space:** With a covered porch and large open deck, sunbathers and barbecuers alike will enjoy relaxing outdoors.
- **Kitchen:** This room is perfect for relaxing or enjoying a home-cooked meal.
- **Den:** This den doubles as an office, or can be converted into an entertainment center for a movie night.
- **Master Suite:** This luxurious master suite features one of the three large bathrooms in the home.
- **Garage:** This two-car garage is ideal for multi-car families or those with a lot of sports equipment to store.

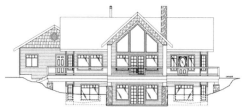

Rear Elevation

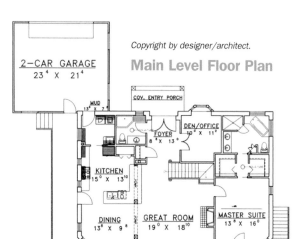

Copyright by designer/architect.

Main Level Floor Plan

Lower Level Floor Plan

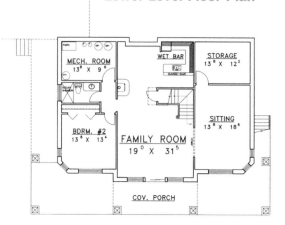

Plan #151021

Dimensions: 75'2" W x 89'6" D
Levels: 2
Heated Square Footage: 3,385
Main Level Sq. Ft.: 2,633
Upper Level Sq. Ft.: 752
Bedrooms: 4
Bathrooms: 4
Foundation: Crawl space, or slab
CompleteCost List Available: Yes
Price Category: F

Images provided by designer/architect.

From the fireplace in the master suite to the well-equipped game room, the amenities in this home will surprise and delight you.

Features:

- Great Room: A bank of windows on the far wall lets sunlight stream into this large room. The fireplace is located across the room and is flanked by the built-in media center and built-in bookshelves. Gracious brick arches create an entry into the breakfast area and kitchen.

- Breakfast Room: Move easily between this room with 10-foot ceiling either into the kitchen or onto the rear covered porch.

- Game Room: An icemaker and refrigerator make entertaining a snap in this room.

- Master Suite: A 10-ft. boxed ceiling, fireplace, and access to the rear porch give romance, while the built-ins in the closet, whirlpool tub with glass blocks, and glass shower give practicality.

Main Level Floor Plan

Upper Level Floor Plan

Copyright by designer/architect.

Main Level Floor Plan

Images provided by designer/architect.

CAD FILE AVAILABLE CAD

Plan #151482

Dimensions: 58'6" W x 60'6" D
Levels: 2
Heated Square Footage: 3,248
Main Level Sq. Ft.: 2,021
Upper Level Sq. Ft.: 1,227
Bedrooms: 5
Bathrooms: 3
Foundation: Crawl space or slab; basement or walkout for fee
CompleteCost List Available: Yes
Price Category: G

Upper Level Floor Plan

Copyright by designer/architect.

Plan #571043

Dimensions: 50' W x 36' D
Levels: 2
Heated Square Footage: 3,312
Main Level Sq. Ft.: 1,656
Upper Level Sq. Ft.: 1,656
Bedrooms: 4
Bathrooms: 2½
Foundation: Basement
Material List Available: Yes
Price Category: G

Images provided by designer/architect.

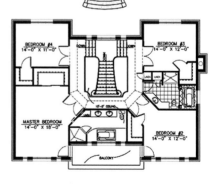

Main Level Floor Plan

Rear Elevation

Upper Level Floor Plan

Copyright by designer/architect.

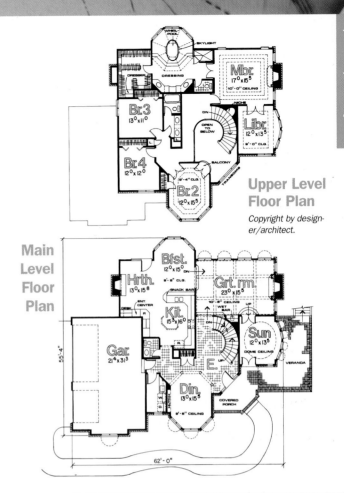

Upper Level Floor Plan

Copyright by designer/architect.

Main Level Floor Plan

Plan #121065

Dimensions: 62' W x 55'4" D

Levels: 2

Heated Square Footage: 3,407

Main Level Sq. Ft.: 1,719

Upper Level Sq. Ft.: 1,688

Bedrooms: 4

Bathrooms: 2½

Foundation: Basement; crawl space for fee

Materials List Available: Yes

Price Category: G

Images provided by designer/architect.

This home, as shown in the photograph, may differ from the actual blueprints. For more detailed information, please check the floor plans carefully

Main Level Floor Plan

Upper Level Floor Plan

Plan #151011

Dimensions: 59'6" W x 74'4" D

Levels: 2

Heated Square Footage: 3,437

Main Level Sq. Ft.: 2,184

Upper Level Sq. Ft.: 1,253

Bedrooms: 5

Bathrooms: 4

Foundation: Crawl space or slab; basement or daylight basement for fee

CompleteCost List Available: Yes

Price Category: F

Images provided by designer/architect.

CAD FILE AVAILABLE

Copyright by designer/architect.

Plan #161031

Dimensions: 99'8" W x 68'8" D

Levels: 2

Square Footage: 5,381

Main Level Sq. Ft.: 3,793

Lower Level Sq. Ft.: 1,588

Bedrooms: 4

Bathrooms: 3½

Foundation: Basement, or walkout

Materials List Available: Yes

Price Category: I

Images provided by designer/architect.

If you're looking for a compatible mixture of formal and informal areas in a home, look no further!

Features:

- Great Room: Columns at the entry to this room and the formal dining room set a gracious tone that is easy around which to decorate.

- Library: Set up an office or just a cozy reading area in this quiet room.

- Hearth Room: Spacious and inviting, this hearth room is positioned so that friends and family can flow from here to the breakfast area and kitchen.

- Master Suite: The luxury of this area is capped by the access it gives to the rear yard.

- Lower Level: Enjoy the 9-ft.-tall ceilings as you walk out to the rear yard from this area.

Entry

Rear View

Main Level Floor Plan

Copyright by designer/architect.

Deck

Bedroom
16'8" x 12'

Hearth Room   Breakfast
23' x 16' irr.

Master Bedroom
15'8" x 22"

Bath

Bath

Hall

Bedroom
16'8" x 12'

Kitchen
17'7" x 14'8"

Laun.

Great Room
16' x 21'6"

Dressing

walk-in closet

Three Car
Garage
20' x 33'4"

Dining Room
13'6" x 15'3" irr.

Foyer

Porch

Library
12'4" x 16'2" irr.

walk-in closet

Basement Level Floor Plan

Bedroom
12' x 10'

Rec Room
44'1" x 31'2" Irreg.

Unfinished Basement

Bath

Bar

SMARTtip

Paint or Polyurethane Clear Finish?

It usually does not pay to strip the finish off a painted door in the hope of obtaining a wood-grained look. It is extremely difficult to remove all of the paint, and the effort spent stripping, sanding, staining, and sealing isn't worth the time and expense. It is best either to paint the door in a traditional color, such as white, to provide a fresh look, or to coat it with an opaque stain over the existing finish. Consider adding a brass kick plate or letter slot for an elegant touch.

Rear Elevation

Left Elevation

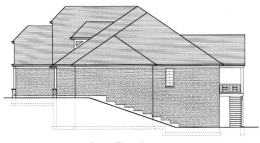

Right Elevation

Dining Room

sto 12x10

garage 34 x 24

sto 10x9

deck

br 3 15 x 14

porch

sit 11 x 11

eating 16 x 16

porch 18 x 12

sun 16 x 12

br 4 14 x 11

mbr 18 x 18

kit 15x14

family 26 x 20

br 2 15 x 14

util

12' clg

dining 16 x 16

foy 12x8

living 16 x 16

pantry 12 x 8

porch 40 x 8

Images provided by designer/architect.

Plan #211067

Dimensions: 96' W x 90' D
Levels: 1
Heated Square Footage: 4,038
Bedrooms: 4
Bathrooms: 4½
Foundation: Crawl space
Materials List Available: Yes
Price Category: I

Copyright by designer/architect.

Over 3,500 sq. ft.

CAD FILE AVAILABLE

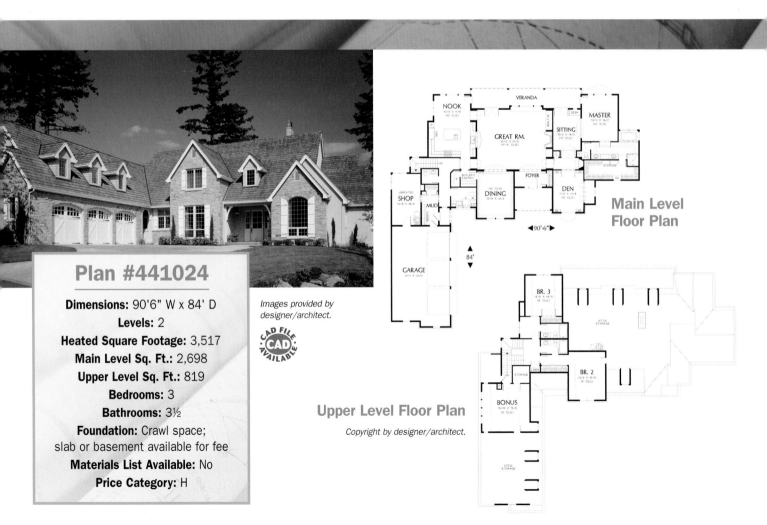

Images provided by designer/architect.

Plan #441024

Dimensions: 90'6" W x 84' D
Levels: 2
Heated Square Footage: 3,517
Main Level Sq. Ft.: 2,698
Upper Level Sq. Ft.: 819
Bedrooms: 3
Bathrooms: 3½
Foundation: Crawl space; slab or basement available for fee
Materials List Available: No
Price Category: H

CAD FILE AVAILABLE

NOOK

VERANDA

GREAT RM.

SITTING

MASTER

SHOP

BUTLER'S PANTRY

FOYER

DEN

MUD

DINING

GARAGE

Main Level Floor Plan

BR. 3

ATTIC STORAGE

BONUS

BR. 2

ATTIC STORAGE

Upper Level Floor Plan

Copyright by designer/architect.

Plan #151060

Dimensions: 80'11" W x 95'8" D

Levels: 1

Heated Square Footage: 3,554

Bedrooms: 3

Bathrooms: 3

Foundation: Crawl space, slab basement, or walkout

CompleteCost List Available: Yes

Price Category: F

Images provided by designer/architect.

Copyright by designer/architect.

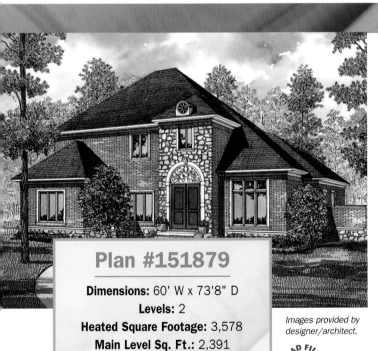

Plan #151879

Dimensions: 60' W x 73'8" D

Levels: 2

Heated Square Footage: 3,578

Main Level Sq. Ft.: 2,391

Upper Level Sq. Ft.: 1,187

Bedrooms: 5

Bathrooms: 4

Foundation: Crawl space or slab; basement or walkout for fee

CompleteCost List Available: Yes

Price Category: H

Images provided by designer/architect.

Main Level Floor Plan

Upper Level Floor Plan

Copyright by designer/architect.

Plan #161028

Dimensions: 84'6" W x 69'4" D
Levels: 1
Heated Square Footage: 3,570
**Optional Finished Basement
Sq. Ft.:** 2,367
Bedrooms: 3
Bathrooms: 3½
Foundation: Basement
Materials List Available: No
Price Category: H

From the gabled stone-and-brick exterior to the wide-open view from the foyer, this home will meet your greatest expectations.

Images provided by designer/architect.

Features:

- Great Room/Dining Room: Columns and 13-ft. ceilings add exquisite detailing to the dining room and great room.

- Kitchen: The gourmet-equipped kitchen with an island and a snack bar merges with the cozy breakfast and hearth rooms.

- Master Suite: The luxurious master bed room pampers with a separate sitting room with a fireplace and a dressing room boasting a tub and two vanities.

- Additional: Two bedrooms include a private bath and walk-in closet. The optional finished basement solves all your recreational needs: bar, media room, billiards room, exercise room, game room, as well as an office and fourth bedroom.

Rear Elevation

Main Level Floor Plan

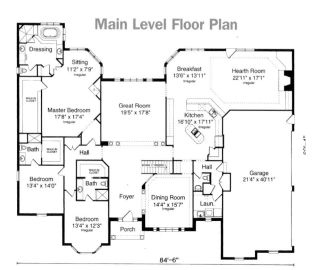

Basement Level Floor Plan

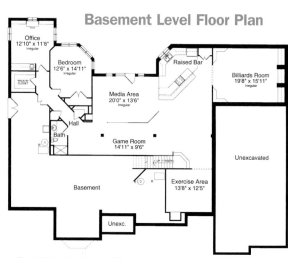

Copyright by designer/architect.

Images provided by designer/architect.

Plan #151822

Dimensions: 108'10" W x 73'10" D
Levels: 1
Heated Square Footage: 3,602
Bedrooms: 4
Bathrooms: 3½
Foundation: Crawl space or slab; basement or walkout for fee
CompleteCost List Available: Yes
Price Category: G

- **Master Suite:** Who cares about the spacious bedroom when such a master bath exists? It features an enormous walk-in closet, his and her vanities, an extra-large glass shower, and a whirlpool tub, which is illuminated through glass blocks.

- **Secondary Bedrooms:** All three bedrooms feature their own walk-in closet and access to a private full bathroom. Bedroom 4 is a small version of a master suite, with its own full bathroom with whirlpool tub and separate stall shower.

Perfect for the modern family, this home is both spacious and efficiently designed.

Features:

- **Outdoor Space:** This large porch is great for welcoming guests in or sitting outside for a chat with the neighbors. The rear grilling porch, with entrances from the great room and bedroom 4, adds to the entertaining area available to you.

- **Great Room:** Flanked by windows, a fireplace, and built-in storage, this great room is waiting for occupants and guests to enjoy it.

- **Kitchen:** This kitchen features ample work and storage space, a large island, a walk-in closet, and a long snack bar, which provides a transition into both the breakfast room and the great room. An adjacent butler's pantry leads into the formal dining room, providing easy transitions between meal preparation and serving.

Copyright by designer/architect.

Plan #441012

Dimensions: 65' W x 55' D
Levels: 1
Heated Square Footage: 3,682
Main Level Sq. Ft.: 2,192
Basement Level Sq. Ft.: 1,490
Bedrooms: 4
Bathrooms: 4
Foundation: Walkout
Materials List Available: Yes
Price Category: H

CAD FILE AVAILABLE

Images provided by designer/architect.

Accommodating a site that slopes to the rear, this home is not only good-looking but practical.

Features:

- **Den:** Just off the foyer is this cozy space, complete with built-ins.
- **Great Room:** This vaulted gathering area features a lovely fireplace, a built-in media center, and a view of the back yard.

- **Kitchen:** This island kitchen is ready to handle the daily needs of your family or aid in entertaining your guests.
- **Lower Level:** Adding even more livability to the home, this floor contains the games room with media center and corner fireplace, two more bedrooms (each with a full bathroom), and the wide covered patio.

Rear Elevation

Main Level Floor Plan

Basement Level Floor Plan

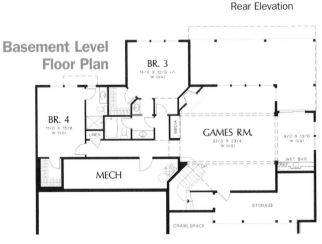

Copyright by designer/architect.

Plan #161035

Dimensions: 75' W x 64'11" D
Levels: 1.5
Heated Square Footage: 3,688
Main Level Sq. Ft.: 2,702
Upper Level Sq. Ft.: 986
Bedrooms: 4
Bathrooms: 3½
Foundation: Basement
Materials List Available: No
Price Category: H

Images provided by designer/architect.

You'll appreciate the style of the stone, brick, and cedar shake exterior of this contemporary home.

Features:

• Hearth Room: Positioned for an easy flow for guests and family, this hearth room features a bank of windows that integrate it with the yard.

• Breakfast Room: Move through the sliding doors here to the rear porch on sunny days.

• Kitchen: Outfitted for a gourmet cook, this kitchen is also ideal for friends and family who can perch at the island or serve themselves at the bar.

• Master Suite: A stepped ceiling, crown moldings, and boxed window make the bedroom easy to decorate, while the two walk-in closets, lavish dressing area, and tub in the bath make this area comfortable and luxurious.

Main Level Floor Plan

Upper Level Floor Plan

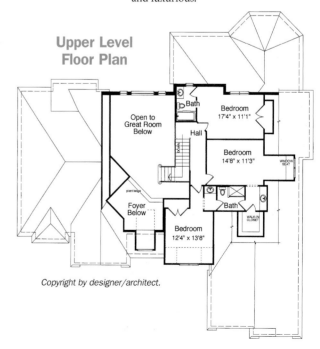

Copyright by designer/architect.

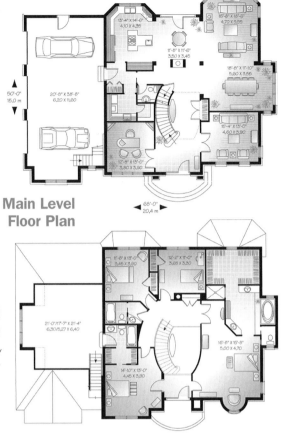

Main Level Floor Plan

Plan #181253

Dimensions: 68' W x 50' D

Levels: 2

Heated Square Footage: 3,614

Main Level Sq. Ft.: 1,909

Upper Level Sq. Ft.: 1,705

Bedrooms: 4

Bathrooms: 3½

Foundation: Basement; crawl space or slab for fee

Material List Available: Yes

Price Category: H

Images provided by designer/architect.

Upper Level Floor Plan

Copyright by designer/architect.

Plan #151502

Dimensions: 81'7" W x 97'2" D

Levels: 1

Heated Square Footage: 3,654

Bedrooms: 3

Bathrooms: 3

Foundation: Slab

CompleteCost List Available: Yes

Price Category: H

Images provided by designer/architect.

Copyright by designer/architect.

Upper Level Floor Plan

Copyright by designer/architect.

Main Level Floor Plan

Plan #151080

Dimensions: 92'5" W x 64' D
Levels: 1.5
Heated Square Footage: 3,740
Main Level Sq. Ft.: 2,651
Upper Level Sq. Ft.: 1,089
Bedrooms: 4
Bathrooms: 4½
Foundation: Crawl space or slab; basement or walkout for fee
CompleteCost List Available: Yes
Price Category: F

Images provided by designer/architect.

CAD FILE AVAILABLE

Main Level Floor Plan

Upper Level Floor Plan

Copyright by designer/architect.

Plan #261001

Dimensions: 77'8" W x 49' D
Levels: 2
Heated Square Footage: 3,746
Main Level Sq. Ft.: 1,965
Upper Level Sq. Ft.: 1,781
Bedrooms: 4
Bathrooms: 3½
Foundation: Basement
Materials List Available: No
Price Category: H

Images provided by designer/architect.

Main Level Floor Plan

Copyright by designer/architect.

Images provided by designer/architect.

Plan #161033

Dimensions: 78'2" W x 74'6" D

Levels: 2

Heated Square Footage: 5,125

Main Level Sq. Ft.: 2,782

Upper Level Sq. Ft.: 1,027

Optional Basement Level Sq. Ft.: 1,316

Bedrooms: 4

Bathrooms: 3½

Foundation: Basement

Materials List Available: Yes

Price Category: H

Upper Level Floor Plan

Optional Basement Level Floor Plan

Copyright by designer/architect.

Upper Level Floor Plan

Plan #371092

Dimensions: 71'6" W x 70'8" D

Levels: 2

Heated Square Footage: 3,836

Main Level Sq. Ft.: 2,981

Upper Level Sq. Ft.: 855

Bedrooms: 5

Bathrooms: 4

Foundation: Slab

Materials List Available: No

Price Category: H

Images provided by designer/architect.

CAD FILE AVAILABLE

Upper Level Floor Plan

Front View

Main Level Floor Plan

Images provided by designer/architect.

CAD FILE AVAILABLE

Upper Level Floor Plan

Copyright by designer/architect.

Plan #181267

Dimensions: 69' W x 75' D
Levels: 2
Heated Square Footage: 3,899
Main Level Sq. Ft.: 1,995
Upper Level Sq. Ft.: 1,904
Bedrooms: 3
Bathrooms: 2½
Foundation: Basement
Materials List Available: Yes
Price Category: H

Main Level Floor Plan

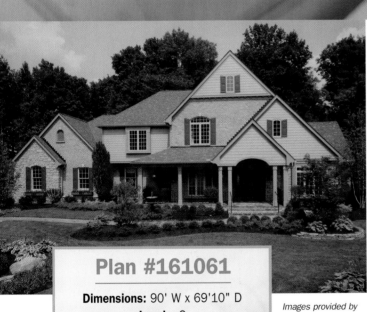

Plan #161061

Dimensions: 90' W x 69'10" D
Levels: 2
Heated Square Footage: 3,816
Main Level Sq. Ft.: 2,725
Upper Level Sq. Ft.: 1,091
Bedrooms: 4
Bathrooms: 3½
Foundation: Basement, walkout basement
Materials List Available: No
Price Category: H

Images provided by designer/architect.

Upper Level Floor Plan

Copyright by designer/architect.

Plan #121019

Dimensions: 70' W x 60' D
Levels: 2
Heated Square Footage: 3,775
Main Level Sq. Ft.: 1,923
Upper Level Sq. Ft.: 1,852
Bedrooms: 4
Bathrooms: 3½
Foundation: Basement; crawl space or slab for fee
Materials List Available: Yes
Price Category: H

Images provided by designer/architect.

The grand exterior presence is carried inside, beginning with the dramatic curved staircase.

Features:

• Ceiling Height: 8 ft.

• Den: French doors lead to this sophisticated den, with its bayed windows and wall of bookcases.

• Living Room: A curved wall and a series of arched windows highlight this large space.

• Formal Dining Room: This room shares the curved wall and arched windows found in the living room.

• Screened Porch: This huge space features skylights and is accessible by another French door from the dining room.

• Family Room: Family and guests alike will be drawn to this room, with its trio of arched windows and fireplace flanked by bookcases.

• Kitchen: An island adds convenience and distinction to this large, functional kitchen.

• Garage: This spacious three-bay garage provides plenty of space for cars and storage.

Main Level Floor Plan

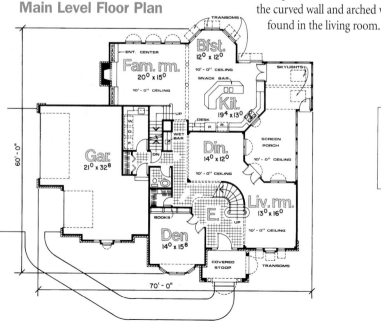

Upper Level Floor Plan

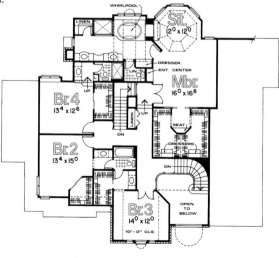

Copyright by designer/architect.

Main Level Floor Plan

Plan #181267

Dimensions: 69' W x 75' D
Levels: 2
Heated Square Footage: 3,899
Main Level Sq. Ft.: 1,995
Upper Level Sq. Ft.: 1,904
Bedrooms: 3
Bathrooms: 2½
Foundation: Basement
Materials List Available: Yes
Price Category: H

Images provided by designer/architect.

CAD FILE AVAILABLE

Upper Level Floor Plan

Copyright by designer/architect.

Main Level Floor Plan

Plan #161061

Dimensions: 90' W x 69'10" D
Levels: 2
Heated Square Footage: 3,816
Main Level Sq. Ft.: 2,725
Upper Level Sq. Ft.: 1,091
Bedrooms: 4
Bathrooms: 3½
Foundation: Basement, walkout basement
Materials List Available: No
Price Category: H

Images provided by designer/architect.

Upper Level Floor Plan

Copyright by designer/architect.

Plan #121019

Dimensions: 70' W x 60' D
Levels: 2
Heated Square Footage: 3,775
Main Level Sq. Ft.: 1,923
Upper Level Sq. Ft.: 1,852
Bedrooms: 4
Bathrooms: 3½
Foundation: Basement;
crawl space or slab for fee
Materials List Available: Yes
Price Category: H

Images provided by designer/architect.

The grand exterior presence is carried inside, beginning with the dramatic curved staircase.

Features:

• Ceiling Height: 8 ft.

• Den: French doors lead to this sophisticated den, with its bayed windows and wall of bookcases.

• Living Room: A curved wall and a series of arched windows highlight this large space.

• Formal Dining Room: This room shares the curved wall and arched windows found in the living room.

• Screened Porch: This huge space features skylights and is accessible by another French door from the dining room.

• Family Room: Family and guests alike will be drawn to this room, with its trio of arched windows and fireplace flanked by bookcases.

• Kitchen: An island adds convenience and distinction to this large, functional kitchen.

• Garage: This spacious three-bay garage provides plenty of space for cars and storage.

Main Level Floor Plan

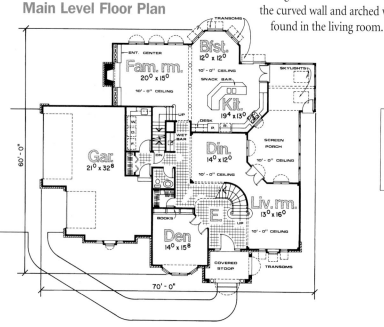

Upper Level Floor Plan

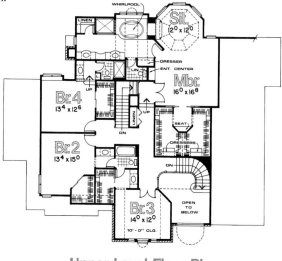

Copyright by designer/architect.

Plan #121023

Dimensions: 85'5" W x 74'8" D
Levels: 2
Heated Square Footage: 3,904
Main Level Sq. Ft.: 2,813
Upper Level Sq. Ft.: 1,091
Bedrooms: 4
Bathrooms: 3½
Foundation: Basement
Materials List Available: Yes
Price Category: H

Images provided by designer/architect.

Spacious and gracious, here are all the amenities you expect in a fine home.

Features:

• Ceiling Height: 8 ft. except as noted.

• Foyer: This magnificent entry features a graceful curved staircase with balcony above.

• Sunken Living Room: This sunken room is filled with light from a row of bowed windows. It's the perfect place for social gatherings both large and small.

• Den: French doors open into this truly distinctive den with its 11-ft. ceiling and built-in bookcases.

• Formal Dining Room: Entertain guests with style and grace in this dining room with corner column.

• Master Suite: Another set of French doors leads to this suite that features two walk-in closets, a tub flanked by vanities, and a private sitting room with built-in bookcases.

Main Level Floor Plan

Upper Level Floor Plan

Copyright by designer/architect.

Plan #481028

Dimensions: 86'8" W x 53' D
Levels: 1
Heated Square Footage: 3,980
Main Level Sq. Ft.: 2,290
Lower Level Sq. Ft.: 1,690
Bedrooms: 3
Bathrooms: 2½
Foundation: Walkout basement
Material List Available: No
Price Category: H

Images provided by designer/architect.

• Lower Level: For fun times, this lower level is finished to provide a wet bar and a recreation room. Two bedrooms, which share a full bathroom, are also on this level. Future expansion can include an additional bedroom.

Rear View

This home, with its Southwestern flair, invites friends and family in for some down-home hospitality.

Features:

• Foyer: A 12-ft-high ceiling extends an open welcome to all. With a view through the great room, the open floor plan makes the home feel large and open.

• Kitchen: This spacious gourmet kitchen opens generously to the hearth room, which features an angled fireplace. A two-level island, which contains a two-bowl sink, provides casual seating and additional storage.

• Master Suite: This romantic space features a 10-ft.-high stepped ceiling and a compartmentalized full bath that includes his and her sinks and a whirlpool tub.

Copyright by designer/architect.

Lower Level Floor Plan

Plan #391049

Dimensions: 78' W x 52'4" D
Levels: 1
Heated Square Footage: 4,064
Bedrooms: 4
Bathrooms: 3
Foundation: Basement
Material List Available: Yes
Price Category: E

This home proves that elegance can be comfortable. No need to sacrifice one for the other. Here, a peaked roofline creates a well-mannered covered front porch and classical columns announce the beauty of the dining room.

Features:

- **Living Areas:** High windows and a fireplace light up the living room, while an open hearth room shares the glow of a three-sided fireplace with the breakfast area and kitchen.

- **Kitchen:** To please the cook there's a built-in kitchen desk, cooking island, food-preparation island, double sinks, and pantries.

- **Master Suite:** To soothe the busy executive, this first-floor master suite includes a lavish bath and a nearby study.

- **Recreation:** The lower level entertains some big plans for entertaining—a home theater, wet bar, and large recreation room with a double-sided fireplace.

- **Bedrooms:** Two additional bedrooms with excellent closet space and a shared full bath keep family or guests in stylish comfort.

Living Room

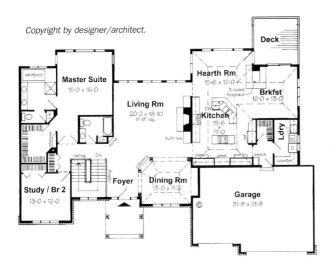

Copyright by designer/architect.

Basement Level Floor Plan

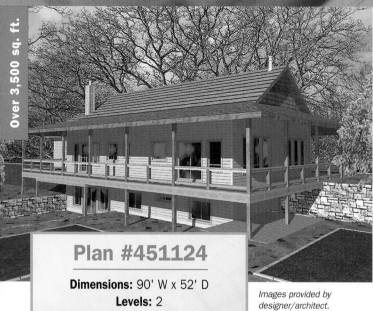

Main Level Floor Plan

8' COVERED PORCH

DINING 14'8" X 13'6" VAULTED

KITCHEN 11'1" X 15'6"

MASTER SUITE 15'8" X 15'2"

W-I-C 10'X6'-2"

LIVING ROOM 21'8" X 17'6" VAULTED

2-CAR GARAGE 29'8" X 27'4"

OFFICE 12'0" X 12'0"

BDRM. #2 15'8" X 15'6"

8' COVERED PORCH

8' COVERED PORCH

8' COVERED PORCH

Plan #451124

Dimensions: 90' W x 52' D
Levels: 2
Heated Square Footage: 4,016
Main Level Sq. Ft.: 2,008
Lower Level Sq. Ft.: 2,088
Bedrooms: 4
Bathrooms: 3
Foundation: Walkout – insulated concrete form
Material List Available: No
Price Category: I

Images provided by designer/architect.

CAD FILE AVAILABLE

Lower Level Floor Plan

Copyright by designer/architect.

8' COVERED PORCH

BDRM. #3 12'0" X 11'6"

BDRM. #4 12'0" X 11'6"

RECREATION ROOM 19'10" X 23'6"

SHOP/STORAGE 21'8" X 13'6"

WET BAR 8'8" X 9'0"

WEIGHT ROOM 19'4" X 11'0"

WINE 4'8" X 7'6"

Plan #611050

Dimensions: 44'10" W x 82'10" D
Levels: 2
Heated Square Footage: 4,224
Main Level Sq. Ft.: 2,343
Upper Level Sq. Ft.: 1,881
Bedrooms: 5
Bathrooms: 3½
Foundation: Slab
Material List Available: No
Price Category: I

Images provided by designer/architect.

CAD FILE AVAILABLE

Rear View

Main Level Floor Plan

82'-10"

44'-10"

Upper Level Floor Plan

Copyright by designer/architect.

Main Level Floor Plan

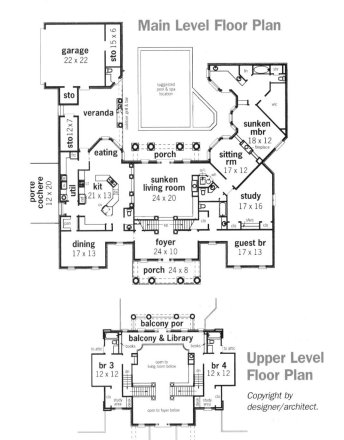

garage 22 x 22

sto 15 x 6

sto

veranda

sto 12 x 7

eating

porte cochere 12 x 20

util

kit 21 x 13

suggested pool & spa location

outdoor grill & bar

porch

sunken living room 24 x 20

sunken mbr 18 x 12

sitting rm 17 x 12

study 17 x 16

dining 17 x 13

foyer 24 x 10

guest br 17 x 13

porch 24 x 8

Images provided by designer/architect.

CAD FILE AVAILABLE
CAD

Plan #211076

Dimensions: 95' W x 90' D
Levels: 2
Heated Square Footage: 4,242
Main Level Sq. Ft.: 3,439
Upper Level Sq. Ft.: 803
Bedrooms: 4
Bathrooms: 4 full, 3 half
Foundation: Raised slab
Materials List Available: Yes
Price Category: I

balcony por

balcony & Library

to attic

books

books

to attic

br 3 12 x 12

open to living room below

br 4 12 x 12

study area

study area

open to foyer below

Upper Level Floor Plan

Copyright by designer/architect.

Plan #531020

Dimensions: 74' W x 97' D
Levels: 1
Heated Square Footage: 4,271
Bedrooms: 4
Bathrooms: 3½
Foundation: Slab
Material List Available: No
Price Category: I

Images provided by designer/architect.

CAD FILE AVAILABLE
CAD

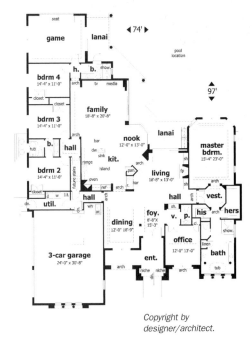

seat

game

lanai

◄ 74' ►

pool location

bdrm 4 14'-4" x 11'-0"

closet

closet

h. b. show.

tv

media

97'

family 18'-8" x 20'-8"

lanai

bdrm 3 14'-4" x 11'-0"

b.

hall

nook 12'-0" x 13'-0"

living 18'-8" x 13'-0"

master bdrm. 15'-4" x 23'-0"

bdrm 2 14'-4" x 11'-0"

bar

dw

sink

kit.

island

range

oven

ref

future stairs

vest.

closet

dn.

util.

hall

wh

ac

dining 12'-0" x 18'-9"

foy. 8'-8" x 15'-3"

v. p.

his

hers

3-car garage 24'-0" x 30'-8"

ent.

office 12'-0" x 13'-0"

bath

ac

hall

bath

linen

ref

cl.

bar

sink

38'-10"

bonus 13'-4" x 20'-4"

stepped clg.

Bonus Area Floor Plan

Copyright by designer/architect.

Plan #161093

Dimensions: 70'8" W x 64' D
Levels: 1
Heated Square Footage: 4,328
Main Level Sq. Ft.: 2,582
Lower Level Sq. Ft.: 1,746
Bedrooms: 3
Bathrooms: 3½
Foundation: Walkout
Materials List Available: Yes
Price Category: I

Detailed stucco and stone accents impart warmth and character to the exterior of this one level home.

Images provided by designer/architect.

Features:

- Great Room: This gathering room, which features a fireplace and a decorative ceiling, offers an extensive view of the rear yard.

- Kitchen: Spacious and up-to-date, this extra-large combination gourmet kitchen and breakfast room is an ideal area for doing chores and hosting family gatherings.

- Main Level: The extravagant master suite, with its private bathroom and dressing area, the library with built-in shelves, and the formal dining room round out the

main floor. Accented by a wood rail, the extra-wide main stairway leads to the lavish lower level.

- Lower Level: The two additional bedrooms, adjoining bathroom, media room, billiard room, and exercise room comprise this fantastic finished lower level.

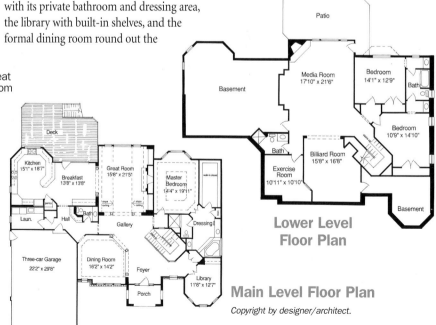

Lower Level Floor Plan

Main Level Floor Plan

Copyright by designer/architect.

Dining Room

Master Bedroom

Great Room

Foyer

Images provided by designer/architect.

Plan #291014

Dimensions: 102' W x 54' D
Levels: 2
Heated Square Footage: 4,372
Main Level Sq. Ft.: 3,182
Upper Level Sq. Ft.: 1,190
Bedrooms: 3
Bathrooms: 3 full, 2 half
Foundation: Basement
Materials List Available: No
Price Category: I

Cottage-like architectural details and an abundance of windows add warmth and personality to this generously designed home.

Features:

- **Entry:** Welcome family and friends from a shaded porch into this grand foyer. A curving stairway ahead and a vaulted library to the left make an elegant impression.

- **Kitchen:** The heart of any home, this kitchen will be the center of all your entertaining. Plenty of workspace, a nearby pantry, and an island complete with cooktop will appease chefs of any skill level. The kitchen's proximity to the dining room, the living room, and the sunlit morning room, as well as to a small back porch, creates a simple transition for any kind of dining.

- **Master Suite:** This area is a sybaritic retreat where you can shut out the frenzied world and simply relax. The attached master bath includes dual walk-in closets, his and her sinks, a standing shower, and a separate tub-perfect for busy mornings and romantic evenings.

- **Second Floor:** Great for guests or growing siblings, both secondary bedrooms have ample closet space and private bathrooms. A bonus room over the three-car garage and laundry area can fulfill whatever need you have. Create a quiet study environment or a fully featured entertainment area.

Main Level Floor Plan

Copyright by designer/architect.

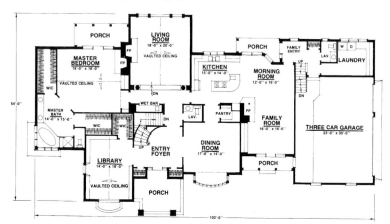

Upper Level Floor Plan

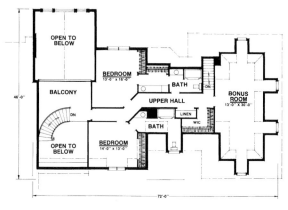

Plan #161030

Dimensions: 98'6" W x 61'5" D
Levels: 2
Heated Square Footage: 4,562
Main Level Sq. Ft.: 3,364
Upper Level Sq. Ft.: 1,198
Bedrooms: 4
Bathrooms: 3½
Foundation: Basement
Materials List Available: Yes
Price Category: I

You'll be charmed by this impressive home, with its stone-and-brick exterior.

Features:

- **Great Room:** The two-story ceiling here adds even more dimension to this expansive space.

- **Hearth Room:** A tray ceiling and molding help to create a cozy feeling in this room, which is located so your guests will naturally gravitate to it.

- **Dining Room:** This formal room features columns at the entry and a butler's pantry for entertaining.

- **Master Suite:** A walk-in closet, platform whirlpool tub, and 2-person shower are only a few of the luxuries in the private bath, and tray ceilings and moldings give extra presence to the bedroom.

- **Upper Level:** A balcony offers a spectacular view of the great room and leads to three large bedrooms, each with a private bath.

Images provided by designer/architect.

Main Level Floor Plan

Upper Level Floor Plan

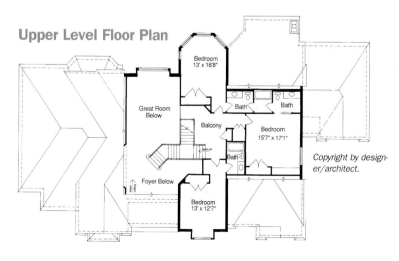

Copyright by designer/architect.

Plan #451217

Dimensions: 103'6" W x 53'11" D
Levels: 1
Heated Square Footage: 4,711
Main Level Sq. Ft.: 2,470
Lower Level Sq. Ft.: 2,241
Bedrooms: 4
Bathrooms: 3
Foundation: Walkout basement
Materials List Available: No
Price Category: I

This Craftsman-style home is spacious and filled with wonderful amenities you will enjoy.

Features:

- Deck: This large deck area wraps around the back of the house and opens up to the great room and master suite.

- Great Room: Tall windows and a built-in fireplace make this room a wonderful location to entertain guests, both inside and outside on the adjoining deck.

- Kitchen: With its center cooktop island and eating bar, this kitchen is a great area for any home cook. The nearby nook and formal dining room are located for easy food and dish transportation.

- Master Suite: You'll love the location of this master suite, with its direct access to the deck at the back of the home. Inside, the large bedroom area opens to the bath with its dual-sink vanity and two walk-in closets.

Main Level Floor Plan

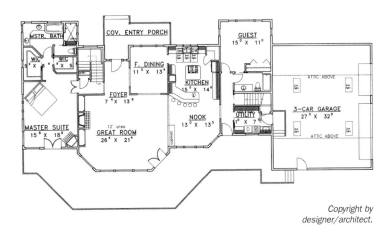

Copyright by designer/architect.

Lower Level Floor Plan

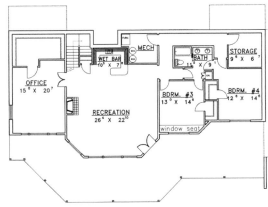

Plan #121049

Dimensions: 82' W x 60'8" D

Levels: 2

Heated Square Footage: 3,335

Main Level Sq. Ft.: 2,054

Upper Level Sq. Ft.: 1,281

Bedrooms: 4

Bathrooms: 3½

Foundation: Slab; basement for fee

Materials List Available: Yes

Price Category: G

Images provided by designer/architect.

This home, as shown in the photograph, may differ from the actual blueprints. For more detailed information, please check the floor plans carefully.

This charming European-style home creates a welcoming environment with its covered porch, two-story foyer, and attractive accommodations.

CAD FILE AVAILABLE

Features:

• **Living Room:** Bask in the quiet glow of abundant natural light; cozy up to the smoldering fireplace; or gather with the family in this large, relaxing area.

• **Kitchen:** This design creates a great balance between workspace and play space. The kitchen surrounds the household chef with workspace without feeling closed-

in. A breakfast bar opens into the large breakfast area, making life a little simpler in the mornings.

• **Master Suite:** This spacious room is yours for the styling, a private space that features a walk-in closet and full bath, which includes his and her sinks, a standing shower, and a large tub.

• **Second Floor:** "Go to your room" sounds much better when that room is separated by a story. Identically sized bedrooms with ample closet space save you from family squabbles. The second floor has everything you need, with a full bathroom and computer loft.

Copyright by designer/architect.

Main Level Floor Plan

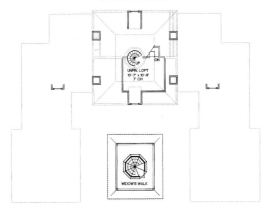

Upper Level Floor Plan

Third Floor Bedroom Floor Plan

Main Level Floor Plan

Plan #551193

Dimensions: 125' W x 74' D

Levels: 2

Heated Square Footage: 4,650

Main Level Sq. Ft.: 2,595

Upper Level Sq. Ft.: 2,055

Bedrooms: 5

Bathrooms: 4½

Foundation: Crawl space; slab, basement or walkout for fee

Material List Available: N

Price Category: I

Images provided by designer/architect.

Upper Level Floor Plan

Copyright by designer/architect.

Main Level Floor Plan

Copyright by designer/architect.

Plan #551195

Dimensions: 85' W x 61' D

Levels: 2

Heated Square Footage: 4,720

Main Level Sq. Ft.: 2,240

Upper Level Sq. Ft.: 2,480

Bedrooms: 4

Bathrooms: 3½

Foundation: Crawl space; slab, basement or walkout for fee

Material List Available: No

Price Category: I

Images provided by designer/architect.

Upper Level Floor Plan

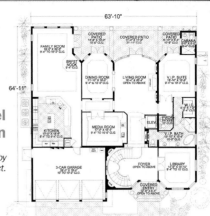

Main Level Floor Plan

Copyright by designer/architect.

Upper Level Floor Plan

Front View

Plan #611198

Dimensions: 63'10" W x 64'11" D
Levels: 2
Heated Square Footage: 5,536
Main Level Sq. Ft.: 2,924
Upper Level Sq. Ft.: 2,612
Bedrooms: 5
Bathrooms: 5 Full, 2 Half
Foundation: Slab
Material List Available: No
Price Category: J

Images provided by designer/architect.

CAD FILE AVAILABLE

Plan #611080

Dimensions: 57'3" W x 121' D
Levels: 2
Heated Square Footage: 5,872
Main Level Sq. Ft.: 3,147
Upper Level Sq. Ft.: 2,725
Bedrooms: 5
Bathrooms: 5½
Foundation: Slab
Material List Available: No
Price Category: J

Images provided by designer/architect.

CAD FILE AVAILABLE

Main Level Floor Plan

Upper Level Floor Plan

Copyright by designer/architect.

Plan #441030

Dimensions: 117'6" W x 63'6" D
Levels: 2
Heated Square Footage: 5,180
Main Level Sq. Ft.: 3,030
Upper Level Sq. Ft.: 2,150
Bedrooms: 6
Bathrooms: 5
Foundation: Crawl space;
slab or basement available for fee
Materials List Available: YES
Price Category: J

Images provided by designer/architect.

There's no doubt, this home plan is pure luxury. The plan incorporates a wealth of space on two levels, plus every amenity a family could desire.

CAD FILE AVAILABLE

Features:

• **Great Room:** Defined by columns, this room with fireplace and built-in cabinet has an 11-ft.-high ceiling. There is access to the rear patio through French doors.

• **Kitchen:** Furnished with multiple work-stations, this kitchen can accommodate a cook and helpers. The island is equipped with a sink and dishwasher. The secondary sink occupies the half-wall facing the family room. The walk-in pantry beside the dining room supplements storage.

• **Main Level:** The main level is host to rooms devoted to special interests-the office, complete with storage units and a French door to the front porch, and the crafts or hobby room, furnished with an L-shaped work surface.

• **Upper Level:** The upper level of the home accommodates three bedrooms, two bath rooms, the full-service laundry room, and

the master suite, which is a dream come true. The master bedroom is divided into sitting and sleeping areas. French doors open it to a private deck. A two-sided fireplace warms both the sitting area and the master bath. The highlight of the spacious bath is the oval tub, which is tucked beneath a bay window.

Rear View

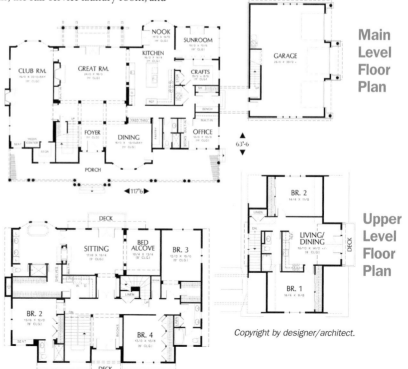

Main Level Floor Plan

Upper Level Floor Plan

Copyright by designer/architect.

Plan #611069

Dimensions: 61'8" W x 75' D
Levels: 2
Heated Square Footage: 5,445
Main Level Sq. Ft.: 2,900
Upper Level Sq. Ft.: 2,545
Bedrooms: 6
Bathrooms: 4
Foundation: Slab
Material List Available: No
Price Category: J

- **Secondary Bedrooms:** Five additional bedrooms, each with their own private full bathroom, complete this home. Two bedrooms are located on the first level, with the remaining three on the upper level with the master suite.

Rear View

Luxury abounds in this six-bedroom home, great for larger families.

CAD FILE AVAILABLE

Features:

- **Living Room:** This spacious open room includes a bar and wine storage for entertaining family and friends. The two-story area boasts a dramatic fireplace and access to the covered porch at the back of the home.

- **Family Room:** The kitchen's open snack bar faces this room, which will become a favorite for the family to enjoy. On nice days or evenings you can step through the double doors and onto the covered porch.

- **Master Suite:** This private oasis features a large sleeping area, a sitting area, a covered terrace, and an exercise room complete with a sauna and a steam room. The large master bath features a whirlpool tub, dual vanities, and a separate shower.

Main Level Floor Plan

Upper Level Floor Plan

Images provided by designer/architect.

Plan #151033

Dimensions: 81'6" W x 93'2" D
Levels: 2
Heated Square Footage: 5,548
Main Level Sq. Ft.: 3,276
Upper Level Sq. Ft.: 2,272
Bedrooms: 5
Bathrooms: 4½
Foundation: Crawl space or slab; basement option for fee
CompleteCost List Available: Yes
Price Category: I

From the exercise room to the home theatre, you'll love the spaciousness and comfort in this beautifully-designed home.

Features:

- **Family Room:** Everyone can gather around the stone fireplace and built-in media center.

- **Hearth Room:** Open to the breakfast/kitchen area, this room also has a lovely gas fireplace.

- **Computer Areas:** Set up work areas in the computer room, as well as the kid's nook.

- **Dining Room:** Sit by the bay window or go through the swinging door to the adjoining hearth room.

- **Master Suite:** Somewhat secluded, the bedroom has a vaulted 10-ft. boxed ceiling while the bath features a TV, whirlpool tub, a separate shower, and corner vanities.

- **Porch:** The rear screened-in porch lets in extra light through skylights on its roof.

Main Level Floor Plan

Upper Level Floor Plan

Copyright by designer/architect.

Plan #151557

Dimensions: 117'8" W x 84'8" D
Levels: 2
Heated Square Footage: 6,388
Main Level Sq. Ft.: 5,338
Upper Level Sq. Ft.: 1,050
Bedrooms: 4
Bathrooms: 4 full, 2 half
Foundation: Crawl space or slab
CompleteCost List Available: Yes
Price Category: K

The exquisite design and extensive amenities of this home make it a dream-come-true.

CAD FILE AVAILABLE

Features:

- **Entry:** This two-story entry gives the home an open feeling. It separates the formal living room from the dining room. The stairs lead to a balcony, which overlooks the enormous great room.

- **Kitchen:** This expansive kitchen adjoins both the breakfast nook and the hearth room. It is located near the guest suite, providing an abundance of options. The walk-in pantry is a bonus.

- **Master Suite:** This main-level master suite has a large sitting bay and private access to the study. Enter through the French doors to a luxurious master bath complete with a double vanity and whirlpool tub.

- **Upper Level:** Located above the four-car garage, this large bonus room contains skylights and stairs that lead to the hearth room. Two secondary bedrooms, each with a full bathroom, are located on this level.

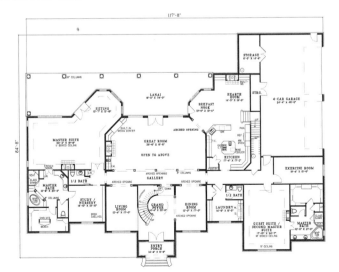

Main Level Floor Plan

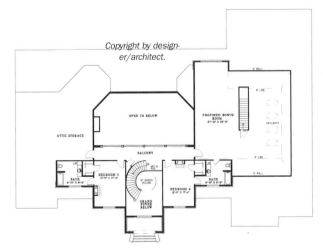

Copyright by designer/architect.

Upper Level Floor Plan

Images provided by designer/architect.

Plan #441015

Dimensions: 130'3" W x 79'3" D

Levels: 1

Heated Square Footage: 4,732

Bedrooms: 4

Bathrooms: 3 full, 2 half

Foundation: Walkout basement

Materials List Available: Yes

Price Category: I

An artful use of stone was employed on the exterior of this rustic hillside home to complement other architectural elements, such as the angled, oversize four-car garage and the substantial roofline.

CAD FILE AVAILABLE

Features:

- **Great Room:** This massive vaulted room features a large stone fireplace at one end and a formal dining area on the other. A built-in media center and double doors separate the great room from a home office with its own hearth and built-ins.

- **Kitchen:** This kitchen features a walk-in pantry and snack counter and opens to a skylighted outdoor kitchen. Its appointments include a cooktop and a corner fireplace.

- **Home Theatre:** This space has a built-in viewing screen, a fireplace, and a double terrace access.

- **Master Suite:** This private space is found at the other side of the home. Look closely for expansive his and her walk-in closets, a spa tub, a skylighted double vanity area, and a corner fireplace in the salon.

- **Bedrooms:** Three family bedrooms are on the lower level; bedroom 4 has a private bath room and walk-in closet.

- **Garage:** This large garage has room for four cars; don't miss the dog shower and grooming station just off the garage.

Main Level Floor Plan

Copyright by designer/architect.

Entry

Basement Level Floor Plan

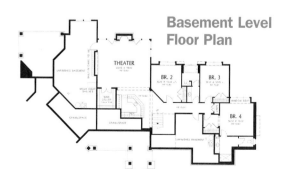

Master Bath

Rear View

Foyer

Dining Room

Great Room

Plan #121103

Dimensions: 68' W x 66' D
Levels: 2
Heated Square Footage: 3,992
Main Level Sq. Ft.: 2,040
Upper Level Sq. Ft.: 1,952
Bedrooms: 4
Bathrooms: 3½
Foundation: Basement; crawl space, slab or walkout for fee
Material List Available: Yes
Price Category: H

The exterior of this beautiful home will make your guests feel welcome.

Features:

• Entry: You'll love the first impression this elegant two-story entry makes. The living room, dining room, and den are all conveniently located near the entry, wonderful for entertaining.

• Kitchen: Separated from the family room by a raised bar, this kitchen is wonderful for watching the children while preparing meals. The adjacent breakfast nook is lined with windows, so you can enjoy some morning sunshine with your coffee.

• Family Room: Built-in shelves and a fireplace make this room perfect for relaxing with your loved ones after a long day.

• Master Suite: This master suite includes the amenities you've always wanted. The bedroom area is connected to a sitting room with built-in shelves and a fireplace. The bathroom includes a whirlpool tub, two separate vanities, and two spacious walk-in closets.

Main Level Floor Plan

Upper Level Floor Plan

Copyright by designer/architect.

Plan #441028

Dimensions: 53'6" W x 73' D
Levels: 2
Heated Square Footage: 3,165
Main Level Sq. Ft.: 1,268
Upper Level Sq. Ft.: 931
Lower Level Sq. Ft.: 966
Bedrooms: 4
Bathrooms: 3½
Foundation: Slab
Materials List Available: Yes
Price Category: G

Images provided by designer/architect.

Arts and Crafts style meets hillside design. The result is this stunning design, which fits perfectly on a sloped site.

CAD FILE AVAILABLE

Features:

- **Porch:** This covered porch introduces the front entry but also allows access to a mud-room and the three-car garage beyond.

- **Great Room:** This room is vaulted and has a fireplace, media center, and window seat in a corner window area—a cozy place to read or relax.

- **Dining Room:** The recess in this room is ideal for a hutch, and the double French doors open to the wide lower deck.

- **Upper Level:** This floor holds the two family bedrooms with walk-in closets, the shared bathroom, and the master suite. A spa tub and vaulted salon with private deck appoint the suite.

- **Lower Level:** This floor features another bedroom, with its full bathroom; the recreation room, which has a fireplace and wet bar; and the wine cellar.

Lower Level Floor Plan
Copyright by designer/architect.

Main Level Floor Plan

Upper Level Floor Plan

Plan #481031

Dimensions: 98' W x 72' D

Levels: 1

Heated Square Footage: 4,707

Main Level Sq. Ft.: 2,518

Basement Level Sq. Ft.: 2,189

Bedrooms: 4

Bathrooms: 3½

Foundation: Walkout basement

Material List Available: No

Price Category: I

The stucco-and-stone siding on this home makes it stand out in the neighborhood.

Images provided by designer/architect.

Features:

- **Great Room:** This large entertaining area features a built-in media center and a see-through fireplace into the hearth and kitchen area. The large bay windows allow an abundance of natural light to illuminate the 12-ft.-high space.

- **Kitchen:** This open island kitchen boasts an eating area with sliding glass doors leading to a deck. The space is open into the hearth area, and its fireplace adds warmth to the whole space.

- **Master Suite:** Located on the main floor for privacy and convenience, this retreat boasts a stepped ceiling in the sleeping area. The master bath features dual vanities, a separate shower, and a compartmentalized lavatory.

- **Lower Level:** This space features three bed rooms, two full bathrooms, the family room, and the bar and game area. The fireplace in the family room will be a cozy place to relax.

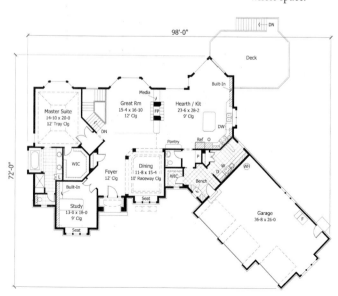

Basement Level Floor Plan

Copyright by designer/architect.

Rear Elevation

Plan #661289

Dimensions: 113'8" W x 97'4" D
Levels: 1
Heated Square Footage: 5,342
Bedrooms: 4
Bathrooms: 4 Full, 2 Half
Foundation: Slab
Material List Available: No
Price Category: J

This Mediterranean-style one-story home has it all and then some.

Features:

- **Kitchen:** This large island kitchen features space for two refrigerators and two cooking areas, and a large walk-in pantry. The nook area adjoining the kitchen is a great space to enjoy a meal while looking out onto the patio.

- **Family Room:** The family room has large sliding glass doors that make the covered patio and family room feel as though it is one large entertainment area.

- **Theater:** This home theater is located through the double doors off of the family room. The entertainment houses a split-level floor to accommodate theater-seating layouts.

- **Master Suite:** The master wing of this home includes a large library with a bay window, an exercise room, and a juice bar. This master suite has a large sitting area, access to the covered patio, an island tub, two vanities, and a spacious walk-in closet.

Images provided by designer/architect.

Copyright by designer/architect.

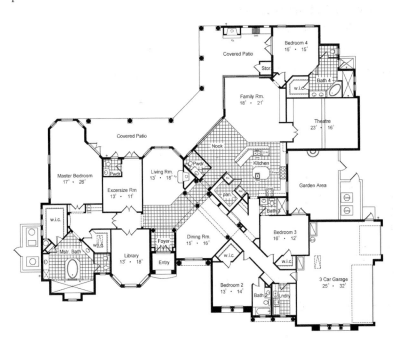

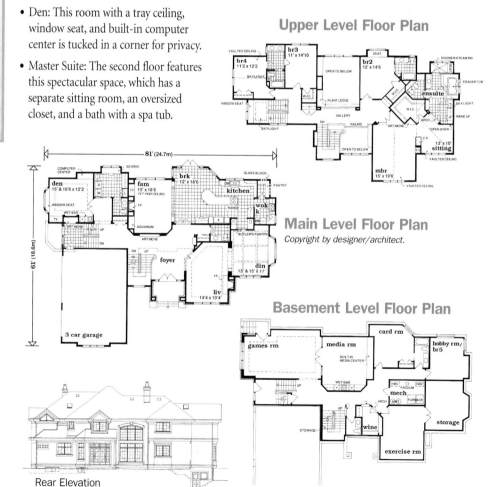

Plan #401050

Dimensions: 81' W x 61' D
Levels: 2
Heated Square Footage: 6,841
Main Level Sq. Ft.: 2,596
Upper Level Sq. Ft.: 2,233
Finished Basement Sq. Ft.: 2,012
Bedrooms: 4
Bathrooms: 3 full, 2 half
Foundation: Basement
Materials List Available: Yes
Price Category: K

This grand two-story European home is adorned with a facade of stucco and brick, meticulously appointed with details for gracious living.

Features:

- **Foyer:** Guests enter through a portico to find this stately two-story foyer.

- **Living Room:** This formal area features a tray ceiling and a fireplace and is joined by a charming dining room with a large bay window.

- **Kitchen:** A butler's pantry joins the dining room to this gourmet kitchen, which holds a separate wok kitchen, an island work center, and a breakfast room with double doors that lead to the rear patio.

- **Family Room:** Located near the kitchen, this room enjoys a built-in aquarium, media center, and fireplace.

- **Den:** This room with a tray ceiling, window seat, and built-in computer center is tucked in a corner for privacy.

- **Master Suite:** The second floor features this spectacular space, which has a separate sitting room, an oversized closet, and a bath with a spa tub.

Images provided by designer/architect.

Upper Level Floor Plan

Main Level Floor Plan
Copyright by designer/architect.

Basement Level Floor Plan

Rear Elevation

Let Us Help You
Plan Your Dream Home

Whether you've always dreamed of building your own home or you can't find the right house from among the dozens you've toured, our collection of Best-Selling House Plans can help you achieve the home of your dreams. You could have an architect create a one-of-a-kind home for you, but the design services alone could end up costing up to 15 percent of the cost of construction—a hefty premium for any building project. Isn't it a better idea to select from among the hundreds of unique designs shown in our collection for a fraction of the cost?

What Does Creative Homeowner Offer?

In this book, Creative Homeowner provides hundreds of home plans from the country's best architects and designers. Our designs are among the most popular available. Whether your taste runs from traditional to contemporary, Victorian to early American, you are sure to find the best house design for you and your family. Our plans packages include detailed drawings to help you or your builder construct your dream house. **(See page 342.)**

Can I Make Changes to the Plans?

Creative Homeowner offers three ways to help you achieve a truly unique home design. Our customizing service allows for extensive changes to our designs. **(See page 343.)** We also provide reverse images of our plans, or we can give you and your builder the tools for making minor changes on your own. **(See page 346.)**

Can You Help Me Manage My Costs?

To help you stay within your budget, Creative Homeowner has teamed up with the leading estimating company to provide one of the most accurate, complete, and reliable building material take-offs in the industry. **(See page 344.)** If that is too much detail for you, we can provide you with general construction costs based on your zip code. **(See page 346.)** Also, many of our plans come with the option of buying detailed materials lists to help you price out construction costs.

How Can I Begin the Building Process?

To get started building your dream home, fill out the order form on page 347, call our order department at 1-800-523-6789, or visit our We site, ultimateplans.com. If you plan on doing all or part of the work yourself, or want to keep tabs on your builder, we offer best-selling building and design books at www.creativehomeowner.com.

Our Plans Packages Offer:

"Square footage" refers to the total "heated square feet" of this plan. This number does not include the garage, porches, or unfinished areas. All of our home plans are the result of many hours of work by leading architects and professional designers. Most of our home plans include each of the following:

Frontal Sheet

This artist's rendering of the front of the house gives you an idea of how the house will look once it is completed and the property landscaped.

Detailed Floor Plans

These plans show the size and layout of the rooms. They also provide the locations of doors, windows, fireplaces, closets, stairs, and electrical outlets and switches.

Foundation Plan

A foundation plan gives the dimensions of basements, walk-out basements, crawl spaces, pier foundations, and slab construction. Each house design lists the type of foundation included. If the plan you choose does not have the foundation type you require, our customer service department can help you customize the plan to meet your needs.

Roof Plan

In addition to providing the pitch of the roof, these plans also show the locations of dormers, skylights, and other elements.

Exterior Elevations

These drawings show the front, rear, and sides of the house as if you were looking at it head on. Elevations also provide information about architectural features and finish materials.

Interior Elevations and Details

Interior elevations show specific details of such elements as fireplaces, kitchen and bathroom cabinets, built-ins, and other unique features of the design.

Cross Sections

These show the structure as if it were sliced to reveal construction requirements, such as insulation, flooring, and roofing details.

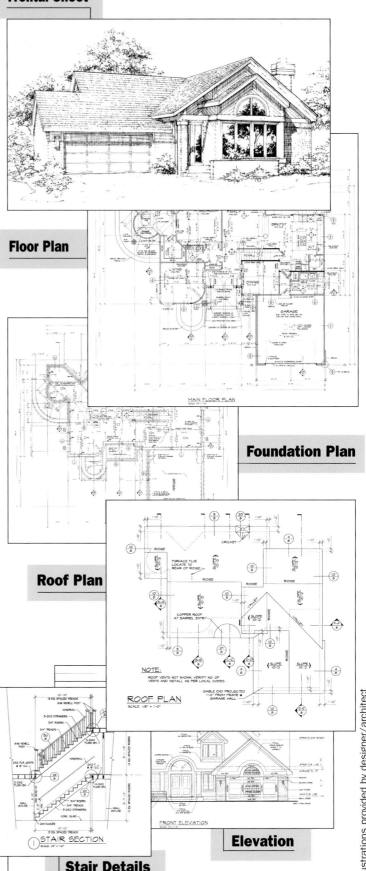

Frontal Sheet

Floor Plan

Foundation Plan

Roof Plan

Cross Sections

Stair Details

Elevation

Illustrations provided by designer/architect

Customize Your Plans in 4 Easy Steps

1 Select the home plan that most closely meets your needs. Purchase of a reproducible master is necessary in order to make changes to a plan.

2 Call 1-800-523-6789 to place your order. Tell our sales representative you are interested in customizing your plan. To receive your customization cost estimate, our modification company will contact you (via fax or email) requesting a list or sketch of the changes requested to one of our plans. There is a $50 nonrefundable consultation fee for this service. If you decide to continue with the custom changes, the $50 fee is credited to the total amount charged.

3 Fax or email your request to our modification company. Within three business days of receipt of your request, a detailed cost estimate will be provided to you.

4 Once you approve the estimate, a 75% retainer fee is collected and customization work begins. Preliminary drawings typically take 10 to 15 business days. After approval of the design, the balance of your customization fee is due before modified plans can be shipped. You will receive five sets of blueprints, a reproducible master, or CAD files, depending on which package was purchase.

Modification Pricing Guide

Categories	Average Cost For Modification
Add or remove living space	Quote required
Bathroom layout redesign	Starting at $150
Kitchen layout redesign	Starting at $120
Garage: add or remove	Starting at $600
Garage: front entry to side load or vice versa	Starting at $300
Foundation changes	Starting at $220
Exterior building materials change	Starting at $200
Exterior openings: add, move, or remove	$75 per opening
Roof line changes	Starting at $600
Ceiling height adjustments	Starting at $280
Fireplace: add or remove	Starting at $90
Screened porch: add	Starting at $300
Wall framing change from 2x4 to 2x6	Starting at $250
Bearing and/or exterior walls changes	Quote required
Non-bearing wall or room changes	$65 per room
Metric conversion of home plan	Starting at $495
Adjust plan for handicapped accessibility	Quote required
Adapt plans for local building code requirements	Quote required
Engineering stamping only	Quote required
Any other engineering services	Quote required
Interactive illustrations (choices of exterior materials)	Quote required

Note: Any home plan can be customized to accommodate your desired changes. The average prices above are provided only as examples of the most commonly requested changes, and are subject to change without notice. Prices for changes will vary according to the number of modifications requested, plan size, style, and method of design used by the original designer. To obtain a detailed cost estimate, please contact us.

Terms & Copyright

These home plans are protected under the terms of United States Copyright Law and may not be copied or reproduced in any way, by any means, unless you have purchased reproducible masters, which clearly indicate your right to copy or reproduce. We authorize the use of your chosen home plan as an aid in the construction of one single-family home only. You may not use this home plan to build a second or multiple dwellings without purchasing another blueprint or blueprints, or paying additional home plan fees.

Architectural Seals

Because of differences in building codes, some cities and states now require an architect or engineer licensed in that state to review and "seal" a blueprint, or officially approve it, prior to construction. Delaware, Nevada, New Jersey, New York, and some other states require that all plans for houses built in those states be redrawn by an architect licensed in the state in which the home will be built. We strongly advise you to consult with your local building official for information regarding architectural seals.

Before Customization

After

Turn your dream home into reality with

UltimateEstimate

When purchasing a home plan with Creative Homeowner, we recommend you order one of the most complete materials lists in the industry.

1 What comes with an Ultimate Estimate?

Quote

- Basis of the entire estimate.

- Detailed list of all the framing materials needed to build your project, listed from the bottom up, in the order that each one will actually be used.

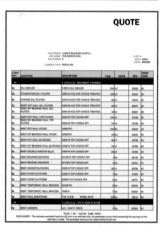

Comments

- Details pertinent information beyond the cost of materials.

- Includes any notes from our estimator.

Express List

- A version of the Quote with space for SKU numbers listed for purchasing the items at your local lumberyard.

- Your local lumberyard can then price out the materials list.

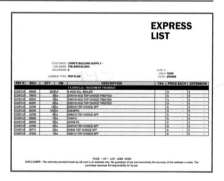

Construction-Ready Framing Diagrams

- Your "map" to exact roof and floor framing.

Millwork Report

- A complete count of the windows, doors, molding, and trim.

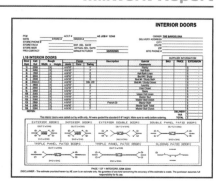

Man-Hour Report

- Calculates labor on a line-by-line basis for all items quoted and presented in man-hours.

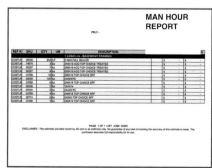

2 Why an Ultimate Estimate?

Accurate. Professional estimators break down each individual item from the blueprints using advanced software, techniques, and equipment.

Timely. You will be able to start your home-building project quickly — knowing the exact framing materials you need and how to get them with Lowe's.

Detailed. Work with your Lowe's associate to select the remaining products needed for your new home and get a final, accurate quote.

3 So how much does it cost?

Pricing is determined by the total square feet of the home plan — including living area, garages, decks, porches, finished basements, and finished attics.

Square Feet Range	UE Tier*	Price
Up to 5,000 total square feet	XB	$345.00
5,001 to 10,000 total square feet	XC	$545.00

*Please see the Plan Index to determine your plan's Ultimate Estimate Tier (UE Tier).
Note: All prices subject to change.

4 What else do I need to know?

Call our toll-free number (800-523-6789), or visit **ultimateplans.com** to order your Ultimate Estimate.

Turn your dream home into reality.

Decide What Type of Plan Package You Need

How many Plans Should You Order?

Standard 8-Set Package. We've found that our 8-set package is the best value for someone who is ready to start building. The 8-set package provides plans for you, your builder, the subcontractors, mortgage lender, and the building department.

Minimum 5-Set Package. If you are in the bidding process, you may want to order only five sets for the bidding round and reorder additional sets as needed.

1-Set Study Package. The 1-set package allows you to review your home plan in detail. The plan will be marked as a study print, and it is illegal to build a house from a study print alone. It is a violation of copyright law to reproduce a blueprint without permission.

Buying Additional Sets

If you require additional copies of blueprints for your home construction, you can order additional sets within 60 days of the original order date at a reduced price. The cost is $35.00 for each additional set. For more information, contact customer service.

Reproducible Masters

If you plan to make minor changes to one of our home plans, you can purchase reproducible masters. These plans are printed on bond or vellum paper that is easy to alter. They clearly indicate your right to modify, copy, or reproduce the plans. Reproducible masters allow an architect, designer, or builder to alter our plans to give you a customized home design. This package also allows you to print as many copies of the modified plans as you need for the construction of one home.

CAD (Computer Aided Design) Files

CAD files are the complete set of home plans in an electronic file format. Choose this option if there are multiple changes you wish made to the home plans and you have a local design professional able to make the changes. Not available for all plans. Please contact our order department or visit our Web site to check the availability of CAD files for your plan.

Mirror-Reverse Sets/Right-Reading Reverse

Plans can be printed in mirror-reverse—we can "flip" plans to create a mirror image of the design. This is useful when the house would fit your site or personal preferences if all the rooms were on the opposite side than shown. As the image is reversed, the letter-ing and dimensions will also be reversed, meaning they will read backwards. Therefore, when ordering mirror-reverse drawings, you must order at least one set of the original plan unreversed. A $50.00 fee per plan order will be charged for mirror-reverse (regardless of the number of mirror-reverse sets ordered). Some plans are available in right-reading reverse, this feature will show the plan in reverse, but the writing on the plan will be readable. A $150.00 fee per plan order will be charged for right-reading reverse (regardless of the number of right-reading reverse sets ordered). Please contact our order department or visit our Web site to check the availibility of this feature for your chosen plan.

EZ Quote: Home Cost Estimator

EZ Quote is our response to one of the most frequently asked questions we hear from customers: "How much will the house cost me to build?" EZ Quote: Home Cost Estimator will enable you to obtain a calculated building cost to construct your home, based on labor rates and building material costs within your zip code area. This summary is useful for those who want to get an idea of the total construction costs before purchasing sets of home plans. It will also provide a level of comfort when you begin soliciting bids. The cost is $29.95 for the first EZ Quote and $19.95 for each additional one. Available only in the U.S. and Canada.

Materials List

Available for most of our plans, the Materials List provides you an invaluable resource in planning and estimating the cost of your home. Each Materials List outlines the quantity, dimensions, and type of materials needed to build your home (with the exception of mechanical systems). You will get faster, more-accurate bids from your contractors and building suppliers. A Materials List may only be ordered with the purchase of at least five sets of home plans.

CompleteCost Estimator

CompleteCost Estimator is a valuable tool for use in planning and constructing your new home. It provides more detail than a materials list and will act as a checklist for all items you will need to select or coordinate during your building process. CompleteCost Estimator is only available for certain plans (please see Plan Index) and may only be ordered with the purchase of at least five sets of home plans. The cost is $125.00 for CompleteCost Estimator.

Ultimate Estimate (See page 344).

Order Toll Free by Phone	**Order Online**	**Canadian Customers**
1-800-523-6789	**www.ultimateplans.com**	**Order Toll Free 1-800-393-1883**
By Fax: 201-760-2431		
	Mail Your Order	**Mail Your Order (Canada)**
Orders received 3PM ET, will be processed and shipped within two business days.	Creative Homeowner Attn: Home Plans 24 Park Way Upper Saddle River, NJ 07458	Creative Homeowner Canada Attn: Home Plans 113-437 Martin St., Ste. 215 Penticton, BC V2A 5L1

Before You Order

Our Exchange Policy

Blueprints are nonrefundable. However, should you find that the plan you have purchased does not fit your needs, you may exchange that plan for another plan in our collection within 60 days from the date of your original order. The entire content of your original order must be returned before an exchange will be processed. You will be charged a processing fee of 20% of the amount of the original order, the cost difference between the new plan set and the original plan set (if applicable), and all related shipping costs for the new plans. Contact our order department for more information. Please note: reproducible masters may only be exchanged if the package is unopened and CAD files cannot be exchanged and are nonrefundable.

Building Codes and Requirements

All plans offered for sale in this book and on our Web site (www.ultimateplans.com) are continually updated to meet the latest International Residential Code (IRC). Because building codes vary from area to area, some drawing modifications and/or the assistance of a professional designer or architect may be necessary to comply with your local codes or to accommodate specific building site conditions. We strongly advise you to consult with your local building official for information regarding codes governing your area.

Multiple Plan Discount

Purchase **3** different home plans in the **same order** and receive **5% off** the plan price.

Purchase **5** or more different home plans in the **same order** and receive **10% off** the plan price. (Please Note: Study sets do not apply.)

Blueprint Price Schedule

Price Code	1 Set	5 Sets	8 Sets	Reproducible Masters or PDF Files	CAD	Materials List
A	$410	$470	$545	$660	$1,125	$85
B	$465	$540	$615	$740	$1,310	$85
C	$525	$620	$695	$820	$1,475	$85
D	$575	$670	$745	$870	$1,575	$95
E	$625	$730	$805	$925	$1,675	$95
F	$690	$790	$865	$990	$1,800	$95
G	$720	$820	$895	$1,020	$1,845	$95
H	$730	$830	$905	$1,045	$1,900	$95
I	$995	$1,095	$1,170	$1,290	$2,110	$105
J	$1,190	$1,290	$1,365	$1,490	$2,300	$105
K	$1,195	$1,295	$1,370	$1,495	$2,300	$105
L	$1,240	$1,335	$1,410	$1,535	$2,400	$105

Note: All prices subject to change

Ultimate Estimate Tier (UE Tier)

UE Tier*	Price	
XB	$345	* Please see the Plan Index to determine your
XC	$545	plan's Ultimate Estimate Tier (UE Tier).

Shipping & Handling

	1–4 Sets	5–7 Sets	8+ Sets or Reproducibles	CAD
US Regular (7–10 business days)	$18	$20	$25	$25
US Priority (3–5 business days)	$35	$40	$45	$45
US Express (1–2 business days)	$45	$60	$80	$50
Canada Express (3–4 business days)	$100	$100	$100	$100
Worldwide Express (3–5 business days)		** Quote Required **		

Note: All delivery times are from date the blueprint package is shipped (typically within 1-2 days of placing order).

Order Form Please send me the following:

Plan Number: _____ **Price Code:** _____ (See Plan Index.)

Indicate Foundation Type: (Select ONE. See plan page for availability.)
❏ Slab ❏ Crawl space ❏ Basement ❏ Walk-out basement
❏ Optional Foundation for Fee _____ $_____
(Please enter foundation here)
Please call all our order department or visit our website for optional foundation fee

Basic Blueprint Package   Cost
❏ CAD Files $_____
❏ Reproducible Masters $_____
❏ 8-Set Plan Package $_____
❏ 5-Set Plan Package $_____
❏ 1-Set Study Package $_____
❏ Additional plan sets:
  __ sets at $35.00 per set $_____
❏ Print in mirror-reverse: $50.00 per order $_____
  Please call all our order department or visit our website for availibility
❏ Print in right-reading reverse: $150.00 per order $_____
  Please call all our order department or visit our website for availibility

Important Extras
❏ Ultimate Estimate (See Price Tier above.) $_____
❏ Materials List $_____
❏ CompleteCost Materials Report at $125.00 $_____
  Zip Code of Home/Building Site _____
❏ EZ Quote for Plan #_____ at $29.95 $_____
❏ Additional EZ Quotes for Plan #s_____
  at $19.95 each $_____
Shipping (see chart above) $_____
SUBTOTAL $_____
Sales Tax (NJ residents only, add 7%) $_____
TOTAL $_____

Order Toll Free: 1-800-523-6789 By Fax: 201-760-2431
Creative Homeowner (Home Plans Order Dept.)
24 Park Way
Upper Saddle River, NJ 07458

Name _____
(Please print or type)
Street _____
(Please do not use a P.O. Box)
City _____ State _____
Country _____ Zip _____
Daytime telephone ( ) _____
Fax ( ) _____
(Required for reproducible orders)
E-Mail _____

Payment ❏ Bank check/money order. No personal checks.
Make checks payable to Creative Homeowner

❏ VISA ❏ MasterCard ❏ American Express Cards ❏ Discover

Credit card number _____
Expiration date (mm/yy) _____
Signature _____

Please check the appropriate box:
❏ Building home for myself ❏ Building home for someone else

SOURCE CODE CA425

Copyright Notice

Index

For pricing, see page 347.

Index

For pricing, see page 347.

UltimateEstimate

The fastest way to get started building your dream home

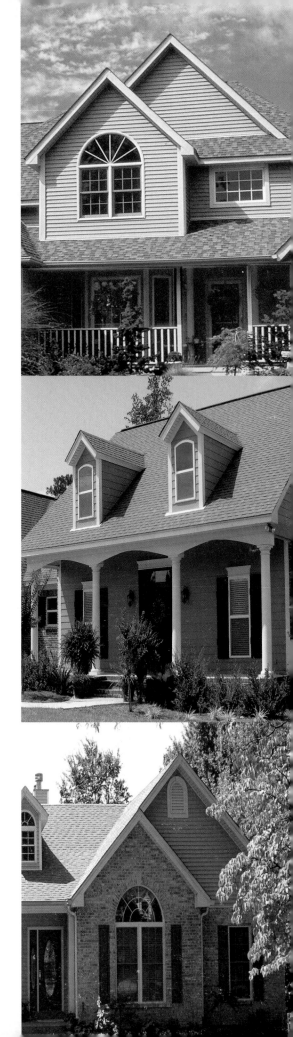

One of the most complete materials lists in the industry. Work with our order department to get you started today.

CRE▲TIVE HOMEOWNER®

To learn more, go to page 344 or go to UltimatePlans.com and select Ultimate Estimate located under "Quick Links" for complete details on this program.